D1743556

Jim Haynes is a first-generation Aussie whose mother migrated from the UK as a child during the Depression. His father arrived on a British warship at the end of World War II, met his mother and stayed. 'My parents always insisted we were Australian, not British,' says Jim.

Educated at Sydney Boys High School and Sydney Teachers' College, he taught for six years at Menindee, on the Darling River, and later at high schools in northern New South Wales and in London. Jim has also worked in radio and as a nurse, cleaner and sapphire salesman and was a professional entertainer and recording artist for 25 years. He has two degrees in literature from the University of New England and a master's degree from the University of Wales in the UK.

Jim was awarded the Order of Australia Medal in 2016 'for service to the performing arts as an entertainer, author, broadcaster and historian'. He has written and compiled 30 books, released many albums of songs, verse and humour, and broadcast his weekly Australiana segment on Macquarie Radio for twenty years. He lives at Moore Park in Sydney with his wife, Robyn.

ALSO BY JIM HAYNES

Great Furphies of Australian History
Adventurers, Pioneers and Misfits
The Big Book of Australia's War Stories
Best Australian Drinking Stories
Great Australian Scams, Cons and Rorts
Australia's Most Unbelievable True Stories
The Big Book of Australian Racing Stories
The Best Gallipoli Yarns and Forgotten Stories
Australia's Best Unknown Stories
The Best Australian Yarns
The Best Australian Bush Stories
The Best Australian Sea Stories
The Best Australian Trucking Stories
The Great Australian Book of Limericks
The Best Australian Racing Stories
The Big Book of Verse for Aussie Kids

GREAT AUSTRALIAN RASCALS, ROGUES AND RATBAGS

AUSTRALIA'S MOST COLOURFUL CRIMINAL CHARACTERS

JIM HAYNES

ALLEN&UNWIN
SYDNEY•MELBOURNE•AUCKLAND•LONDON

First published in 2022

Copyright © Jim Haynes 2022

All rights reserved. No part of this book may be reproduced or transmitted in
any form or by any means, electronic or mechanical, including photocopying,
recording or by any information storage and retrieval system, without prior
permission in writing from the publisher. The Australian *Copyright Act 1968*
(the Act) allows a maximum of one chapter or 10 per cent of this book, whichever
is the greater, to be photocopied by any educational institution for its educational
purposes provided that the educational institution (or body that administers it) has
given a remuneration notice to the Copyright Agency (Australia) under the Act.

Allen & Unwin
Cammeraygal Country
83 Alexander Street
Crows Nest NSW 2065
Australia
Phone: (61 2) 8425 0100
Email: info@allenandunwin.com
Web: www.allenandunwin.com

*Allen & Unwin acknowledges the Traditional Owners of the Country on which we
live and work. We pay our respects to all Aboriginal and Torres Strait Islander
Elders, past and present.*

A catalogue record for this
book is available from the
National Library of Australia

NATIONAL
LIBRARY
OF AUSTRALIA

ISBN 978 1 76106 790 7

Set in 12/15 pt Minion Pro by Midland Typesetters, Australia
Printed and bound in Australia by Griffin Press

10 9 8 7 6 5 4 3 2 1

MIX
Paper from
responsible sources
FSC® C009448

The paper in this book is FSC® certified.
FSC® promotes environmentally responsible,
socially beneficial and economically viable
management of the world's forests.

For Rebecca Kaiser

'Si finis bonus est, totum bonum erit'

CONTENTS

INTRODUCTION

'Our crime against criminals lies in the fact that we treat them like rascals.'

Friedrich Nietzsche

It is a fact of life that we tend to sentimentalise and romanticise criminals, especially as time passes.

In writing about criminal characters from the past, there is a tendency to concentrate on the personal lives, tragic circumstances and redeeming characteristics of the individual, rather than look at the damage they did to others, and the often horrific nature of the acts they committed.

The further we go back in history, the more romantic, heroic and legendary these 'criminals' become.

For example, it is now far too late to find out what the robber and outlaw Robin Hood was *really* like, or even if he ever existed. He is, in all probability, just an amalgamation of various renegades who became 'local heroes' by bucking the system and annoying the local authorities, whose job it was to keep law and order. If there ever was a real Robin Hood, he was long ago fictionalised out of existence and replaced, in our culture, by a mythical cartoon cliché.

American culture is littered with examples of criminals being romanticised and hero-worshipped. Clyde Barrow was responsible for the murder of thirteen innocent people, but false history and Hollywood have created the romance of 'Bonnie and Clyde—victims of a cruel and unfair society'. Henry McCarty was a ruthless thug who murdered eight men, some in cold blood. He is remembered as a (fictionalised) dashing and daring gunfighter, alias William Bonney, aka 'Billy the Kid'. McCarty was 21 when he was shot dead by sheriff Pat Garrett, but 'Billy the Kid' lives on as one of the most ridiculously inaccurately portrayed 'legends of the west'.

Here in Australia we have done a similar thing with Ned Kelly. All the factual evidence tells us that Ned was a self-obsessed thug, whose family on both sides were habitual criminals. Far from being a 'Robin Hood', Ned and his family stole from anyone they could and were the 'neighbours from hell'. Ned was a bully who recklessly endangered many innocent people's lives, murdered in cold blood, and then attempted to justify himself with a pack of lies and garbled nonsense in his Jerilderie letter.

Yet, in less than 150 years, Ned Kelly has become a mythical figure, transformed by film-makers, writers and artists (who are either misguided or deliberately wish to perpetuate the fictional version of the story) into an heroic, legendary freedom fighter and an iconic symbol of the Australian rebel spirit and republicanism.

Perhaps the inspiration we derive from the myths is what really counts. Much of our Western culture, or any nation's culture for that matter, is derived from myths and legends, the truth of which is long lost in the mists of time.

In our Western Judeo-Christian culture, the stories and myths of Ancient Greece, Roman and Norse mythology mix with the Old Testament stories to give us a sense of ourselves and guidelines and references for our beliefs and philosophies. The English language is full of words and phrases that reference that rich mythological mix, and often we cannot distinguish the history from the mythology.

In this book I have attempted to get as close as possible to telling the truth, and exposing the mythology, in fifteen stories concerning criminals from Australia's past.

The characters range from the most despicable examples of humanity to those whose courage has to be admired and whose so-called 'crimes' were seemingly unjustly punished.

I have grouped the fifteen stories under the rather arbitrary headings of 'rascals', 'rogues' and 'ratbags'. This is merely based on my personal opinion that the crimes of the 'rascals' were less heinous than those of the 'rogues' and the motivations of the 'rascals' were less evil than those of the 'rogues'. In the 'rascals' section there are several quite admirable human beings, two of whom can be called 'high achievers'. None of them was guilty of violent crimes.

The 'rogues' are those who I find it hard to admire or forgive. One was a murderer and another shot and killed a man and had people murdered. The others in the section are, to my mind, among the least likeable characters I have ever written about.

Those in the 'ratbags' section are perhaps the most interesting, in that their lives were extraordinarily unusual and their crimes often farcical, even comical in certain cases. In several instances, mental illness and insanity were obviously partly the cause of their abnormal behaviour, and for that they can be pitied.

Readers will quite possibly disagree with my classifications, and that is fine. In preparing this collection I have switched certain stories from category to category a number of times.

Five of the stories have a transported convict as their subject, and I would argue that two of the other stories concern characters who were greatly influenced by their convict heritage.

When you realise that more than 162,000 convicted criminals were sent to the colonies of Australia, this is hardly surprising. The population of Sydney in 1850, for example, was 39,000. Over the previous six decades 80,000 convicts had arrived in the settlement. The percentage of Sydney's residents who were convicts, ex-convicts or the children of convicts was, therefore, obviously a substantial majority.

The other eight stories, three from the 19th century and five from the 20th century, have a diverse range of *dramatis personae*. Two of the stories have soldiers who served in World War I as their subject. Then there is the incredibly successful entrepreneur, the obese butcher from Wagga Wagga, the poet and newspaper owner who was tarred and feathered, the celibate Irish Catholic who tried to murder a member of the royal family, the bunch of white-shoe-brigade petty criminals from the Gold Coast, the transgendered wife murderer, and the very famous and much-admired Irish American journalist.

Only one of the fifteen, Tom Skeyhill, was never officially charged with a crime, yet I find him to be one of the most despicable and dishonest characters in the collection.

Most of the fifteen have at least some redeeming features, some talents to be admired, or some glimmer deep down in their personality that reveals kindness to their fellow men and women. In some of them, however, these redeeming features and saving graces are massively outweighed, even made insignificant, by their crimes, cruelty, lack of respect for their fellow human beings and, often, a mind-boggling selfishness and lack of remorse.

I have attempted at all costs to avoid fictionalising any of them.

I have to confess to the fact that I deplore the modern trend to fictionalise history. I get annoyed by those so-called 'biographies' in which the author assumes to know the thoughts and the words spoken, often hundreds of years ago, by long-dead characters.

'Oh, look, Mr Banks,' said Captain Cook peering through his tele-scope, 'I can see land!' Grrrrrrr . . .

I am getting older, crankier and less tolerant, I know, but that sort of nonsense can only make the 'history' into a farce.

If there are written accounts of speeches, diaries, journals and newspaper reports, we should attempt to use them honestly and try to make an accurate history, always remembering that the accounts we have may be false or inaccurate. We cannot know the thoughts, spoken words and motivations of characters from the past unless they themselves have at least put them in writing.

If there is doubt, then it is an author's responsibility to say so. It's not hard to say, 'Many believe he was attempting to . . .' or, 'The newspaper stated . . .'.

Authors are, of course, allowed to have theories and opinions but they should always make it clear that is what they are. Authors who put what *they* believe *might have happened* into the mouths of dead people are just writing fiction, not history. (Here endeth the sermon.)

I hope my efforts at researching, unravelling and explaining the lives of these criminal characters from Australia's past will provide some insight into the times in which they lived and the reasons why they became the people they were. I hope readers will be enlightened, entertained and, at times, amused by them.

Every one of us has a story, and I hope you find these fifteen stories as fascinating and interesting as I did.

PART ONE
THE RASCALS

'Rascally: . . . meanly tricky or dishonest . . . often in humorous disparagement, without serious implication.'

Webster's New International Dictionary, 1929 edition

'Self-denial is not a virtue: it is only the effect of prudence on rascality.'

George Bernard Shaw, *Man and Superman*, 1903

1

MARY BRYANT—WHO WENT HOME

'. . . from whence it is hardly possible for persons to return without permission.'

The Ones Who Got Away

Escape attempts began as soon as the convicts of the First Fleet came ashore at Sydney Cove. There were no prison bars to contain the 775 convicts and, needless to say, all the efforts of the guards and marines could not possibly prevent cunning or desperate bids for freedom—and there were many.

Probably the first man to escape by sea was French-born convict Peter Parris, sentenced to death for burglary in Exeter in 1783 and transported on the *Scarborough*.

French explorer La Perouse was camped at Botany Bay for many weeks after the First Fleet arrived at Sydney Cove and, within days of the convicts being set ashore, escapees began visiting his camp, some seeking asylum or places in his crew. La Perouse told Lieutenant William Dawes, who visited him at Botany Bay, that he turned them all away, with scant rations sufficient to get them back to Sydney Cove.

La Perouse was a man of his word, but it does seem odd that the French-born Peter Parris disappeared within days of the colony being established, never to be seen or heard from again. My guess is that he died with the rest of the La Perouse expedition, after the two ships were wrecked on Vanikoro in the Santa Cruz Islands, some 300 miles (480 kilometres) north of Vanuatu. Whether La Perouse knew Parris was taken on board or not, who can say?

In the earliest days of the settlement some of the more naive convicts attempted to flee overland and met their death in the bush from starvation or fatal encounters with various Indigenous tribes, so it would have quickly become known that the only 'sane' and practical way to escape was by sea. Escape of any kind was highly unlikely to succeed, but life could be grim for the convicts, whether they stayed or ran. After all, the whole point of sending convicts to 'Botany Bay' was that the Lords Commissioners of the Treasury knew it was a place 'from whence it is hardly possible for persons to return without permission'.

'Hardly possible' perhaps, but not *entirely* impossible.

In September 1790, a former seaman and highwayman, John Tarwood, stole a leaky boat from the South Head lookout station and set off for Tahiti with four other convicts.

Judge Advocate Collins, in his journal for September of that year, noted:

In the night of the 26th a desertion of an extraordinary nature took place. Five male convicts conveyed themselves, in a small boat called a punt, from Rose Hill undiscovered. They there exchanged the punt, which would have been unfit for their purpose, for a boat, though very small and weak, with a mast and sail, with which they got out of the harbour. On sending to Rose Hill, people were found who could give an account of their intentions and proceedings, and who knew that they purposed steering for Otaheite. They had each taken provisions for one week; their cloaths and bedding; three iron pots, and some other utensils of that nature. They all came out in the last fleet, and took this method of speedily accomplishing their sentences of transportation, which were for the term of their natural lives.

The 'last fleet' referred to here is the Second Fleet which arrived in June 1790. The convicts involved had only taken three months to decide they didn't like the prospect of spending life sentences in New South Wales. Tahiti is, however, a long way in a leaky boat and, five years later, in August 1795, the four survivors of this daring escapade were found by Captain Broughton of the *Providence*, alive but somewhat emaciated at Port Stephens, where they had survived due to the generosity of the Indigenous people.

Collins recorded the event:

> Captain Broughton . . . found and received on board four white people, (if four miserable, naked, dirty, and smoke-dried men could be called white,) runaways from this settlement . . . John Tarwood, George Lee, George Connoway, John Watson . . . (Joseph Sutton having died) . . . They told a melancholy tale of their sufferings in the boat; and . . . spoke in high terms of the pacific disposition and gentle manners of the natives . . . Each of them had had names given him, and given with several ceremonies. Wives also were allotted them, and one or two had children . . . They told us a ridiculous story, that the natives appeared to worship them, often assuring them, when they began to understand each other, that they were undoubtedly the ancestors of some of them who had fallen in battle, and had returned from the sea to visit them again.

A few years later, sometime during the first decade of the colony, a group of convicts undertook one of the most bizarre escapes. They stole a boat and escaped from the settlement at Sydney, but headed south. Seven of them were found in 1798, living on an island near Western Port, in what was later named Bass Strait. The man who found them, a very surprised George Bass, was supposedly the first European to explore the area. The men had been abandoned there by the rest of the runaway group. Bass, who was exploring in a whaleboat with six convict rowers, set five of the men ashore with directions to Sydney, a compass and rations, and took the two weakest on board for the return trip to Sydney. Those set ashore were never seen again.

Naturally Bass asked them what were they doing on an island off the south coast of the continent, with no means of leaving. They replied that they had been trying to sail to China but had been abandoned by the rest of the group. Perhaps those who left them on the island perished attempting to find China—somewhere in the Great Southern Ocean!

Some 40 years later, in an act of daring piracy, a bunch of desperate convicts stole a ship—the brig *Cyprus*—and sailed to New Zealand, Tonga, Japan and China. They were caught and sent to be tried in London and several were hanged for piracy. There were other daring escape attempts in the meantime.

This is the story of an escape that occurred when the settlement was just three years old, almost exactly six months after John Tarwood and his four companions set out in a leaky boat for Tahiti.

Unlike the spontaneous or opportunistic and doomed attempt by Tarwood and his mates, the escape of William and Mary Bryant, their two children and seven convict companions was carefully planned and well prepared. The Bryants and their crew knew exactly where they were headed. Unlike Tarwood, they also knew how to get there.

Against all odds, in 1791, the convict Mary Bryant not only escaped, but eventually successfully returned to her home in Cornwall; what's more, she received a pardon and financial aid.

Mary Broad

Mary Broad was born in 1765 into a fishing family in the town of Fowey at the mouth of the River Fowey, about 6 miles from St Austell in Cornwall. At nineteen she moved to the much larger town of Plymouth, some 30 miles to the east, seeking work.

There she evidently fell into bad company and criminal activity. In company with Catherine Fryer and Mary Hayden, she robbed and violently assaulted a spinster named Agnes Lakeman on a public street in Plymouth. Mary appeared, listed as 'Mary Braund', with the other two at the Exeter Assizes in 1786, charged with stealing goods valued at £1 and 11 shillings, including Agnes's silk bonnet valued at 1 shilling. On 20 May 1786, all three were found guilty and sentenced to death by hanging. A month later this was commuted to seven years transportation and Mary was taken from Exeter Gaol to the hulk *Dunkirk*, at Plymouth. There she awaited transportation to the planned 'Botany Bay' convict colony.

Mary was described in the convict records as being 'marked with smallpox with one knee bent but not lame'. She was 5 feet 4 inches in height, with grey eyes, brown hair and a sallow complexion. She spent almost a year on the *Dunkirk*, during which time, probably in December 1786, she became pregnant, evidently to a man named Spence. Sometime in April 1787 the prisoners from the *Dunkirk* hulk were transferred to Portsmouth and embarked on the transports of the First Fleet. Mary was sent aboard the *Charlotte*, which carried 100 male convicts and 24 female prisoners.

During the voyage, she formed a relationship with William Bryant, the convict given the responsibility for distributing provisions to the other prisoners. She had possibly known William from her days on the *Dunkirk*, where he had been incarcerated for almost three years. It seems he was given a similar position of responsibility on the *Dunkirk* and was considered a good man who could be trusted.

William, a Cornish fisherman and smuggler, was aged 26 when sentenced to death, commuted to seven years transportation to America, in 1784, for 'resisting revenue officers'. As the American option had already been lost to Britain when the American War of Independence ended a year earlier, William spent the first three years of his sentence on the hulks, where he more than likely met Mary Broad, although he was not, it seems, the father of her first child.

The First Fleet reached Rio de Janeiro on 3 August and remained there a month. Arthur Phillip had served with distinction in the Portuguese navy for four years (1774–1778), including as captain of the 26-gun frigate, *Nossa Senhora do Pilar,* during the war against Spain. He was welcomed as an old friend and war hero when he arrived back at Rio flying his commodore's pennant from the mast top of HMS *Sirius*.

In September 1787, four days after the fleet departed Rio de Janeiro, Surgeon John White reported in his journal: 'On the evening of the 8th, between the hours of three and four, Mary Broad, a convict, was delivered of a fine girl.'

In October, when the fleet reached Cape Town, the child was officially named after the ship on which she was born—and baptised 'Charlotte Spence'.

The *Charlotte* arrived in Botany Bay on 20 January and, six days later, made her way to Port Jackson with the rest of the fleet. The convicts were disembarked over the next two weeks, the female convicts from the *Charlotte* being among the last to go ashore, on 7 February.

Four days later, on Sunday 10 February, after the church service, the Reverend Johnson baptised three children and married five couples. One of those couples was William Bryant and Mary Broad, although the name registered is 'Mary Brand', possibly because her court records at the Exeter Assizes had her listed as 'Mary Braund'.

Spellings were quite arbitrary in the 1780s and it is possible that an 'n' inserted itself into the pronunciation of 'Broad' at the assizes, making it 'Braund' which then transmuted to 'Brand'.

William's privileged position continued in Port Jackson, where he was given a hut apart from the other convicts and was made the fisherman for the colony. He was also put in charge of the colony's small boats.

One reason for the hut being set apart from the other convicts on the eastern side of the Tank Stream was to prevent an easy trade in black-market fish developing. However, on 4 February 1789, William was caught selling some of his catch. He was dismissed from his post as fisherman, lost his hut, and received 100 lashes. Mary was forced to deliver her second child, a son named Emanuel, in the convict camp at The Rocks.

The Plan

William continued in a lesser role, maintaining the colony's small boats and helping with the fishing, as he was the most skilled and capable man for the job. He took extra care to maintain the government cutter, as he had a plan for escape, but he cunningly waited until there were no ships in the colony capable of pursuit.

Collins tells us that the plan to escape was suspected:

William Bryant . . . was, at the latter end of the month, overheard consulting in his hut after dark, with five other convicts, on the prac-ticability of carrying off the boat in which he was employed. This circumstance being reported to the governor, it was determined that all his proceedings should be narrowly watched, and any scheme of that nature counteracted. The day following this conference, however, as he was returning from fishing with a boat-load of fish, the hook of the fore tack giving way in a squall of wind, the boat got stern-way, and filled, by which the execution of his project was for the present prevented.

As the escape was meticulously organised, it is tempting to think that perhaps the overturning of the fishing boat (which was actually officially 'the Governor's six-oared cutter') was part of the plan. After the boat was overturned in the squall, Bryant restored it to first-class order with new sails, new masts and a complete refit—all at government expense. He and Mary stashed away 100 pounds of rice, the same of flour and also salt pork, water, tents and tools, under the floor of their hut.

They waited until there were no ships in Sydney Harbour capable of pursuit. The *Sirius* had been wrecked at Norfolk Island on 19 March 1790 and the *Supply* was on its way to Norfolk Island, when the Dutch supply ship *Waaksamheyd* sailed out of Port Jackson on 28 March 1791.

The *Waaksamheyd* (*Vigilance*) was a 'snaw brig' (also called a 'snow')—a two-masted merchant ship—which had been chartered from Batavia by Captain Ball, who had sailed there in the *Supply* in April 1790. The *Waaksamheyd* had arrived in December 1790 with much-needed supplies, having lost most of her crew to fever on the way. After difficult negotiations between Governor Phillip and her captain, Detmer Smit, she was then chartered to take the crew of *Sirius* back to Britain for the statutory court martial, after the loss of that vessel on the reef on Norfolk Island. (None of the officers of the *Sirius* were found to be negligent—there is no safe anchorage at Norfolk Island and a sudden storm drove the *Sirius* onto the reef while she was being unloaded.)

William Bryant knew he was technically a free man: he had served his time. However, Governor Phillip, who was waiting for the convict indents to arrive, had no record of which convicts had served their time and which had not.

William approached Captain Smit for help and outlined his escape plans to the Dutchman. Sailing and rowing a small open boat to Timor meant a voyage of 3250 miles. Smit told Bryant that Captain Bligh had made the journey from Tahiti to Timor in a similar boat, and, for whatever reason we cannot be sure, supplied Bryant with a compass, quadrant, two guns, ammunition and detailed charts of the Great Barrier Reef.

At midnight on 28 March 1791, the same day that the *Waaksam-heyd* sailed off to Britain, William and Mary Bryant with two infant children and seven other convicts rowed out through Sydney Heads and turned north. David Collins records:

> In the course of the night of the 28th, Bryant, whose term of trans-portation, according to his own account, expired some day in this month, eluded the watch that was kept upon him, and made his escape, together with his wife and two children (one an infant at the breast) and seven other convicts, in the fishing-boat, which, since the accident at the latter end of the last month, he had taken care to keep in excellent order. Their flight was not discovered until they had been some hours without the Heads.
>
> They were traced from Bryant's hut to the Point, and in the path were found a hand-saw, a scale, and four or five pounds of rice, scat-tered about in different places, which, it was evident, they had dropped in their haste . . . The names of these desperate adventurers were,
> Came in the first fleet,
> William Bryant, His sentence was expired.
> Mary Braud his wife, and two children, She had 2 years to serve.
> James Martin, He had 1 year to serve.
> James Cox, He was transported for life.
> Samuel Bird, He had 1 year and 4 months to serve.
> Came in the second fleet,
> William Allen, He was transported for life.
> Samuel Broom, He had 4 years and 4 months to serve.
> Nathaniel Lilly, He was transported for life.
> William Morton, He had 5 years and 1 month to serve.
> So soon as it was known in the settlement that Bryant had got out of reach, we learned that Detmer Smith, the master of the Waaksamheyd, had sold him a compass and a quadrant, and had furnished him with a chart, together with such information as would assist him in his passage to the northward. On searching Bryant's hut, cavities under the boards were found, where he had secured the compass and such

other articles as required concealment . . . It was conjectured that they would steer for Timor, or Batavia . . . The situation of these people was very different from that of Tarwood and his associates, who were but ill provided for an undertaking so perilous . . .

The Voyage to Kupang

There were two written accounts of the voyage, but only one has survived. It was written in three different styles of handwriting on 23 small pieces of paper, varying in size. It is the story of the journey as told by James Martin, perhaps with the help of Allen, Broom and Lilly, while the four men, having ended their journey back in London, were in Newgate Prison, between June 1792 and 2 November 1793 when they were released. It is also possible that a prison staff member wrote sections of the document from dictation by Martin.

This first-hand account became part of the collection of Jeremy Bentham (1747–1832), the political philosopher and social reformer who promoted 'Utilitarianism', the theory that an action is right if it results in the happiness of the greatest number of people in society. Bentham opposed transportation as a punishment for crime, arguing that its results were haphazard and its effects could not be observed by other members of society, so that it was not an effective deterrent to crime.

Bentham promoted the concept of the panopticon prison, where a single central gaoler/inspector could observe from a central tower, at any time, any of the inmates housed in solitary cells in a circular cell block without being seen himself. Bentham wrote a treatise on the subject titled 'Panopticon Versus New South Wales'.

As part of the development of his theory, through the 1790s and into the 19th century, Bentham collected evidence of what he saw as the failure of transportation as a punishment. He had a 'fair copy' made of Martin's documented account of the voyage, on ten sheets of his own notepaper, with corrected spelling. In 2014, Tim Causer, Research Associate at the Bentham Project at University College, London, published the results of his extensive study of the documents, along with accurate transcriptions of the original writings and the 'fair copy'.

Martin's narrative, titled *The Memorandoms of James Martin*, gives a rather brief (3500 words), but often detailed, account of the

3250-mile voyage from Sydney to Kupang, on the Dutch-governed island of Timor, and the subsequent events that led the four men to Newgate Prison.

After two days sailing and rowing, having left Sydney Harbour, the fugitives put ashore at what was probably Glenrock Lagoon, about 4 miles south of Newcastle, where:

> . . . we found a quantity of fine burning Coal, we remained there 2 Nights & 1 day and found a great many Cabbage trees, some of which we cut down and procured the Cabbage. The Natives came down to whom we gave some Cloaths and other articles, and they went away very well satisfied. The land appeared much better than at Sidney Cove, here we got a great many fishes . . .
>
> *The Memorandoms of James Martin*, fair copy, page 2

After that friendly encounter, however, most meetings with the locals were hostile and coming ashore for water, wood and food became a hazardous venture. It is interesting to note that the fugitives were, undoubtedly, the first Europeans to discover the rich coal fields of what would become Newcastle.

Two days later, further north:

> . . . we made a very fine harbour, seeming to run up the Country for many Miles and very commodious for the Anchorage of Shipping; here we found plenty of fresh water, we hawled our boat a shore to repair her bottom with some Bees-wax and Resin which we had a small quantity of. But on the same Night we were drove off by the Natives, which meant to destroy us, we launched our boat and rode off in the stream quite out of reach of them . . .
>
> . . . we rowed lower down, thinking to land some miles below. On Monday morning we attempted to land, and we found a place convenient for to repair our boat, we accordingly put some of our things part being ashore when the Natives came in great numbers armed with Spears and Shields &c . . . we fired a Musket thinking to affright them but they paid no attention to it . . . we were forced to take to our boat and get out of their reach as fast as we could . . .
>
> *The Memorandoms of James Martin*, fair copy, pages 2–3

This was almost certainly Port Stephens, where they eventually found a safe island, 10 miles further up. They stayed two days and made repairs to the boat.

Leaving Port Stephens, a wind from the southwest drove them north along the coast, but then strengthened and took them out to sea and they did not make landfall for a full three weeks. Travelling along what today is the north coast of New South Wales, they tried to land a few times but the surf was too big. At one point they entered a bay and two of the men swam ashore to attempt to find wood and water, only to retreat having managed to get just a few pieces of wood due to the presence of 'Natives which they saw in numbers'.

On the other side of the bay, however, they managed to get the boat ashore and do some repairs, before tacking out to sea and continuing the voyage. ·

They were almost starving by now and they ran into a storm. Waves broke over the boat and it began taking water and was riding so low that they threw overboard all unnecessary items and clothing.

In searching for a place to land, they lost an anchor and were driven ashore in heavy surf. The boat and the escapees survived the forced landing and they were able to light a fire and find shellfish to eat. Having driven off the locals with a musket shot, they relaunched the boat and survived another storm at sea that lasted three days and forced them to bail continuously.

They next went ashore at a place they called White Bay, which they calculated was at 27 degrees south latitude. This was almost certainly Moreton Bay.

Here they saw two Aboriginal women on shore with a fire stick and, having landed, they convinced the women to give them fire, but were then forced to fire a musket to scare away the rest of the locals. The fugitives then used two of the natives' huts as shelter for two nights and dried their clothes. When the surf abated they once more put to sea:

> . . . we were drove out to Sea by a heavy Gale of Wind & Current,
> expecting every Moment to go to the Bottom next Morning saw no
> Land the Sea running Mountains high we were Under a Close Reeft
> Mainsail & kept so untill Night & then . . . all the Night with her Head

> to the Sea thinking every Moment to be the Last the Sea Coming in so
> heavy upon us every now & then that two Hands was Obliged to keep
> Bailing out & it Rained very hard all that Night and the next Morning.
>
> *The Memorandoms of James Martin*, fair copy, page 5

Running before the storm, they came to an area of reefs and saw land. At this stage they had only a gallon of fresh water and uncooked rice on board. In spite of the heavy surf and reefs they decided to attempt a landing and, safely negotiating the dangerous conditions, the boat came to rest on a sandy beach. It was Lady Elliot Island, at the southern end of the Great Barrier Reef.

Here their luck was about to change for the better. It was now mid-May and there were green sea turtles on the island, as it was the season in between egg laying and hatching.

> ... being almost starving we put on a little rice to cook when we landed
> on this Island we had but one Gallon of fresh water for there was not
> a drop to be had on this Island ... after the tide fell we went to look
> for some shell fish but found a great quantity of very fine large Turtles
> which was left upon the reef, we turned 5 of them and hawled them
> upon the beach ... we killed one of the Turtles and had a noble meal
> that night it rained very hard when we spread our mainsail & filled
> our two Breakers full of water. We staid on the island 6 days during
> that time we killed 12 Turtles and some of them we took and dried
> over the Fire to take to Sea with us ...
>
> *The Memorandoms of James Martin*, fair copy, page 6

Living on shellfish and dried turtle meat they miraculously negotiated the Great Barrier Reef, stopping at many small islands for water. They then set off across the Gulf of Carpentaria.

Having several times outsped the small bark canoes of the mainland Aboriginal people, they now met with, and had to outrun, the more sophisticated canoes of the warriors of the Torres Strait:

> ... we ran down the Gulph 9 or 10 Miles and saw several small Islands
> on which were several of the Natives in 2 Canoes ... they seemed to
> stand in a posture of defence against us we fired a Musket over them &

immediately they began firing their Bows and Arrows at us we immediately hoisted up our Sails and rowed away from them but as God would have it none of their arrows came into the Boat but dropped along side.

The Memorandoms of James Martin, fair copy, page 7

Further along the coast they found a source of fresh water which was in sight of a village of some twenty large huts. They took on board some water and spent the night just off shore. Next morning they returned to take on more water:

... but as we were making towards the shore we saw two very large Canoes coming towards us we did not know what to do for we were afraid to meet them there seemed to be about 30 or 40 men in each Canoe they had sails seemed to be made of matting one of the canoes then she hoisted her Sails and made after us as soon as we saw that we tacked about with what water we had determined to cross the Gulph which was about 500 Miles but as God would have it we out run them they followed us till we lost sight of them, having but little fresh water and no wood to make a fire with but in four days and a half we made the other side of the Gulph ... we saw a small river which we made to and got plenty of fresh water; we put off to sea the same night then we concluded the best way to shape our course would be for the Island of Timor with what little water we had which we made in 36 Hours we ran along the Island of Timor till we came to the Dutch Settlements.

The Memorandoms of James Martin, fair copy, page 8

Recaptured

At Kupang, the Dutch Governor Timotheus Wanjon treated them with compassion and charity and evidently believed their story about being castaways from the shipwreck of a whaling vessel. The escapees were taken to Government House and fed and clothed and, over the next two months, several of the men found paid work. Then, however, they were arrested and imprisoned after the truth became known to Governor Wanjon.

William Bryant had written an account of their travels, which included the bogus story of the shipwreck. This was kept by Wanjon and later given to William Bligh, when he visited the settlement for a second time, in command of HMS *Providence*, in October 1792. It has since been lost.

When Bligh, and the other seventeen surviving loyal crew members of the *Bounty* mutiny, had arrived at Kupang in June 1789, after their epic voyage of 4000 miles from the island of Tofua, it was Timotheus Wanjon, then acting for his father-in-law Governor van Este, who welcomed and helped them.

Bligh was told by Wanjon that an unnamed member of the 'castaway' group had informed on them, in a fit of pique and jealousy at being treated less well than the rest.

James Martin's version is that William Bryant, after an argument with Mary: 'went and informed against himself, wife, Children and all of us; we were immediately taken prisoners and put in the Castle'.

Tim Causer finds this hard to believe, commenting that it, 'seems doubtful given the penalty for absconding from transportation'. We must remember, however, that Bryant's sentence had expired when he stole the boat and escaped. It is quite likely that he felt he would be spared the death penalty on that technicality. It has also been suggested that the argument with Mary was about the future of the Bryant 'family' and the marital status of the pair, now that they were no longer in New South Wales. This can only be conjecture.

David Collins suggests that the group eventually gave themselves away: 'by their language to each other, and by practising the tricks of their former profession, gave room for suspicion; and being taken up, their true characters and the circumstances of their escape were divulged'.

In *A Complete Account of the Settlement at Port Jackson*, published in London in 1793, Captain Watkin Tench of the marines, who knew the fugitives as convicts in Sydney and later travelled with the survivors from Cape Town to England on HMS *Gorgon*, suggests: 'their behaviour giving rise to suspicion, they were watched; and one of them at last, in a moment of intoxication, betrayed the secret'.

James Martin claims that, after the truth was revealed, they were all interrogated and then kept as prisoners, although they were allowed the freedom of the town for a day—two at a time, on strict rotation, until September.

Now there is another twist to the tale and, once again, it involves the mutiny on the *Bounty*.

HMS *Pandora*, commanded by Captain Edward Edwards, left England in November 1790 to hunt down the mutineers. In Tahiti fourteen were captured and some were kept in an iron cage on deck as the ship made her way home. Near the tip of Cape York, the *Pandora* hit the outer edge of the Great Barrier Reef and sank. Thirty-one crew and four mutineers drowned. Eighty-nine crew and ten mutineers survived a hazardous voyage across the Arafura Sea in four open boats and arrived at Kupang on 16 September 1791. For a third time, Dutch Governor Timotheus Wanjon provided aid and assistance to unfortunate British refugees and fugitives.

At this point, Captain Edwards questioned the escaped convicts, who confessed.

Edwards arranged for a Dutch vessel, the *Nambang*, to take the prisoners, now in chains, to the fever-ridden port of Batavia, and during the voyage they survived the most savage storm Martin had ever known.

The prisoners spent six weeks in chains on a Dutch guard ship while they waited for Edwards to arrange transport to Cape Town. It was at Batavia that Mary lost both her husband and her infant son to disease. William died first and little Emanuel six days later. Both were buried at Batavia.

Mary, Charlotte and the seven surviving male convicts were taken to the Cape of Good Hope on three different ships of the Dutch East India fleet. During the voyage Samuel Bird and the group's extremely capable navigator, William Morton, who had guided them 3250 miles, both lost their lives to fever and disease contracted at Batavia. James Cox, whose sentence was 'life', disappeared as the ship carrying him passed through the Sunda Strait. Captain Edwards reported Cox 'drowned after falling overboard' but the *Pandora*'s surgeon, George Hamilton, wrote that he 'jumped overboard in the night, and swam to the Dutch arsenal at Honroost'.

Mary, Charlotte and the four surviving men arrived at Cape Town on 18 March 1792, where they were transferred to HMS *Gorgon* for the final voyage home. Ironically the *Gorgon* had arrived from New South Wales and was taking a detachment of marines, who had served in the penal colony, home to England.

The five surviving escaped convicts were greeted, almost as old friends, by the marines and their wives and children. Captain Watkin Tench, of the marines, recorded his thoughts: 'I confess that I never looked at these people, without pity and astonishment. They had miscarried in a heroic struggle for liberty; after having combated every hardship, and conquered every difficulty.'

He recalled that William Bryant and Mary Broad had travelled to Port Jackson with him on the *Charlotte* and had:

> . . . both of them been always distinguished for good behaviour. And I could not but reflect with admiration, at the strange combination of circumstances which had again brought us together, to baffle human foresight, and confound human speculation.

During the voyage home the weather was extremely hot. Lieutenant Clark of the marines recorded that, in May, the soldiers' children were dying and 'going very fast the hot weather is the reason of it'.

It was here, in the same part of the Atlantic Ocean where she was born, that little Charlotte died. She was buried at sea on 6 May 1792. She was four years and six months old.

Mary was now the sole survivor of her little family.

Home
The arrival of the survivors of the daring escape from 'Botany Bay' was big news in London. The press took up the story and many notable citizens appealed to the Home Office for clemency.

On 30 June 1792, having been taken to Newgate Prison five days earlier, they were remanded in custody awaiting sentencing, by Magistrate Nicholas Bond. The *Evening Mail*, of 22 July 1792, reported him as saying that he had: 'never experienced so disagreeable a task as being obliged to commit them to prison, and assured them as far as lay in his power he would assist them'.

The prisoners were reported to have declared they preferred death to a return to 'Botany Bay' and the *London Chronicle* of 3 July 1792 declared that: 'His Majesty, who is ever willing to extend his mercy, surely never had objects more worthy of it.'

However, on 7 July, the five faced court and were not punished for the escape but merely ordered 'to remain on their former sentences until they should expire'.

At this point James Boswell took up their cause. Boswell, the 9th Laird of Auchinleck, was a Scottish diarist, lawyer and reformer, who was also famously the biographer of Dr Samuel Johnson. He wrote to the Home Secretary, Henry Dundas, in August, asking that 'nothing harsh shall be done to the unfortunate adventurers from New South Wales'. In November, Boswell visited Evan Nepean, Under-Secretary for State in the Home Department, and asked for clemency and the prisoners' release.

Others disagreed.

David Collins, who, as the colony's judge advocate, knew only too well the difficulties involved in keeping law and order in a far-flung penal settlement. He believed that showing sympathy to the group set a bad example and compromised the safe conduct of the colony. Writing four years later, after several others had attempted to steal boats and escape from Sydney Cove, he stated:

> . . . instead of meeting with the compassion and lenity which were expressed in England for their sufferings, [they should have] been sent back and tried in New South Wales, for taking away the boat, and other thefts which they had committed, it was probable that others might have been deterred from following their example.

Responding to pleas for clemency and forgiveness, Nepean told Boswell that: the 'Government would not treat them with harshness, but at the same time would not do a kind thing to them, as that might give encouragement to others to escape'.

This really pleased neither side and sent mixed messages to those expecting a definitive reaction. The official cautious attitude meant that Mary Bryant was finally released ten months later, on 6 May 1793, six weeks after her original sentence had expired. She was, however, given an unconditional pardon.

Until she returned home to Fowey, Mary stayed in accommodation paid for by Boswell, in Great Titchfield Street, about a mile from Boswell's home. He also paid for her passage home on board the coastal passenger ship *Ann and Elizabeth* on 13 October 1793. Boswell also attempted to raise money for Mary by asking people in Cornwall to contribute to a charity fund for her wellbeing. Unfortunately, her family were best known locally for stealing sheep, and the appeal raised very little money.

Boswell sent regular payments of money to Mary. These amounted to £10 per annum and were sent via the Reverend John Baron, the vicar at Lostwithiel, several miles from Fowey. The payments were conditional on Mary 'behaving herself'.

Although Boswell was a known womaniser who frequented brothels, both before and after his wife died in 1789, there is no hint of any immoral dealings between him and Mary. Certain of his friends (and quite a few of his enemies!) teased him and hinted at 'ulterior motives' in cartoons, but there is no evidence of any such thing, and he kept fighting to have the four male convicts freed after Mary had been released and returned to Cornwall.

In May, just after Mary's release, he again petitioned Nepean to have the men pardoned or, failing that, to allow them to serve their time in the Royal Navy. In August he visited them in Newgate to reassure them he was doing all in his power to have them released. On 2 November he visited the Home Secretary's office and spoke to the First Clerk, Mr Pollock, about the plight of the four prisoners.

When Boswell returned home from the visit to the Home Secretary's office that day, he was surprised to be informed that the four men had come to his house while he was away, seeking to thank him for their release. They had been discharged from prison by proclamation, though not pardoned.

Three of the surviving male convicts had skills as sailors or fishermen and likely returned to their home towns. William Allen told Boswell he would go to sea on a merchant ship as soon as he was released. Nathaniel Lilly was a Londoner and a skilled net maker with a wife and four kids, who was already busy making nets to support his family while in Newgate. Samuel Broom, who used the alias John Butcher, was a 50-ish bachelor from Kidderminster who apparently was offered a job at the local pub on his release. (The oft-told tale of him joining the army and returning to New South Wales is a complete fiction, first told in the novel *A First Fleet Family*, in 1896.) Irishman

James Martin was a skilled mason and bricklayer from County Antrim, with a wife and son in Exeter. Boswell was sure his skills could earn good money either in London or back in Ireland.

James Boswell continued to support Mary Bryant until he died on 19 May 1795 at age 55, as a result of what today would be called 'acute and chronic post-gonorrheal urethral stricture and infection'; in other words 'complications from venereal disease'.

After the Bryant family and seven other convicts successfully made off in the government fishing boat, colonial authorities were constantly anxious about escape attempts and a regulation was introduced prohibiting the building of vessels longer than 14 feet (4.2 metres). Out of necessity this regulation was later relaxed, but a strict control was kept on boat-building, and ships were not allowed to anchor in those places in the harbour where they could be easily seized by footloose convicts.

In spite of speculation about a 'Mary Bryant' being married at Breage, 44 miles away from Fowey, in 1807, and a 'Mary Broad' being found not guilty of stealing at the Old Bailey, 275 miles away from Fowey, in 1806, there is not a shred of evidence to link either with our heroine.

The last that history knows of the resilient Mary Bryant is a letter of thanks received by James Boswell in November 1794, sent from her home in Cornwall. Put simply, all we can say about Mary Broad/Braund/Brand/Bryant is that she was the first female convict to escape from New South Wales and return to Britain, she travelled some 14,400 miles by sea, lost a husband and two children in the process, was sent to prison, was pardoned . . . and went home.

2

GEORGE BARRINGTON— THE CELEBRITY CONVICT

'. . . never pilfered any man of his fair name.'

The Bloody Code

George Barrington was the most famous criminal ever sent to 'Botany Bay', as the British public called the penal settlement at Sydney in its early days.

While it is true that our nation's first European citizens were either criminals or those guarding them, it is not accurate to think of them as a bunch of 'cut-throats' and 'cold-blooded murderers'. Although there were quite a few 'hardened criminals' among their ranks, those sent here were mostly petty thieves and miscreants convicted of minor crimes. There were, let us not forget, 222 crimes for which you could be sentenced to death, and some of them were rather trivial by 21st century standards.

As well as the obvious crimes of violence, and things like thieving, robbery, poaching, piracy and treason, there was 'being out at night with a blackened face', 'damaging a bridge', 'begging without a licence', 'maiming cattle', 'stealing from a shipwreck', 'writing a threatening letter', 'being in the company of gypsies for a month' and the wonderful 'impersonating an Egyptian'. (These last two actually referred to joining a band of gypsies to escape from justice for some alleged crime, and behaving 'like a gypsy' when you were not one.) You could be hanged for any of those—as well as another 200 or so other crimes.

So, although the vast majority of convicts were 'criminals' of some kind, it didn't take much to get yourself sentenced to be hanged or transported.

About 75 per cent of those sentenced to death were reprieved and had their sentences commuted to prison terms, or transportation— most of the 'real' criminals who were caught were among the 25 per cent who *were* hanged! There were 10,300 convicted criminals hanged in England and Wales in the century from 1790 to 1890. I don't have the figures for Ireland and Scotland but we can safely assume the rates were similar!

In the late 18th century, when New South Wales was established as a convict settlement, it was up to the jury to decide not only guilt, but also the value of any goods allegedly stolen in cases of theft and robbery. If a person was found guilty of stealing goods valued at more than a shilling, they could be hanged.

This explains why many convicts seem to have been transported for stealing items of little value. If the jury took pity on the thief, or felt he or she deserved another chance in life and was perhaps the victim of poverty and circumstance, they could value the goods stolen at under a shilling and thus save the convicted person's life. The penalty for stealing goods valued at under a shilling was transportation.

Which brings us to the strange case of the most famous convict ever sent to 'Botany Bay', George Barrington.

The 'Genteelest Thief'

George was something of a celebrity, and certainly the best-known criminal of his day.

He was once caught in the act and charged with attempting to steal a golden snuff box from the Russian Count Gregory Orlov at the Covent Garden Theatre. It was valued at £30,000. He was convicted of stealing a gold watch and chain at Enfield racetrack, obviously worth rather more than a bob! He stole expensive jewels and goods valued at well over a shilling many times.

Why didn't Barrington hang?

Well, he had a silver tongue and was so famous in his day that society women reputedly boasted about being robbed by the dashing, handsome and elusive 'prince of rogues'. He mixed in the best circles and was the talk of the town in London and the darling of the press, who often attributed all sorts of imaginary crimes and adventures to the notorious and charming gentleman thief.

According to the newspaper accounts of the day, Barrington was a sort of amalgam of the Scarlet Pimpernel, Robin Hood and Beau Brummell. He met with the best of society and picked pockets at the Royal Court during the Queen's birthday celebrations in 1775. He was also a master of disguise and often dressed as a minister of religion for his thieving acts, and even stole jewellery while wealthy women were wearing it. Many of his victims, including Orlov, did not testify against him.

London society was agog at the exploits of this famous thief and expert pickpocket. He was so well liked that, although he was arrested more than a dozen times and convicted at least eight times, he was pardoned on more than one occasion and 'let off' lightly by judges on quite a few other charges. Often he was able to talk his way out of being convicted at all. His silver tongue, fashionable dress and genteel manners would frequently convince a jury that it was 'all a terrible mistake' or a misunderstanding, or even that he had merely found misplaced items and was returning them!

Barrington was not, however, 'to the manor born', he was simply a very good actor and an excellent thief.

George was born in 1755, somewhere near Dublin, possibly at the village of Maynooth where his mother worked as a midwife.

He claimed to be the illegitimate son of Captain Barrington, the commander of a nearby British garrison, but we should not take that too seriously. At different times in his life, both Barrington and the newspapers of the day claimed that he was the illegitimate son of various noblemen, even royalty.

He was more than likely the son of a silversmith named Waldron, and although his early life in Ireland is confused by various romantic versions, it appears his parents gave him some early education and he served some time as an apprentice to an 'apothecary', or village doctor and pharmacist, until a minister of the Church of Ireland saw some promise in him and arranged a scholarship to the famous 'Blue Coats', a charity grammar school attached to Trinity College in Dublin.

At the age of sixteen he was involved in a fight with another school-boy and resorted to stabbing his opponent with his penknife.

(All literate men, scholars and students carried a 'penknife' in those days—the term originally applied to a very small clasp knife used to make a quill pen from a goose, duck or chicken feather by shaping and forming a nib. Carrying a penknife on your watch chain was a status symbol—it showed you could write.)

Barrington was given a severe flogging by the headmaster for his crime and took it rather badly. He actually retaliated by committing the first of many robberies, to wit, stealing 12 guineas and the headmaster's gold watch and absconding. Some accounts say he was expelled, which he no doubt was, but he did, in fact, expel himself by running off to Dublin with the watch and cash, and embarking on a life of crime.

He soon joined a 'theatre company', which was actually a group of petty criminals and strolling players whose leader was John Price, a conman and thief who was already wanted by the police in England. Price taught young George to pick pockets and he was so good at it that he and Price set out in partnership on their own, picking pockets and thieving, first in Dublin and then in London.

When Price was finally tracked down, arrested and transported to the American colonies in 1773, Barrington continued his career solo and used his acting skills and good manners to enter society, posing as a gentleman or even a nobleman. It is said that he 'stole the hearts of influential friends as readily as their purses'.

He was arrested but escaped conviction several times, often because those he robbed refused to press charges. Finally, however, in 1776, he was arrested for stealing a pair of silver studs, a silk purse, half a guinea and 3 shillings and sixpence from a widow, Ann Dudman, in the pit of the Drury Lane Playhouse, and sentenced to three years working on the coal hulks on the Thames.

This must have come as quite a shock to the 21-year-old Barrington, who appeared in court tastefully and expensively dressed with a gold-tipped cane and gold buckles on his shoes. He was described in one newspaper as 'the genteelest thief ever to have been seen at the Old Bailey', although it was also reported that a witness stated that 'the genteelest thief' lived in lodgings in the markedly down-market inner London neighbourhood of Charing Cross.

As it was, officially, his first offence, George was free within twelve months due to his excellent behaviour and influential friends. He went straight back to mixing in the best of circles and stealing—and was back in court within six months. Giving his profession as 'surgeon' (I assume that was based on his brief apprenticeship to an apothecary as a boy), he was convicted of stealing £3, a watch, a silk watch string and a glass seal from one Elizabeth Ironmonger on 15 March 1778 in the crowded St Sepulchre's Church, while 'a special sermon was being delivered'.

This time he received a five-year sentence on the hulks and, while serving the sentence, Barrington hit a low point in his life and showed the first signs of a mental instability that would return in later years. He attempted to escape and when he failed to do so, he attempted suicide, using his penknife. While recovering from his wounds he contracted tuberculosis and almost died.

The authorities once more took pity on the gentleman thief and he was freed and pardoned, again due to the efforts of friends, on the condition that he left England and never returned.

George went back to Ireland but, unfortunately, found that he was still wanted there for earlier crimes so, after more robberies in Ireland, he headed to Scotland, and eventually, after a few more robberies in that kingdom, he completed the circuit and fled back to London. There, rather inevitably, in 1783, he was arrested for breaking the terms of his pardon and served a year in prison.

On his release Barrington returned to his former life, mixing with and stealing from 'the brightest luminaries in the globe of London'. Although he was arrested quite a few more times, his connections and his gentlemanly bearing, manners and eloquence usually led to his acquittal.

His luck ran out in 1790 when he appeared at the Old Bailey charged with stealing a gold watch and chain at Enfield racecourse. Although the most famous defence counsel in London, William Garrow, defended him eloquently, he was convicted. The newspapers recorded that Barrington's speech in his own defence easily surpassed that of his attorney as a splendid piece of oration. According to the gentlemen of the press gallery, the emotional impact of his final pleas, which included a detailed list of reasons why he should not be executed, brought tears to the eyes of the jury.

Even though he was found guilty, he was sentenced only to transportation, not hanging, and for only seven years; not the fourteen years, or life, that he could easily have received, and undoubtedly deserved.

Although the newspapers carried colourful stories of Barrington organising breakouts and escaping from Newgate Prison disguised as a woman, he was actually sent to New South Wales, along with 2000 other convicts, on what was called the Third Fleet. Barrington was aboard the convict transport ship *Active*—one of the eleven ships that left in the first three months of 1791.

Bound for Botany Bay

The *Active* left Portsmouth on 27 March 1791, carrying 175 male convicts, and arrived in the colony of New South Wales 183 days later, on 26 September 1791. Of the original complement, 154 made it alive. The loss of 21 out of 175 'passengers' during the voyage was about the average death rate for the Third Fleet, but it was well over three times the average death rate for Britain's population at that time. Being transported was a risky business.

Barrington's arrival in the settlement caused quite a stir and Governor Phillip, it seems, had no idea what to do with a gentleman convict, whose conduct he described as 'irreproachable'. After giving the matter some thought, the governor decided to make him a policeman and put him in charge of the government stores at Parramatta.

In 1792 Phillip granted Barrington a conditional pardon. This was not the usual 'ticket of leave' that convicts received for good behaviour—it was actually a pardon.

In 1796 this was made an absolute pardon by Governor Hunter who, at the same time, appointed Barrington the Chief Constable of the settlement at Parramatta and granted him 30 acres (12 hectares) of land. Barrington had a fine house built and then bought another 50 acres on the Hawkesbury River and farmed there with the help of convicts assigned to him as workers and servants.

By all known accounts Barrington never committed one crime in his newfound home, and it seems the fresh air in sunny New South Wales cured him of any criminal inclinations for good.

He did, however, like a drink and, in 1800, he resigned his post as Chief Constable due to a serious 'infirmity', which may have been alcoholism or perhaps mental illness of some kind. He was allowed to keep half his salary as a pension.

Soon his mental health was so poor that a commission was appointed to look after his affairs and care for him. He died on 27 December 1804. He wasn't quite 50 years old.

Barrington's fame lasted long after his death. He is credited with so many adventures, crimes and daring deeds that he would have needed to live three lifetimes to have done them all.

While on the voyage out to Sydney he was credited by sections of the British press with having prevented a mutiny. One London newspaper published a long sentimental letter, purportedly from Barrington to his long-suffering wife, begging forgiveness and swearing repentance, although he certainly never wrote it.

Although absent from Britain, his notoriety lingered on, and stories about him continued to sell newspapers. Many copies were sold of a popular broadside ballad, 'The Jolly Lad's Trip to Botany Bay', in which a group of convicts laugh about being transported and swear that the first thing they will do in New South Wales is take over the colony and appoint a king, 'for who knows but it may be the noted Barrington'.

Fake News

Despite being credited with many publications, letters, journals and theatre pieces, there is little doubt that George Barrington wrote none of them. He certainly never wrote the books that appeared in his name. Two books, supposedly written by him, *The History of New South Wales* (1802) and *A Voyage to New South Wales* (1803), were selling in London shops in the last years of his life and another, entitled *A History of New Holland,* was published four years after his death.

All those books sold very well in Britain and no one to this day knows who wrote any of them, though one seems to have been based heavily on the published journals of Judge Advocate David Collins.

No doubt some enterprising journalists and publishers of the day conspired to cash in on Barrington's name and, using the journals published legitimately—written by Collins, Arthur Phillip, Surgeon John White and Captain Watkin Tench of the marines—simply plagiarised and paraphrased them. It sounds all too familiar, doesn't it? Fake news is nothing new.

As well as not writing any of the books attributed to him, Barrington was also certainly not the author of the much-quoted speech supposedly given by him as a prologue at the opening of the first Australian theatre in 1796.

There were also suggestions that George Barrington was an artist! The two books, *A History of New South Wales* and *A Voyage to New South Wales,* contain images showing views of the harbour and the settlement of Sydney and these were credited to him.

However, a study of the seven engravings in these two volumes shows that several are crude 'mirror' images of views that appear in Collins's publication, originally engraved by James Heath in London from drawings by convict artist Thomas Watling. This indicates that the images in Collins's book were copied directly onto a new engraving plate so that, when printed, the images appear reversed. Others are believed to be rough copies of other drawings and engravings now lost.

The so-called 'Barrington' images are mostly poorly executed engravings which resemble vaguely accurate views of Sydney only when reversed. The figures of people, cows and trees imposed into the engravings are poorly drawn and out of scale.

It is almost an insult to poor old George Barrington to suggest they are based on drawings or paintings by him. As there is no evidence that he ever drew or painted, we cannot accuse him of being a poor artist. They are the work of someone else . . . who was a poor artist.

Also, of course, there is no suggestion that Barrington knew about, or benefited from, these publications. He might have been a thief and a liar, but he is credited with having said, in his own defence and to avoid hanging, that he 'never pilfered *any* man of his fair name'. That, at least, seems to be true.

3

HARRY READFORD—PIONEER CATTLE THIEF

'. . . not a cattle-stealer, although he might have stolen some.'

Hybrid Vigour

Of all the rascally acts of outback skulduggery in our colonial past, the sheer audacity of Harry Readford's theft of 1000 head of cattle probably takes the prize for daring and originality, not to mention skill and bushmanship!

Henry Arthur Readford (or Redford), known all his adult life as 'Harry', was born in December 1841 near Mudgee, the youngest of the eleven surviving children of a Yorkshire convict and his Australian-born wife, herself the daughter of two convicts.

It has often occurred to me, in researching and writing convict-related stories from our past, that the hybrid vigour and risk-taking energy that was poured into the melting pot of our convict-bred population was, in fact, the elemental factor in creating our post–European settlement Australian character and culture.

Where else would men and women from all corners of Britain and Ireland have been forced into partnership with people they would never have otherwise met? In the Britain and Ireland of the 18th and 19th centuries, people rarely moved far from their birthplace, they married and reproduced locally, most often within their village or the local areas of large cities like London and Dublin and Glasgow. Cities then were really a collection of villages, anyway.

However, as convicts (and soldiers and sailors), Irishmen, for example, married, or at least mated with, women from all parts of Scotland, England, Wales... and parts of Ireland they would never have visited in their lives. Convict women from Yorkshire, the Hebrides, London, Wales, the Isle of Wight and the Isle of Man bore children to men from Lincolnshire, the Midlands, the Highlands, County Cork and God-knows-where-else in Britain and Ireland. And, of course, once they reached the colonies there were unions with Indigenous peoples and others from around the world, though that is not the focus of my musings here.

If you add to this hybrid vigour the fact that most convicted criminals were risk-takers of some sort, you start to realise how the origins and upbringing of the first few generations of 'convict-bred' Australians were likely to produce a 'new breed' of Anglo-Celts. Strangely, it is also true that the convict system could achieve social reform and create a new, more egalitarian and less restrictive society, by simply putting people in a place where their past was irrelevant to whatever they might achieve once they were free.

Henry 'Harry' Readford and his siblings were perfect examples of this.

Their father, Yorkshireman Thomas Readford (listed in convict records as Thomas Ratford and Retford and in other places as Radford and Redfern), was born in 1791 and transported for seven years to New South Wales on the *Marquis of Wellington*, which left London on 1 September 1814. He was a labourer, who was, at the York Assizes in March of that year, 'charged with burglariously entering a Cellar, part of the Dwelling-House of Mrs. Charlotte Richardson, situate in College-street, York, and stealing therefrom four hides of Leather, the property of Edward Hogarth'.

Thomas and his accomplice then sold the leather to a shoemaker, John Dale, who copped fourteen years for receiving stolen goods!

Thomas is a good example of the convicts who, once freed in the colony, put the past behind them and got on with creating a better life and raising a family. He and his wife, Jemima, produced eleven healthy children, eight of whom survived their childhood. By the time the last of them, our subject, Henry, was born in 1841, Thomas was 40 and Jemima was 41 and they were a respected family and had established successful rural properties, businesses and hotels, from Emu Plains and the Hawkesbury Valley, to Mudgee and the Castlereagh district.

Jemima Readford, née Smith, was a 'currency lass', an Australian-born child of convicts, born in Sydney on 2 February 1801. Jemima's parents were slightly more 'colourful characters' than her husband, Thomas Readford. She was the daughter of Edwin Turleigh (or Turley) Smith and Jane Maher.

Edwin's crime was highway robbery, which occurred when he was about 34 years old.

Although he is registered in convict records as a native of Dublin, he and two other men (one named James Smith, possibly a relative, and Humphrey Moore) were tried 160 miles (260 kilometres) further south, at the Cork Assizes, on 17 October 1794. Their crime was the robbing of John Autchinson, on the highway, of 31 guineas and they were sentenced to be hanged on 25 October.

According to the *Caledonian Mercury* of 3 November 1794, Humphrey Moore (alias Mendoza, alias John Brown) and Edwin Smith received a reprieve from Mr Sergeant Chatterton on the day they were to hang. I assume James Smith was hanged.

Edwin arrived in Sydney on 11 February 1796, on a convict transport, the East Indiaman *Marquis of Cornwallis*. The vessel had departed Portsmouth carrying 36 soldiers and family members of the New South Wales Corps. At Cork she took on board 163 male and 70 female convicts.

The voyage of the *Marquis of Cornwallis* is notable for an attempted mutiny by more than 40 convicts, allegedly assisted by Sergeant Ellis of the New South Wales Corps. A letter dated 22 October 1795, written at St Helena by an officer on board, appeared in the *Edinburgh Advertiser* in January 1796. In recounting the details of the mutiny, which occurred near the Cape Verde Islands, the unnamed officer recalled:

Capt. Hogan rushed down the fore hatchway, followed by Mr. Richardson and three more of the officers and myself, armed with a pair of pistols and cutlass each, where began a scene which was not by any means pleasant. We stuck together in the hatchway and discharged our pistols amongst them . . . seeing their comrades drop in several places . . . their courage failed them, and they called out for quarter. I broke my cutlass in the affray, but met with no accident myself. There were none killed upon the spot, but seven have since died of their wounds. The serjeant [Ellis] was severely punished, and is since dead.

Forty-two convicts were flogged and left in chains for the duration of the voyage as a result of the mutiny. We have no record of whether Edwin was among them or not.

Two months after Edwin arrived in Sydney, Jane Maher (also 'Marr'), aged 30, was tried in Dublin in April for 'stealing money from a brothel patron' and sentenced to seven years transportation.

Jane was (rather oddly) described in the records as being an 'abbess of the lower description' and 'keeper of a nunnery', which evidently meant that she was the madame of a brothel. We can only assume that a previous history of prostitution, and a certain amount of survival skill and 'nous', led her to being able to manage such an establishment.

She was transported aboard the ship *Britannia* which arrived in the colony on 27 May 1797. Like the *Marquis of Cornwallis,* the voyage of the *Britannia* is one of the more notable and much-written-about voyages of the estimated 948 that conveyed convicts to Australia:

The combination of a callous and brutal master and a weak, incompetent surgeon made the voyage of the first *Britannia* one of the worst in the history of transportation. There was one death to every 17 prisoners embarked, 10 men and one woman dying out of 144 men and 44 women; but the convicts were brutally mistreated and the survivors were landed in a wretched and emaciated state. The *Britannia*'s master, Thomas Dennott, was a sadist who, in consequence, as Governor Hunter declared, 'of some conjecture of mutiny', kept the prisoners confined in irons and flogged them unmercifully. Even the women received three or four dozen cuts from a cane for the most trivial offences.

Charles Bateson, *The Convict Ships,* Brown, Son & Ferguson, Glasgow, 1969

Jane's marriage to Edwin, if there ever was one, is estimated to have occurred in 1798. They certainly lived together from that time until she died in 1802 and they had two daughters, Kezia (born 1798) and Jemima (born 1801).

In a sad postscript to her life, which is also a reminder of how the convict system could improve people's lives quickly once they were free and their past was irrelevant, Jane, who had made a successful business as a baker and now owned property, wrote to her old gaoler in Dublin, seeking a son she'd left behind. The letter was passed to the London *Sun* and appeared in that paper, on 9 April 1802, as being from:

> . . . a woman named Jane Maher, who was transported from thence about six years ago. The subject of it is, a request for an inquiry to be made after a male child she left in Dublin behind her, stating, that having by her industry in the baking business acquired property, she is enabled to provide for the child, and wishes to have it educated, and brought up in a decent manner, and for which she will remit money.

Not bad, for an ex-prostitute who stole money from her clients. Sadly, there is no record of the son being found, and Jane died that year, aged 35.

Her daughter, Jemima Smith, the offspring of two convicts, was married to ex-convict Thomas Readford in 1834; she had already borne him seven children and would bear another four after their marriage was formalised. The last of their children was Henry 'Harry' Readford, cattle thief extraordinaire.

Several of Harry's older brothers became pioneer pastoralists, businessmen, blacksmiths and inn-keepers in the Emu Plains and Hawkesbury districts and around Mudgee and the Hunter Valley. One of them founded successful cattle and sheep properties in the Orana district and another, John Readford, was a highly respected pioneer of the town of Warren, population 1500, situated between the towns of Gilgandra and Nyngan, 67 miles northwest of Dubbo. John settled there, raised a family of eleven, and died there in 1901. He is still remembered as 'The Father of Warren'.

Harry was, it seems, the 'black sheep' of the Readford clan. Whereas his father was a reformed convict who had stolen four cattle hides, Harry upscaled by stealing 1000 cattle hides, with the cattle still inside them! It also took him a long time, and fifteen months in Boggo Road Gaol, to 'reform' at least to the point where he gave up stealing cattle and horses . . . and a few other things.

Harry's Heist

Harry Readford and two companions (maybe four, we don't really know) stole the cattle from Bowen Downs Station, in North Queensland, took them more than 935 miles down the Channel Country and through outback desert, where no stock had ever been before, and delivered them into the colony of South Australia—where their brands would be unrecognisable and unknown.

It was a feat comparable to the greatest overland cattle treks in our history (or any other nation's history, for that matter) and the skill and audacity demonstrated led to one of the most obvious and famous miscarriages of justice in Queensland history. (And there have been plenty of those!)

The Bowen Downs region was named in honour of Queensland governor Sir George Bowen by the explorer William Landsborough, the man who was sent to find Burke and Wills and later became the Queensland Commissioner for Crown Lands.

In 1860 Landsborough and Nat Buchanan explored the area and, when the district was opened up for settlement and the newly formed government of Queensland issued grazing licences, the two men applied for, and were granted, a pastoral lease over a large tract of country along the Thomson River. They mortgaged the property to the Scottish Australian Investment Company, and Landsborough's friend Edward Cornish. Nat Buchanan became the first manager. He over-landed 3000 cattle to the property in 1862 but, after a few bad seasons Buchanan abandoned his one-eighth share to the Scottish Australian Investment Company and walked out.

So, apart from Landsborough's small share, Bowen Downs was completely owned by the Scottish Australian Investment Company, whose address was Sydney. The company owned fifteen properties in Queensland, ranging in size from 40 square miles (10,000 hectares) to 1500 square miles (400,000 hectares).

Bowen Downs was huge—fronting more than 125 miles of the Thomson River, with Mitchell grass plains stretching away from the river. The property was managed by Robert Morehead and Matthew Young, who were part-owners as well as the Queensland representatives of the Scottish Australian Investment Company, but it was run by overseers. By 1870 the drought had broken, and after several good seasons, the property had restocked very well, with large numbers of 'cleanskins' (unbranded cattle) running wild over the 100 square miles.

Some modern accounts claim that the station carried more than 60,000 head of cattle in 1870. This is fanciful in the extreme, given that in 1862 Nat Buchanan arrived with 3000 head and walked off the property in a time of severe drought, three years later. Cattle don't breed like rabbits and there had been no store cattle to buy during the drought. After several good seasons, 10,000 to 12,000 might be nearer to the mark.

There were quite a few less cattle on Bowen Downs after Harry Readford's audacious plan succeeded, about 1000 less in fact.

A Lot of Bull

Now, readers should be warned, there is a lot of bull involved in this story—a very large, very valuable and very distinctive pedigreed bull named 'The Duke of Marlborough'. In 1871, the 'Duke' almost sent Harry Readford to gaol. It took that famous, or more correctly, infamous, miscarriage of justice to save him.

Harry's mix of convict DNA produced a strong, massively built bushman who stood 6 feet 3 inches tall (1.9 metres). As a boy and young man, Harry worked at various jobs in the bush and on the Hawkesbury River, and by the late 1860s he'd headed north and was living on a small cattle property in central north Queensland where he was involved in a carrier business with three other men, carting goods from the railhead at Tambo to the large cattle property Bowen Downs.

It seems the business was a success for Harry and his friends, William Forrester, William Rooke (or Brooke) and George Dowdney. Harry also supplemented his income by working as a stockman for Forrester, who owned a station called Balaclave, between Harry's small property and Bowen Downs. He also made money by stealing cattle in partnership with local property owner John McKenzie and a man named James McPherson, who also worked for McKenzie.

Apparently, the epic cattle heist and cattle drive through the Channel Country to another colony was dreamed up by Harry after talking to Dowdney and Rooke, who had travelled through that part of the country from South Australia previously. Harry and the others had been stealing cattle successfully for a while, and had almost been caught a few times. So Harry suggested a big 'one off' job that would make them rich.

Cattle duffing had increased dramatically in the 1860s in Queensland, due to higher cattle prices and the issuing of grazing licences over huge areas of good grazing land to large companies whose principals lived in Sydney, Brisbane, Melbourne or Britain.

Many locals, especially those struggling to make a living with smaller holdings, felt aggrieved by the government policy of allowing absentee ownership of land. They also resented the wasteful grazing practices and the poor way that overseers ran these huge properties. They thought locals and 'Australians' should own and profit from the natural resources of the country. (Sound familiar?) These strongly felt sentiments would later save Harry Readford from prison and bring about a miscarriage of justice that shocked the Queensland establishment to its core.

Harry realised that Bowen Downs Station was so big that parts of it were rarely, if ever, visited by stockmen. Harry and his mates were able to build a set of stockyards in a remote corner of the station and herd a large mob of cattle there without anyone ever knowing what they were doing. They also had cattle from Bowen Downs hidden on the McKenzie property.

Early in March 1870 the men started moving the cattle onto William Forrester's property. At this point Harry revealed his 'master plan'— to take a massive mob of cattle across the outback—and McKenzie and McPherson refused to be part of the scheme. They only wanted to continue stealing small numbers of cattle and keep their 'duffing' on a small scale. But Rooke and Dowdney, who had travelled up from South Australia using the same route Harry proposed to take, thought the scheme was possible—they were 'in'.

At Forrester's cattle camp the cleanskins were branded with various local brands to make the herd look like a typical mob of store cattle (cattle rounded up for market or fattening—not breeding stock).

Many of the Bowen Downs herd were already branded 'LC', which stood for 'Landsborough and Cornish', the original partners in the station.

In late March Harry set off with the stolen cattle down Coopers Creek and the Strzelecki Track, via the Channel Country. He was accompanied by Rooke and Dowdney and perhaps two others, stockmen James Johnson and Harold Merrick, for part, or all, of the journey.

As well as the 1000-strong mob, Harry had decided to steal a valuable white bull, known as 'Whitey' or, more officially, 'The Duke of Marlborough'. The bull's presence, it was thought, would keep the herd, which contained many cows and heifers, quiet and tractable. It was a good idea but ultimately a mistake.

Harry Readford never talked much about the experience, although he did, rather strangely, give a newspaper interview after selling the cattle, as we shall see. He revealed, however, that he was nervous for the first month of the trek and climbed a tree or hill every morning to look for any signs of pursuit. After that first month, he knew they were relatively safe—any dangers lay ahead of them—not behind them.

For most of the trek they kept the cattle together, but sometimes they split the herd into three smaller mobs to get better feed. Harry, his accomplices and the cattle covered more than 810 miles in three months, which included detouring around floodwaters and dealing with local Indigenous people, who they found mostly friendly. It is uncertain whether they had Johnson and Merrick with them or managed the whole trek with just three men—it would have been an incredible task for three men to achieve! With five it was still an amazing feat of droving and bushcraft.

What makes the story even more remarkable, and the feat more believable, however, is the fact that they had incredibly good luck with the weather. The Channel Country and Strzelecki Desert were experiencing unusual wet conditions and a 'good season' and the biggest problem the cattle duffers had with water was avoiding it!

They arrived safely in June 1870, at the general store at Strzelecki Creek, also known as Artracoona Native Well, in northeastern South Australia.

Harry, posing as 'Henry Collins', attempted to trade two cows for clothes and provisions at the general store. He told the storekeepers, two brothers named Walke, that the cattle were from a station called Wilbe Wilbe in New South Wales and belonged to him and his brother Lawrence Collins, which explained the 'LC' brand.

Allan Walke was suspicious and demanded the white bull as part of the deal. With the heist almost completed, Harry reasoned they no longer needed the bull—so he exchanged Whitey and two cows for the clothes and sorely needed provisions. Harry signed a receipt 'Henry Collins'.

After resting a few days, the last stage of the journey via Mount Hopeless to Blanchewater Station east of Marree was easily accomplished. Blanchewater was owned by the Hon. John Baker, a conservative member of the South Australian parliament who had briefly been premier—for six days in 1857.

The cattle were sold for £5000 to station manager Mr J. Mules, who may have believed Readford's story or simply been only too happy to buy 1000 head of cattle cheaply in the best season the country had seen since European settlement—no questions asked. There was feed for fattening and the Adelaide market needed beef.

Harry was paid with a promissory note cashable in six months time and made out to 'Henry Collins'. The men then proceeded to Adelaide where the note was sold off at a discounted rate to a money dealer. On their way down through the Flinders Ranges to Adelaide, 'Henry Collins' gave an account of his exploits—part fact, part fiction—to a newspaper reporter in the township of Blinman.

The newspaper reported that Collins, 'the owner of Wilbe Wilbe Station', had overlanded cattle and 'just sold them at Blanchewater after a trek of four months' which had 'involved repeated detours of more than 50 miles to escape floodwaters'.

It wasn't until September that stockmen at Bowen Downs noticed tracks of cattle that had left the station. They followed the tracks to the neighbouring property belonging to John McKenzie.

The police became involved and McKenzie was implicated in the thefts. He and two other men were arrested and charged with stealing 100 head of cattle from Bowen Downs. McKenzie and a man named McGrath were tried at the district court in Roma in early 1871 and, despite an overwhelming case and many witnesses testifying against them, a sympathetic local jury found them not guilty.

It seems amazing that it was only while this investigation was underway in late 1870 that mustering on Bowen Downs led to the realisation that many more cattle were missing and local rumours started circulating that suggested certain 'possibilities'.

Bowen Downs' manager Boyd Morehead (son of one of the joint owners, Robert Morehead) had even been told about a huge mob of cattle being moved through the Channel Country, but the clue had been dismissed as irrelevant as the prosecution of McKenzie and McGrath was in progress.

The information had come from a bushman named John Costello who noticed the tracks of a huge mob around the part of the Channel Country known as Wombunderry Channel, 250 miles south of Bowen Downs. Costello was exploring with the idea of taking out a lease there, which he later did.

Costello assumed, quite rightly, that a mob that big had to have come from Bowen Downs, but his information went unheeded until mustering on the station brought to light the missing numbers and the secret stockyards were discovered in October 1870.

The trail was now six months old and fading, but Bowen Downs sent stockmen Edmund Butler, John Vernon and John Craigie to follow it, track down the missing cattle and unravel the mystery. They found the white bull at Artracoona and traced some of the cattle to the Adelaide markets. South Australian police had already arrested a drover taking cattle branded 'LC' down a stock route to Adelaide. Morehead and Young's agents, auctioneers Elder Smith, found other cattle similarly branded in the Adelaide market.

Morehead travelled to Adelaide by steamer and arrived on 17 February 1871 and the Blanchewater connection was exposed.

A warrant was issued for the arrest of 'Henry Collins' and Harry Readford's name started to be associated with the affair, but the connection wasn't made until John Craigie remembered being in Adelaide on family business in July 1870 and meeting Readford unexpectedly and being surprised to hear him called 'Mr Collins'. Then it was noticed that Collins's description matched Readford.

But where was Harry Readford?

He had left Adelaide soon after meeting Craigie, on 20 July 1870, aboard the steamship *Aldinga*. Returning via Sydney to Mudgee, he had married childhood sweetheart Elizabeth Scuthorpe there in April 1871.

The Trials

Meanwhile, in light of new evidence, McKenzie and McGrath, along with Forrester and two local men, were taken all the way back to Roma to face fresh charges of stealing 200 head from Bowen Downs.

McGrath was tried first.

This time McKenzie confessed and gave evidence for the prosecution. He admitted he had been paid by McGrath to take part in the theft and was present when the cleanskins in the large mob of cattle were branded at Forrester's cattle yards.

Amazingly, the Roma jury found McGrath not guilty and the Crown prosecutor decided not to proceed with the trials of the other men.

Warrants were issued for the arrest of Henry 'Harry' Readford.

Meanwhile, Harry and Elizabeth had used the ill-gotten gains from the cattle theft to buy a pub in Gulgong, near Mudgee. Even though he was wanted in three colonies, no one noticed when Harry used his real name to apply for a liquor licence and had his name published in the Police Gazette in order that police across the colony could check the name to see if he was an appropriate person to own a pub.

If only Harry could have stayed away from trouble, he might have lived a long and happy life as a publican with the now-pregnant Elizabeth and the daughter she was carrying.

Harry, however, was arrested in November 1871 in Gulgong—for helping two men open a stolen safe. One of the men told police the robbery had been Harry's idea and he'd lent them his horse to carry the safe away.

The case against Harry wasn't very strong and he was released, but subsequent checks discovered he was wanted in three colonies and he was re-arrested a week later and charged with the Bowen Downs cattle theft. Taken to Roma in late November, he was charged with 'stealing 100 bullocks 100 cows 100 heifers 100 steers and one bull'.

Harry was in custody a long time and the trial was finally set for February 1873. However, out of 48 jurors empanelled, the prosecution accepted only seven. The frustrated judge—Queensland parliamentarian Charles Blakeney, who was born in Ireland and educated at

Dublin Trinity College—had no choice but to ask the prosecution to reconsider jurors until twelve were chosen.

The evidence, as reported by the *Sydney Morning Herald* on 1 March 1873, was overwhelming against Harry. An expert gave evidence that the handwriting on the receipt for the bull was obviously Harry's: 'Mr. J.K. Cannan was examined as an expert, and gave it as his opinion that the signatures "Henry Redford" to the recognisance [for bail], and "Henry Collins" to the receipt given to Mr. Walke, were written by the same person.'

The white bull was the star witness.

Only a dozen or so of the other cattle had survived and been recovered, most of the rest had already been eaten by hungry South Australians. The Hon. John Baker had stalled attempts by Morehead and his agent to inspect the herd at Blanchewater while he sold off as many of the stolen cattle as he could to local butchers. Still, there was sufficient evidence to prove that the rest of the stolen herd had arrived in South Australia.

The first witness called was Edmund Butler, cattle overseer on the Bowen Downs station, who testified that he bought and branded a white bull in November 1867, from Gracemere Station, near Rockhampton. He further stated that:

The bull outside the Court was the animal he bought at that time, he could not be mistaken as to his identity . . . during the months of March, April, mid May, 1868, a muster of the cattle was made on that part of the Bowen Downs where the bull was kept, and about 1,000 head of cattle, together with the bull in question, were at that time missed from the station.

Butler, as reported in the *Sydney Morning Herald*, then gave the damning evidence of Harry's guilt:

The next time he saw the bull was in South Australia, about 1,000 miles distant from the place where he had been missed: it was at a place called Streletzski Creek, [sic]; he was in the possession of a person named Allan Walke; he (Walke) told witness that he had purchased the bull with two cows from a man who gave his name as Henry Collins; there were with Collins at the time two other men whom he (Walke) knew to be named Doudney [sic] and Brooke; Walke then produced to witness a document which he said was the receipt given to him by Collins for the purchase of the cattle.

Other witnesses corroborated the evidence that the bull was stolen and disposed of by Harry Readford. Bowen Downs stockman John Vernon was the next witness, and he stated:

. . . that he knew the bull outside the Court well, and could identify him amongst a thousand irrespective of his brands as the animal . . . was in his charge from the time he came on the station up to the year 1869, when he disappeared. The next time he saw him after he was missed was in South Australia, in 1871, where he, witness, in company with Butler, found the beast in Walke's possession. The moment he saw the bull he knew him.

Allan Walke was called and said that:

He and his brother kept a general store at Streletzski Creek [sic], and the prisoner, at the time mentioned, with his mates, came there to purchase clothes and stores, after selecting what articles they required, they proposed to sell witness two cows, branded LC: he agreed to purchase the animals provided they would also dispose of a bull they had in their mob, (the bull outside the Court was the animal he alluded to); to this the prisoner and his mates consented, before completing the purchase witness asked who the cattle belonged to, and prisoner replied that they belonged to himself, in conjunction with his brother, who owned a station in an adjoining colony, he gave his name as Henry Collins; witness's brother then drew up a receipt, which the prisoner signed, the document before the Court is the receipt mentioned; he (witness) had no doubt whatever as to the prisoner being the man who sold him the cattle and signed the receipt.

Ownership of the bull was incontrovertibly proven when Mr Robert Morehead's son, Boyd, the manager of Bowen Downs Station from October 1866 to June 1868, stated: 'that he knew the bull outside the

Court to be the property of the owners of that station, and that he never sold the animal to any person, or authorised any other person to sell him'.

James McPherson was then produced as a witness and entertained the courtroom, according to the *Sydney Morning Herald*, which announced that defence attorney Mr Paul's 'examination of this witness occasioned some amusement'.

Having testified that he had helped muster the stolen cattle and helped build the secret cattle yards on Bowen Downs, McPherson stated that, 'the white bull outside the court was amongst the cattle taken at that time' and that, 'ultimately the whole of the cattle were driven off by Readford, McKenzie, and Brooke, towards the southern colonies'.

McPherson also said that he was 'not a cattle-stealer, although he might have stolen some, though not to his knowledge'.

He next admitted that he was previously:

... charged with the offence of stealing these very cattle from Bowen Downs; that he was committed for trial and pleaded not guilty, and was then discharged on the ground of insanity. He then admitted that he was sent to Brisbane as a lunatic, escaped from the reception-house, was rearrested at Armidale, in New South Wales, and was brought up to this Court to give evidence against the prisoner, under a promise of a free pardon if he gave fair evidence at the trial.

Harry Readford's defence was almost non-existent. It consisted of a statement that he was now a married man with a young daughter and had suffered great distress since his arrest, along with bringing to the jury's notice the fact that James McPherson had recently escaped from a lunatic asylum. No witnesses were called by the defence— not one.

The case lasted a total of twelve hours; most of it consisted of hard evidence of Readford's guilt. The *Sydney Morning Herald* reported Justice Blakeney's summing up:

The Judge observed that he trusted that the jury would not be led away by the specious although clever address of the counsel for the prisoner; and that they would dismiss from their minds the hardships said to have been endured by the prisoner, no doubt placed before them with a view to making him a martyr. They should bear in mind the train of circumstances which had been proved respecting the prisoner.

He is found, at the period when this extensive robbery of cattle took place, on the Thomson, the locality from which the cattle were missed. He is shortly afterwards found in South Australia, more than 1000 miles from the scene of robbery, next in the City of Adelaide, under a false name. He is next found in the colony of New South Wales, where he is arrested.

It seemed cut and dried to Blakeney that Harry Readford had to be found guilty, even if McPherson's evidence was ignored, as the defence counsel had suggested:

He next would submit that, supposing that the jury accepted Mr Paul's recommendation, and gave no credence to M'Pherson, yet the case was plain against the prisoner.

The whole case was proven, in Blakeney's mind, by the evidence of the theft of the bull: The bull had been identified beyond all question as the property of Messrs. Morehead and Young; it is also identified as being the one sold by the prisoner to Mr Walke, and the evidence of that gentleman could leave no doubt on any reasonable mind that the prisoner at the bar and the person who sold that animal in South Australia were one and the same person.

The jury took an hour to consider the verdict and then jury foreman, James Nimmo, delivered it to a hushed and packed courtroom.

'Not guilty.'

There was a universal gasp of shock and surprise. Judge Blakeney sat still for several seconds and then asked the jury foreman to repeat the verdict.

'Not guilty.'

Again there were a few seconds of silence and then Judge Blakeney looked at the jury and said, 'Thank God, gentlemen, that verdict is yours, not mine.'

The Aftermath

The greatest 'crime' involved in the whole episode was not the reckless cattle stealing and remarkable journey. It was the mind-boggling effrontery with which jury foreman James Nimmo gave a straight-faced 'not guilty' decision which meant that an obviously guilty-as-sin Harry Readford walked free from the Roma Courthouse.

The press of the various colonies had a field day at the expense of the Queensland judicial system. The *Sydney Morning Herald* reporter reminded the readership of the cost of the trial: 'The costs of the witnesses in this case, I am informed, were over £600.' There were scathing reports ridiculing the verdict in the *Sydney Morning Herald* and *Melbourne Argus*, and the *Brisbane Courier* bemoaned the sad state of justice in the colony of Queensland.

The squattocracy of the Darling Downs were outraged, as were the more socially respectable citizens of Roma. One landowner wrote, 'As a magistrate of the district I beg to add my private testimony to the fact that the feeling in Roma is evidently very much against convictions for cattle stealing and the present jury list contains many names of men quite unfitted to return an honest verdict.'

Although James Nimmo, the jury foreman, had served on juries that had convicted other thieves, the rest of the twelve were suspected of accepting bribes and one had, it transpired, been found guilty of cattle stealing himself!

Judge Blakeney's explanation to the attorney-general commented that, while only the theft of the white bull could be proved beyond any reasonable doubt, he failed 'to see the possibility of obtaining a conviction for cattle stealing in any case before a Roma jury'.

The judge called for a reform of the *Queensland Jury Act*, which he said was defective in that it was framed in such a way that 'respectable people' were barred from jury duty.

The obvious miscarriage of justice caused a furore in Queensland and, in March 1873, was debated in parliament. The result was that the district court was removed from Roma for two years.

Harry Readford was arrested for stealing horses in the St George district twice in 1875, by which time the district court had returned to Roma. Once again he was found not guilty and walked free from Roma Courthouse.

He was arrested again in 1881, for horse stealing from the Hodgson brothers' Eton Vale Station near Cambooya, some 12 miles south of Toowoomba, on the Darling Downs. This region is known for having some of the best grazing country in Australia and the wealthy squattocracy who owned stations in this area were a different breed from those further west around Roma and St George. Also there were plenty more people in the large town of Toowoomba to choose for jury duty.

This time Harry's luck had run out. He was tried in Toowoomba and there he was at last found guilty of an offence and sentenced to eighteen months in Boggo Road Gaol in Brisbane. He served fifteen months and apparently the experience had a sobering effect on his character for, after his release, he led a relatively useful life.

Over the next twenty years, Harry helped explore the country between North Queensland and Darwin, established overland cattle trails throughout the Barkly Tableland, and served as overseer and manager on cattle stations in the area, doing much to establish a viable cattle industry for Queensland. He established the famous Brunette Downs cattle station by overlanding a mob of 3000 head to the area and became the manager of that property.

Old habits die hard, however, and it seems he took to fixing horse races at local meetings and, after a betting coup (more likely a scam) at Tennant Creek races, he had enough money to buy a small holding, which was later added to Brunette Downs. He then moved on to become manager of MacArthur River station, near Borroloola, in the Gulf Country of the Northern Territory.

As a result of the great cattle theft of 1870, several changes were made to the laws in Queensland regarding the empanelling of juries and uniform regulations regarding cattle brands and their registration were written into law. William Landsborough, the man who founded Bowen Downs and had fallen on hard times in the years between, was made an inspector in the new Brands Office.

The most obvious result of the crime was the opening up of crucial stock routes through the Channel Country. Harry Readford had also been the first overlander to realise that cattle fattened perfectly well on saltbush.

Captain Starlight

After the publication of the novel *Robbery Under Arms*, written by Thomas Alexander Browne under the pen name Rolf Boldrewood, Harry Readford became somewhat of a celebrity.

Browne was an unlucky grazier who had established sheep and cattle properties but was beaten by drought at several places, including Swan Hill and Narrandera, before taking a ten-year posting as goldfields commissioner at Gulgong in the 1870s. He was then police magistrate at Dubbo, Armidale and Albury in the 1880s.

As the famous author of *Robbery Under Arms,* published in 1889, Browne retired with his family to Melbourne and became a stalwart of the exclusive Melbourne Club, where he often sat and wrote. He was author of a dozen or so successful novels.

In *Robbery Under Arms* Browne used his experiences as a police magistrate to make a credible and realistic plot. He also used his knowledge of several real people to create the character of the dashing and romantic bushranger and cattle thief, 'Captain Starlight'. Browne always said the Captain Starlight character was made up from stories of different bushrangers of the era.

These included Frank Pearson, who actually used the name 'Captain Starlight' during his career as a bushranger in the late 1860s. Pearson was reputedly involved in daring deeds such as locking police in their own cells, riding his horse into a hotel bar in Barmera, South Australia, and having a shoot-out with police at a store in Enngonia in 1868, during which he mortally wounded one Constable McCabe. Sentenced to death he later had the sentence commuted to life and was released in 1884 having served fifteen years.

Another inspiration was Thomas Smith, known as 'Captain Midnight'. In May 1870, aged twenty, he was sentenced at Bathurst to five years imprisonment for cattle theft. Smith escaped in September 1872 and continued stealing cattle and horses under cover of darkness.

Browne said he also drew on episodes from the lives of bushrangers Ben Hall, Dan Morgan, Frank Gardiner and Johnny Gilbert, as well as Harry Readford. From Harry's life Browne used the cattle drive and the court scene, which occurs in a town called 'Nomah' in the novel.

For some reason Harry Readford, who lived for ten years after the novel appeared, was labelled 'The Real Captain Starlight' in the last decade of his life, although he never applied the name to himself or claimed to be a hero.

Throughout his life Harry was, in fact, an habitual criminal and incorrigible thief and liar. The type of person my mother would have said 'couldn't lay straight in bed'. After all, he was the son of a thief and the grandson of a highwayman and a brothel keeper.

Harry Readford was also a remarkable cattleman, drover, bushman, guide, explorer and, like some of his older brothers, an outback pioneer.

A small, roughly hewn stone pillar marks his grave on Brunette Downs Station and a metal plaque attached to the fence surrounding the grave reads:

Here lies

HARRY REDFORD

alias

CAPTAIN STARLIGHT

Perhaps a small fraction of the dashing Captain Starlight may be Harry Readford immortalised in fiction but, sadly, the real Harry Readford was mortal and he drowned in March 1901, attempting to swim the flooded Corella Creek while exploring from the Gulf Country into the remote Barkly Tableland, 190 miles inland from Brunette Downs.

He was 59 years old.

Captain Starlight would have made it across easily.

4

JOHN BOYLE O'REILLY—THE MOST DISTINGUISHED IRISHMAN IN AMERICA

'Take care of the rest of your Fenians, or Yankees will steal them away.'

The Fenians

In the 19th century when Australia was forming into colonies, there was one group of people who were synonymous with the word 'rascal'—the Irish. They were famous for their rebellions against Britain and her colonies all over the globe, including the far-flung outpost of Western Australia where a daring escape by Irish convicts proved the power of their brotherhood bond.

'Fenian' is a term given to members of the Irish Republican Brotherhood (IRB) and the Fenian Brotherhood in the United States. These organisations were formed after the failed Irish uprising against British rule in 1848. The IRB was formed in 1858 by James Stephens, who had led the ill-fated uprising and then fled to Paris; he returned to Ireland in 1856 to start the *Irish People* newspaper, which first rolled off the presses in 1863. His partner in planning the 1848 uprising was

John O'Mahony, who fled to the United States and started the Fenian Brotherhood there.

Basically, the Fenians believed that Ireland had a natural right to be free and that this could be achieved by violence and armed uprising.

The IRB grew in Ireland during the 1860s. Money was sent from the US and the movement had a cache of weapons and 50,000 willing recruits.

A planned uprising in 1865 was called off, while another insurrection in 1867 was poorly organised and ended in a series of skirmishes. In September 1865, the *Irish People* newspaper was shut down by the government and Stephens and others were arrested and sent to prison. Stephens subsequently escaped to the US.

Anyone suspected of being involved with the Brotherhood was arrested and some units of the British Army based in Ireland, believed to be sympathetic to the cause, were moved out of Ireland.

In 1866 the British government suspended *habeas corpus* in Ireland. This meant that Irish prisoners could be held without being brought to trial and hundreds of men were arrested. Civilians were treated as political prisoners, and men from the army were treated as traitors. The letter 'D', for deserter, was branded on their chests.

Many of these 'traitors' were transported by the British government to Australia.

The colony of Western Australia was the last to receive convicts, having asked for them to be sent when the settlement was struggling to survive due to lack of manpower in the late 1840s. The last convict ship to ever sail to Australia, the *Hougoumont*, carried 62 Irish political prisoners among the 280 convicts. Also on board, acting as an assistant warder of convicts, was Scotland Yard detective and British spy Thomas Rowe. Many of the Irish political prisoners were well educated; some were school teachers and some were journalists, like John Boyle O'Reilly.

O'Reilly the Rebel

John Boyle O'Reilly was born in 1844. He was the second son of William David O'Reilly, who was, for 35 years, the schoolmaster at the national school attached to the Netterville Institution for Widows and Orphans at Dowth Castle, Drogheda, County Meath. John's mother

Eliza O'Reilly (née Boyle) was the orphanage matron and was related to John Allen, a famous Irish rebel involved in the failed uprising of 1803.

Luckily, John's parents were both government employees and the family survived the potato famine that began the year after his birth. John was educated in his father's school until the age of eleven. After his older brother, William, fell ill with tuberculosis, John, who was only eleven years old, took over William's apprenticeship as a compositor with the local newspaper, the *Drogheda Argus*.

John's aunt Christina was married to a sea captain, James Watkinson. They lived at Preston, in Lancashire, and James convinced John to travel back with him to England to live with them, when he was fifteen. He joined the staff of the *Preston Guardian* as a compositor, learned shorthand and became a reporter. In June 1861 he enlisted in the 11th Lancashire Rifle Volunteers and received basic military training. He returned to Ireland in March 1863, and enlisted with the 10th Hussars in Dublin. He had secretly joined the Irish Republican Brotherhood and enlisted in the army as a recruiting agent for the underground organisation. Another rebel and journalist, John Devoy, had hatched the scheme to infiltrate the army and recruit Irish-born soldiers to the rebel cause.

In 1865 the British government moved against the Fenians, closed down the *Irish People* newspaper and uncovered the 'treason' plot that was spreading in the army regiments and threatened to lead to rebellion. Devoy had managed to recruit the majority of three Irish regiments to the IRB before the scheme was uncovered.

O'Reilly was arrested in 1866 for recruiting fellow soldiers to join the Fenians. The Hussars were mostly Englishmen but he had still managed to get more than 80 of them to sign a loyalty oath to join the rebellion. He was court-martialled and sentenced to be shot by firing squad, but the death sentence was commuted to twenty years transportation to Western Australia.

O'Reilly sailed from Portsmouth on 12 October 1867 on the *Hougoumont*. As well as the 280 convicts, there were 108 passengers on board, mostly 'pensioner guards' and their families.

The pensioner guards were retired British military personnel who served as gaolers on convict ships heading to Western Australia from 1850. They were paid for their work on the voyage and given land on arrival, on the proviso that they served twelve days a year, or whenever called upon, once they had settled in the colony. The scheme was designed to bring settlers to the struggling colony, as well as the convicts which it had requested from the British government long after it had ceased transportation to the other Australian colonies.

During the voyage, O'Reilly and another convict, John Sarsfield Casey, produced seven editions of a shipboard magazine called *The Wild Goose: A Collection of Ocean Waifs*, which contained stories, serious articles, advice, poems, songs and humour. There is a complete set of the seven editions in the State Library of New South Wales. The term 'Wild Geese' was given to exiles from Ireland and was originally given to the Irish Jacobite army that agreed to leave Ireland and never return, as part of the Treaty of Limerick of 1691. Most of them lived their lives in France and served in the French Army.

The *Hougoumont* arrived in Western Australia in January 1868 and O'Reilly was appointed as aide to the parish priest and later put in charge of Fremantle Prison's small lending library. Then he was sent south to join a convict work crew, building a road from Bunbury to Busselton. Being educated, he was given the position of clerk and messenger and allowed considerable freedom. He even developed a friendship with warder Henry Woodman and his family.

The local priest was an Irishman, Father Patrick McCabe. He and a settler named James McGuire arranged for O'Reilly to escape and be smuggled away on an American whaling ship, the *Vigilant*. O'Reilly escaped from the work crew on the night of 17 February 1869, met McGuire, and travelled in a small boat up the coast to a deserted beach where he spent the next two weeks hiding and being fed by a local Catholic family while a manhunt took place.

When he rowed out to meet the ship, however, the captain either reneged on the deal or did not see the small boat, so O'Reilly, who was now being hunted by police and Aboriginal trackers, again hid in the dunes while Father McCabe and McGuire made arrangements for another American whaler, the *Gazelle*, to take O'Reilly on board.

Meanwhile, another convict, Thomas Henderson (also known as 'Martin Bowman'), had worked out what was going on and decided to blackmail Father McCabe, McGuire and O'Reilly, forcing them to smuggle him onto the *Gazelle* as well, or be exposed. This time the plan succeeded and both men made it on board.

Father McCabe had arranged for the *Gazelle* to take O'Reilly to Java, but bad weather and whaling kept the vessel in the Indian Ocean. O'Reilly became friendly with the captain, David Gifford, and the third mate, Henry Hathaway. When the ship stopped at the British island of Rodrigues, in the Indian Ocean, 370 miles (590 kilometres) east of Mauritius, a magistrate and police came on board looking for an escaped convict they believed was on the *Gazelle*—and the crew handed over 'Martin Bowman'.

Realising that Bowman would spill the beans and O'Reilly was in danger of being captured at the next port of call, St Helena, also a British possession, Captain Gifford arranged to transfer him onto the American cargo ship *Sapphire*. The transfer was carried out at sea and the *Sapphire* took O'Reilly to the port of Liverpool, in England. There he was secretly transferred to another American ship, the *Bombay*, and, on 23 November 1869, O'Reilly landed at Philadelphia and was warmly greeted by members of the Irish community there.

The time spent whaling on the *Gazelle* had quite an impact on John Boyle O'Reilly's life. He made friendships on board the vessel that would be of great importance to later events. He even had his life saved by Henry Hathaway, after nearly drowning after an accident during a whale chase.

O'Reilly settled in Boston, began writing for the Catholic weekly newspaper, *The Pilot*, and set about planning the escape of his fellow Fenians who were still in Fremantle Prison.

The *Catalpa* Escape

British policy had softened by 1869, and most of the Irish civilian political prisoners at Fremantle had been freed. This reprieve did not apply, however, to military prisoners.

In 1875, John Devoy, who had orchestrated the recruitment of Irish soldiers in British Army units back in the 1860s, been imprisoned and then exiled to the US, came to O'Reilly with a plan to storm Fremantle Prison and rescue the remaining Fenians by force.

One of the Fremantle exiles, James Wilson, had written a desperate plea to Devoy, in June 1874: 'This is a voice from the tomb . . . we have been nearly nine years in this living tomb since our first arrest . . . it is impossible for mind or body to withstand the continual strain that is upon them. One or the other must give way.'

O'Reilly suggested a less drastic plan, similar to the one that had worked for him. Instead of relying on the goodwill and honesty of ships' captains, however, his idea was to raise funds and *buy* a ship for the sole purpose of rescuing the prisoners. That way they could choose a captain who could be trusted—and the ship could easily pose as a legitimate vessel. A whaling ship was the obvious choice.

Devoy and O'Reilly formed a committee to plan the whole venture and set about raising funds with the help of the American Irish Republican Brotherhood, *Clan na Gael*. There was no shortage of donations, which was just as well, as the plan required a large amount of money and manpower.

Devoy knew a shipping agent, John Richardson, who helped them purchase a three-masted barque, the whaling ship *Catalpa*, at a cost of $5200. The ship was bought in the name of one of the committee members, James Reynolds. Richardson also put the committee in touch with his son-in-law, George Smith Anthony, a whaling captain sympathetic to the Irish cause.

The *Catalpa* was set up as an operational whaler and merchant ship and departed from New Bedford, near Boston, at the end of April 1875. Only Captain Anthony and one of the committee—Dennis Duggan, who was on board as the ship's carpenter—knew the real purpose of the voyage.

The ship headed for the Atlantic whaling grounds and then sailed on to the Azores to unload 200 barrels of whale oil. Most of the crew left the ship there and Anthony recruited a new crew and headed for Australia. A savage storm delayed the ship and severely damaged her foremast, but she arrived off Bunbury, south of Perth, on 27 March 1876.

The misfortune Captain Anthony experienced in having the ship damaged in the storm was offset by a stroke of amazing good luck. The *Catalpa* met the trader *Ocean Beauty* in the Indian Ocean and her captain happened to be the former master of the *Hougoumont*, which had carried the Fenians into captivity at Fremantle. Captain Anthony told him they were headed for the whaling grounds off Western

Australia and he happily provided them with navigation charts of the Western Australian coastline.

Meanwhile, in late 1875, two Fenian spies, John Breslin and Thomas Desmond, had travelled to Perth from the US to organise the local side of the rescue operation. Desmond set himself up as a carriage builder in Perth, while Breslin posed as a wealthy American business-man, James Collins, in Fremantle.

The plot worked so well that Breslin, now known as 'Mr Collins', was able to befriend the assistant superintendent of Fremantle Prison, Irishman Joseph Doonan, and be taken on a tour of the establishment. He managed to make contact with six of the twelve remaining Fenian convicts, either personally or through local Irish residents, and explain the plot to them.

Of the other six Fenians, one was in a high-security section of the prison, two were assigned to work out of the district and could not be contacted, and another two had tickets of leave and could not be found either. The twelfth was considered unreliable and a security risk.

When the *Catalpa* berthed at Bunbury on 29 March 1876, Breslin met the ship and he and Captain Anthony took passage to Fremantle on the coastal steamer *Georgette*, which would have a further role to play in the drama. They met Desmond and other sympathisers and made their final plans.

The escape was originally planned for 6 April, but the arrival of several British warships in Fremantle Harbour led to a postponement until 17 April, Easter Monday, when the British ships had departed and the Royal Perth Yacht Club Regatta would be a good distrac-tion. Thomas Desmond was to provide transport and arrange for sympathisers to cut the telegraph lines connecting the colony to the rest of Australia and the world. The *Catalpa* would be waiting offshore from Rockingham Bay, south of Perth, in international waters between Rottnest and Garden islands, having sent a whaleboat ashore to collect the escaped prisoners.

The plan almost came unstuck yet again when Captain Anthony went to send the crucial coded telegram at Bunbury and discovered the telegraph office was closed for Good Friday. Somehow, he was able to locate the telegraph operator's house and get the message sent to Fremantle telegraph office, which was open for business.

Before sunrise on Monday, James Wilson, Robert Cranston and Michael Harrington, who were working outside the prison, slipped away and made their rendezvous with a carriage. Around the same time, James Donagh, Thomas Hassett and Martin Hogan escaped from the prison's minimum-security section and were picked up by another carriage. This had all been arranged by Thomas Desmond.

The two carriages raced to Rockingham, where the whaleboat was waiting.

As they shoved off from the beach, a local timber-cutter named Bell, who had spoken to the men and thought their activities on the beach very suspicious, mounted up and headed for Perth. He arrived at 1 p.m. and informed the police that he had seen an American whaleboat, manned by sailors armed with rifles, take nine men, some in prison clothes, from the beach at Rockingham.

The police only had a small vessel, a single-masted cutter, which put to sea as soon as possible. Within several hours they had also commandeered, by authority of the colonial governor, Sir William Robinson, the schooner-rigged coastal steamer *Georgette*, which headed out to sea with a hastily assembled group of volunteer militiamen from the quaintly named 'Enrolled Pensioner Force'.

Meanwhile, out at sea, the whaleboat came within sight of the *Catalpa* just on sunset, but a sudden fierce squall hit and they lost sight of her and spent the night battling the storm. Next morning the group in the whaleboat relocated the *Catalpa*, but saw the *Georgette* heading towards it and stayed away, lying down in the whaleboat to avoid being seen.

Superintendent Stone of the Water Police, aboard the *Georgette*, hailed the *Catalpa* and requested to be allowed on board to search for escaped convicts. The request was denied, although the fugitives were not yet on board, and the *Georgette* followed the *Catalpa* for several hours until it was forced to return to Fremantle to refuel. As the *Georgette* disappeared towards Fremantle, the police cutter appeared on the horizon and the men in the whaleboat rowed hard and boarded the *Catalpa* as the police approached. The cutter also lingered within sight of the *Catalpa* for some time before heading back to shore.

The governor was now determined to recapture the convicts and had the *Georgette* fitted with a 12-pound howitzer field gun overnight.

Both the police cutter and the *Georgette* set out to find the *Catalpa* the following day, Tuesday 18 April. On board the *Georgette* were the Enrolled Pensioner militia, all eager and armed, along with the howitzer.

The *Catalpa* was spotted on the horizon that afternoon, but it wasn't until 8 a.m. the following day that the *Georgette* overhauled the whaler and fired shots across her stern and bow. Captain Anthony hove-to and parlayed with Superintendent Stone, who demanded to be allowed to board the *Catalpa*. Captain Anthony refused the request.

Superintendent Stone had right on his side, according to British law, and the *Georgette* also had might on her side—a howitzer, and 30 or more eager armed militiamen. Captain Anthony bluffed it out with style. He reminded Stone that they were in international waters; then he pointed to the 'Stars and Stripes' at the masthead and challenged Stone to create a diplomatic incident.

The taunt was intended to remind Stone that several years earlier, the US had sued Britain over a maritime breach of neutrality in the American Civil War. The case had been settled in Geneva on 14 September 1872, with the British government paying £3 million in damages to the US in compensation for building the Confederate commerce-raider *Alabama*, which sank much Union shipping.

Firing on, or attempting to board the *Catalpa* without permission, Anthony declared, would be nothing short of an act of war against the USA. The *Catalpa* then made sail and proceeded westward.

The *Georgette* followed until it was low on fuel, and then turned back to Fremantle as the *Catalpa* disappeared into the vastness of the Indian Ocean.

The complex and daring rescue plan, two years in the making, had worked.

With the successful cutting of the telegraph wires by Thomas Desmond's two recruits, John Durham and Denis McCarthy, it was June before news of the bold escape reached London. Meanwhile, the *Catalpa* managed to avoid British ships and make its way back to the US. Captain Anthony even chased a few whales on the way home, but the *Catalpa* proved to be better at catching escaped convicts than whales—no whales were caught.

John Boyle O'Reilly finally learned of the escape in early June and publicised the event to the world, provoking anger in Britain, jubilation in Ireland and the US, and mixed sentiments in the various colonies of Australia. The *Catalpa* arrived in New York Harbor on 19 August 1876 and was given to Captain Anthony, with shares going to his two chief officers, as a reward for their part in the adventure.

In the colony of Western Australia there was embarrassment and paranoia about a Fenian invasion. Suspicions arose about Irishman Joseph Doonan, the assistant superintendent who had shown Breslin through Fremantle Prison. Poor Doonan unsuccessfully attempted suicide and then resigned. The prison controller and several other officials were sacked, and all tickets-of-leave for Fenians were revoked. Nevertheless, all the Fenians were freed by 1878.

In 2005 a large monument was erected at Rockingham Bay to commemorate the *Catalpa* rescue; it is a statue of six wild geese in flight.

Publisher, Poet and Patriot

Meanwhile, John Boyle O'Reilly had established himself in Boston as a reporter for *The Pilot*. He quickly made a name as an erudite and even-handed journalist, writing intelligently about the failed Fenian raids into Canada in 1870 and riots in New York between Catholic and Protestant Irish immigrants in 1870 and 1871. In 1870 he wrote, in a *Pilot* editorial:

> Why must we carry wherever we go those accursed and contemptible island feuds? Shall we never be shamed into the knowledge of the brazen imprudence of allowing our national hatreds to disturb the peace and safety of respectable citizens of this country?

By 1876 he had married Mary Murphy, a daughter of Irish immigrants, and had become part-owner and editor-in-chief of *The Pilot*, which he took from being a minor Catholic news weekly, to being the second most important newspaper in Massachusetts, behind the famous *Boston Globe*.

He was regarded as the chief spokesman for Irish immigrants in the US, as well as a popular poet, novelist, public speaker, and champion of labour reform and civil rights. He was president of both the literary Papyrus Club and the Boston Press Club and became a close friend of jurist and legal scholar Oliver Wendell Holmes, who would later become Associate Justice of the Supreme Court of the United States. O'Reilly was also a friend to US President Grover Cleveland and Cardinal Gibbons, the head of the Catholic Church in America.

O'Reilly often suffered from insomnia and exhaustion from over-work and died suddenly in 1890, probably from an accidental overdose of his wife's sleeping medicine. His sudden death at the relatively young age of 55 led to a worldwide outpouring of grief and tributes. A civic ceremony of remembrance, held in the New York Metropolitan Opera House, was filled to overflowing and *Harper's Weekly* magazine called him: 'easily the most distinguished Irishman in America . . . one of the country's foremost poets, one of its most influential journalists, an orator of unusual power . . . endowed with such a gift of friendship as few men are blessed with'.

Grover Cleveland, the only president in American history to serve two non-consecutive terms in office, was between his two terms as president when O'Reilly died in 1890. He wrote: 'I have heard with sincere regret that John Boyle O'Reilly is dead. I regarded him as a strong and able man, entirely devoted to any cause he espoused, unselfish in his activity, true and warm in his friendship, and patriotic in his enthusiasm'.

John Boyle O'Reilly left behind his wife and four daughters and was buried in Holyhood Cemetery, Brookline, Norfolk County, Massa-chusetts. There are many monuments to his memory around the world, including one at his birthplace, Dowth, in Ireland and another at Leschenault Peninsula Conservation Park, Australind, Western Australia, where he hid for weeks in the sand dunes waiting to be rescued.

Oliver Wendell Holmes gave him this farewell tribute:

We have been proud of him as an adopted citizen, feeling always that his native land could ill spare so noble a son. His poems show what he might have been had he devoted himself to letters. His higher claim is that he was a true and courageous lover of his country and of his fellow men.

'Farewell' by John Boyle O'Reilly
Farewell! Oh how hard and how sad 'tis to speak
That last word of parting—forever to break

The fond ties and affection that cling round the heart
From home and from friends and from country to part.
'Though it grieves to remember, 'tis vain to regret.
The sad word must be spoken, and memory's spell
Now steals o'er me sadly. Farewell! Oh farewell!

Farewell to thy green hills, thy valleys and plains,
My poor blighted country! In exile and chains
Are the sons doomed to linger. Of God who didst bring
Thy children to Zion from Egypt's proud king,
We implore Thy great mercy! Oh stretch forth Thy hand,
And guide back her sons to their poor blighted land.

Never more thy fair face am I destined to see;
E'en the savage loves home, but 'tis crime to love thee.
God bless thee, dear Erin, my loved one, my own,
Oh! how hard 'tis these tendrils to break that have grown
Round my heart. But 'tis over, and memory's spell
Now steals o'er me sadly. Farewell! Oh, Farewell!

Footnote:

George Smith Anthony's ability to sail the high seas was rather restricted as he was a wanted man by the British, but he did undertake some whaling expeditions before the *Catalpa* was sold. She finished her life as a coal barge in the port of modern-day Belize—which was, ironically, then known as British Honduras.

This was a sad end for the ship whose name became a rallying call for the Irish cause, embarrassing the great naval power of Britain to such an extent that a song about the incident was banned in the colony of Western Australia.

Here is part of the song:

A noble whale ship and commander,
Called the *Catalpa*, they say,
Sailed out to Western Australia
And took six bold Fenians away.
The *Georgette*, all armed with bold warriors,

Went out the brave Yank to arrest,
But she hoisted the star-spangled banner
Saying, 'Now you'll not board me, I guess.'
They landed them safe in Americay
And there they were able to cry,
'Hoist up the green flag and the shamrock,
Hurrah, for Old Ireland we'll die!'

Chorus:
Come all you screw-warders and gaolers
Remember Perth Regatta Day.
Take care of the rest of your Fenians,
Or Yankees will steal them away.

5

JACK DE GARIS—THE PRINCE OF BALLYHOO

'. . . a kindly and good man.'

The Mildura Scheme

The story of Jack De Garis begins with the establishment of the Mildura Irrigation Colony, which was the genesis of the town of Mildura and the district of Sunraysia. It was a 'failure' that eventually succeeded.

In the early 1880s, the Victorian government began examining the idea of irrigation colonies on the Murray River. In 1884 Victorian Solicitor-General and Minister of Public Works Alfred Deakin led a delegation to the United States and met the Canadian brothers George, William and Charles Chaffey, who had successfully established three irrigation communities in California.

Engineer and inventor George Chaffey, the oldest of the brothers, visited Victoria in 1886 and, as a result, the Chaffeys decided the 'Mildura Run' was suitable for an irrigation colony. They sold their Californian interests at a loss in order to invest in this new venture.

The 'Mildura' sheep run was in liquidation. It had a river frontage of 40 miles (64 kilometres) and reached 20 miles (32 kilometres) back with river flats that were subject to frequent flooding. One squatter called it 'the most wretched and hopeless of all the Mallee regions'.

After over a year of negotiations, rejections and delays—during which the Chaffeys negotiated with the South Australian government to secure 250,000 acres (100,000 hectares) at Bookmark Plains, which went on to become the town of Renmark—'The Chaffey Brothers Agreement' was passed by the Victorian colonial government in May 1887.

The Chaffeys took possession of 250,000 acres in August and 50,000 acres were subdivided into cleared 10-acre blocks between irrigation channels; these were offered to potential participants at £5 per acre. A further 200,000 acres were offered at £1 per acre—plus water rights.

In the early years, favourable conditions meant Mildura could rely mostly on river transport, with freight and passengers going downstream for a railway connection to Adelaide, and upstream to Swan Hill and Echuca, for connections to Melbourne.

There were, however, many problems. Pests damaged crops and there were continual problems with the irrigation. When water rates of 15 shillings per acre were introduced in 1891, settlers who had suffered three years of failed crops could not afford to pay and the Chaffeys shut down the pumps. Labourers went on strike for better wages and conditions and were sacked. Many of the men who worked for 'blockers' were never paid.

In December 1895, the company went into liquidation and the Victorian government held a royal commission into its affairs in 1896. Block holders were given tenure over their land with a five-year period to meet their dues and pay their debts. The Mildura Irrigation Trust was created and six commissioners, elected by the growers, ran the trust.

In spite of the problems, failures and upsets, the community struggled on. The allotments that were owned or managed by the Chaffeys were generally successful, proving it was possible to make the scheme work, at least in part. Things improved greatly with the arrival of the railway in 1903.

The Chaffeys' enterprise at Renmark, which had been managed by younger brother Charles while George and William were at Mildura, also failed financially, although the town developed into a successful farming settlement.

George and Charles Chaffey returned to the US after the enquiry, but George's son Ben stayed in Australia and became a successful businessman and noted racehorse owner. William remained in Mildura as a fruit grower until his death in 1926. He was elected president of the Mildura Shire Council in 1903 and mayor in 1920.

Reverend Elisha De Garis

The idea of irrigating the inland attracted its fair share of visionaries and one was Reverend Elisha De Garis, who had migrated with his family as a child from Guernsey, one of the Channel Islands.

Educated at St Peters College, Adelaide, he studied architecture in Melbourne and was ordained as a Methodist minister in 1882, just after his marriage to Elizabeth Buncle, daughter of a successful pioneering agricultural goods manufacturer.

Elisha was so saddened at the effect of drought on his parishioners in farming areas that he became a strong supporter of irrigation. Through his regular articles for the Melbourne *Daily Telegraph*, Elisha lobbied Alfred Deakin to legislate for irrigation communities to be set up—and to visit California and meet the Chaffeys. He became co-founder and chairman of the Central Irrigation League, and created and edited a newspaper called the *Australian Irrigationist*.

In 1888, having resigned from the ministry (although he remained a lay preacher), Elisha joined George Chaffey on yet another proposed irrigation scheme at Werribee, just on the western edge of Melbourne.

Despite complaints from local farmers that there was not adequate water to support the scheme, it went ahead. The local paper was onside, commenting that 'once the Californian expert gets this water on to the land the little irrigation colony at Werribee will burst forth into Eden-like verdure and Paradisial bloom'. George Chaffey promised to build a weir, a pumping station and a farming college.

None of the Chaffeys' schemes succeeded but their enthusiasm was contagious and Mildura and Renmark did eventually become successful 'small farm' districts.

Werribee failed completely. The weir was never built, nor was the college. Only a tenth of the land was ever taken up or became productive. The promised water wasn't delivered, yabbies destroyed the channels and the Depression of the 1890s meant there was no investment capital for schemes like Werribee. The project was wound up in 1896.

In 1891, after three years of trying to manage the Werribee project, Elisha De Garis had moved his family to Mildura, where he worked hard to establish market gardens and build up various businesses in real estate and the growing, processing and marketing of dried fruit.

Elisha's eldest son, Clement John (known as 'Jack' to his family and later 'C.J.' to his friends and business associates), was seven years old when his parents moved to Mildura. Two years later his father requested, and was granted, a special dispensation for Jack to quit school and work in the family business.

Jack De Garis grew up surrounded by the dreams and schemes of the Chaffey brothers and his father's evangelical visions of an irrigated paradise in rural Victoria.

Always enthusiastic and charming, young Jack was given the task of collecting rents for the family real estate business. Historian Travis Sellers tells us:

> In the challenging role of rent collector he was successful as he was unconventional and people soon endeared to his irresistible boyish qualities found it difficult to refuse payment; he also developed a knack of solving troublesome problems.

A Visionary Son

Part of the legend of Jack De Garis is that he saved money from his wages to pay his own school fees and, at fourteen, returned to school from 1899 to 1901, as a boarder at Wesley College in Melbourne where, despite standing only 4 feet 11 inches, he excelled at football.

Other versions of the story say that Jack was urged to attend school again by his father.

Talking about Jack's time at Wesley, Travis Sellers says:

> After a difficult induction he rose from last to dux of his class, became somewhat of a legend with his affectionate smile, and excelled in sports notably cricket and football ('easily the smallest boy who

had ever played in Public School football') where his lack of height (4 feet 11 inches) and weight (6 stone 11 pounds) confounded both his coaches and the opposition.

In 1902 Jack returned to Mildura to run some of the family businesses—he was seventeen years old. Another part of the Jack De Garis legend is that he tripled the profits of the family business within two years of his return.

When his father left town in 1908, to live in Melbourne, Jack was 22 and already married to Rene Vera Corbould. He took over the De Garis enterprises and was soon adding his own ventures to the ones his father had set up.

In 1910 he borrowed £15,000 and built a huge state-of-the-art packing shed to process local fruit. In 1912 he raised £22,000 capital in a venture to take over a failed irrigation colony of 10,000 acres known as Pyap Village Estate in the South Australian Riverland near Loxton, on the Murray River.

The South Australian government had set up Pyap as a communal irrigation colony much earlier, in 1894. Like most other such schemes, it failed. The village struggled on under poor management and was eventually abandoned in 1903. A Melbourne syndicate had attempted to revive the project and failed, going bankrupt in the process.

Jack De Garis raised the capital to buy the village and, using overhead irrigation systems, he turned it into a successful and profitable company town and moved 80 families into the stone cottages.

Jack set up a school, a community library and a recreation centre, and created his own form of 'child endowment' in the form of a 'baby bonus' for settlers—similar to the one set up by the federal government in 1912.

Thirty years after it was initially established, Pyap was a success! The stage was set for Jack De Garis's finest hour.

In 1919 a sudden shortage of cargo space in ships carrying freight to British ports meant that, for four months, dried fruit from Mildura could not reach its primary market. With financial disaster looming for the growers, the Australian Dried Fruits Association (ADFA) called on the one man who they knew could find a solution. That man was their local hero—the district's precocious 'wunderkind'—Mildura's most successful businessman for whom nothing seemed impossible—Jack De Garis.

Jack had a plan that would create a strong local market for their surplus product. He was hired as 'publicity officer' on a salary of £1500 and the ADFA raised a fighting fund with which he was to go into battle—Jack's budget of £20,000 was a huge and unprecedented amount of money for advertising and publicity at the time in Australia. The amount was calculated as one-eighth of a penny per each £1 of turnover from sales of ADFA products.

The promotional stunts, schemes and methods used by Jack De Garis to promote the produce of the Mildura district were certainly imaginative, quirky and way ahead of their time in the Australia of 1919.

His first move in promoting the district was to run a competition to find a name for the local products, an adjective that best described the dried fruits produced in the district.

The winning suggestion was 'Sun-Raysed'.

Jack loved the term and soon hit upon the idea of changing the adjective to a noun to describe the district itself—Sunraysia. In 1920, he bought three regional newspapers, merged them and cemented the term permanently in the nation's consciousness by cleverly calling the paper, which employed more than 90 staff, the *Sunraysia Daily*.

It seemed there was nothing the diminutive dynamo could not do, he oozed charm and confidence. His 'can do' attitude and seemingly endless store of promotional and marketing ideas and schemes were surely almost too grand and expansive to be contained in his small human frame. The ADFA and most of the locals loved him

Jack's projects, gimmicks and awareness campaigns included a series of free recipe books, children's books and information leaflets distributed to schools, cartoons in national and local newspapers, and the establishment of a Sunraysia Cafe in Melbourne, staffed entirely by young girls from the district, all of whom had been, according to Jack's publicity, 'raised on Sunraysia raisins'.

The opening of the cafe was announced by sky-writing, hot air balloons and box kites were flown over all major cities of Australia displaying Sunraysia advertisements, and a competition was launched with a prize of £1000 for whoever could most accurately calculate the number of Sunraysia sultanas in a one-pound packet.

The Mildura Post Office had to take on extra staff as the entries flooded in. People all around Australia bought multiple packets and counted the contents in order to find an average until finally the £1000 went to a woman in Adelaide.

Jack made short films about Mildura and the dried fruits industry, which were played in cinemas across the country before the feature films. There were also 'serialised' guessing competitions and word games that ran in newspapers Australia-wide. This clever technique of getting readers to guess one word a day meant the competitions stretched out over several days or weeks.

A factory was set up in Mildura that turned surplus local fruit into 'Good Little Normie' fruit bars, and cartoon strips on wrappers and in the newspapers followed the adventures of 'Good Little Normie'. Needless to say Little Normie was 'good' because he was consuming healthy Australian-grown dried fruit, instead of other unhealthy confectionary.

A song entitled 'The Sunraysed Waltz', with lyrics by Jack, was heavily promoted and became quite popular. The years 1919 and 1920 saw a huge growth in home entertainment such as pianos, pianolas, sheet music and gramophones. This was partly due to dance hall and theatre closures and fear of crowds during the Spanish influenza pandemic that killed more people than World War I.

The pandemic, however, merely provided Jack De Garis with another bright idea. Posters appeared all over Australia with the slogan:

I fear no more the dreaded 'flu,
For 'Sun-raysed' fruits will pull me through.
(Repeat these lines when steadily eating 'Sun-raysed' fruits and your dread of the influenza will disappear.)

In a few short years between the end of World War I and 1923, super-salesman Jack became an author, songwriter, dramatist, theatre producer, film-maker and aviation pioneer!

When his marriage ended in divorce in 1923, however, he suffered from a drastic change in fortunes.

In 1915 he had written a four-act military drama, *Ambition Run Mad*, which had featured as a serial in the *Mildura Pioneer* newspaper. When he became a newspaper owner, he decided to also be a publisher.

In 1919 Jack organised a fairytale-writing competition as part of the Sunraysia promotional campaign. He then used some of the entries to compile and edit the *Sunraysed Children's Fairy Story Book*. He next launched a competition to find the great Australian novel. This resulted in an avalanche of more than 400 manuscripts arriving at the now quite busy Mildura Post Office.

Between 1920 and 1925, C.J. De Garis Publishing produced several dozen books, novels and verse collections. Jack paid composer Reginald Stoneham to create the melody for his lyrics of 'The Sunraysed Waltz' and the two men were soon collaborating on more songs and a 'musical comedy mystery' stage production—with the odd name of *F.F.F.* It was staged in Adelaide, Melbourne and Perth by the famous entrepreneur Hugh McIntosh and flopped. Theatre manager Claude Kingston, who worked for McIntosh, referred to Jack as 'the Prince of Ballyhoo'.

Jack liked to be referred to as 'an aviation pioneer' but the fact of the matter was that he never actually flew a plane anywhere. He did, however, own several planes that set distance records around Australia while Jack was a passenger in them, but they were flown by professional pilots employed by Jack.

The Victories of Failure
In late 1920 Jack had purchased, sight unseen, a 47,325-acre property at Kendenup, Western Australia. It had previously been a large sheep run owned by the pioneering Hassell family, and then the site of Western Australia's first goldmine, which had failed to produce gold commercially.

Jack flew over to inspect the property and subsequently planned a new settlement that included a factory and dehydrating plant, civic centre, public parks, recreation facilities, 80 cottages, a school and a church.

Jack was in debt for more than £50,000 over the venture, but raised £25,000 by selling the various real estate components and businesses that made up the Pyap Village Estate.

Kendenup was seriously under-capitalised and soon Jack was in financial trouble. As usual his reaction was to spend more money and do more publicity. He left for the US and an advertisement appeared in the *New York Times* on 13 August 1922, attempting to get Americans to invest in Kendenup. It concluded: 'Australia is a great country, and we want as many real Americans as we can get to come and settle there permanently.'

It was obvious that Jack was getting desperate and things were beginning to unravel. Many of the statements in the article were exaggerations at best and lies at worst. Some of them were simply things Jack wanted to believe: he was beginning to make the common error of the over-enthusiastic entrepreneur—he was believing his own publicity.

The inflow of American capital never eventuated, and although £250,000 was promised by one American bank, it never arrived. An Australian bank loaned £30,000 but it was too little too late—the end was inevitable. By December 1923 there were only 30 settlers left at Kendenup, the project had collapsed, and Jack lost everything and was accused of fraud.

A royal commission in Western Australia in 1923 finally exonerated him of any serious crime but his reputation and credibility were in tatters, and his mental stability was deteriorating.

The *Sunraysia Daily* went into receivership and was later sold to a consortium of three politicians, one of whom was the future prime minister Dr Earle Page.

Jack began investing in oil exploration and speculating in land development and real estate in Melbourne with borrowed money. His energy and work ethic were as strong as ever but had taken on a manic dimension. He also somehow managed to find time to write a book, based on his own life and appropriately titled *The Victories of Failure*.

Jack had married his secretary, Violet Austin, one month after his divorce became final. They had a daughter (Jack also had three daughters from his first marriage) and lived at Hawthorn but also rented a house at Mornington, on the southeast shore of Port Phillip Bay, where Jack was involved in drilling for oil.

Towards the end of 1925 Jack's brinkmanship finally failed him. Another land development scheme ran into serious financial trouble, a rather large cheque bounced and a warrant was issued for his arrest.

The Prince of Ballyhoo responded by writing 70 suicide notes and faking his own death by 'drowning' in Port Phillip Bay.

On 5 January 1925 Jack's car was found at Mentone Beach. It contained his clothes and directions to his wife about where to find the suicide notes, but no trace of a body could be found.

The tributes poured in.

When police failed to locate a body, and none was washed up in the bay, some people began to speculate about Jack's ability to creatively handle troublesome situations. Then the whole affair took a sudden change of direction.

The Melbourne *Argus* was first with the news, on 9 January:

MR. C.J. DE GARIS.

REMARKABLE DEVELOPMENT.

WARRANT FOR ARREST ISSUED.

The mystery of the whereabouts of Mr. C.J. De Garis was in no way simplified yesterday, but late in the afternoon events took a remarkable turn. On the information of Frank Northcott, coachbuilder, of 583 Elizabeth street, North Melbourne, Senior-detective Davey, who, with Detective McKerral, is conducting the investigations, issued a warrant for the arrest of C.J. De Garis on a charge of having, on December 22, 1924, obtained £300 by means of a valueless cheque . . .

Although Sergeant Tennant and those who are helping him to patrol the beach and shallows at Mentone in search of a body have practically abandoned hope of finding any trace of the missing man.

The lack of a *corpus delicti* wasn't surprising, for Jack was actually hiding out at various country pubs disguised as an American called 'Mr Leslie' or 'Mr Young'. He then headed to Sydney using the same aliases and no doubt took great pleasure in reading his own obituaries and tributes.

One of the problems associated with being a well-known missing 4-foot 11-inch man is that no amount of padding, wigs and dark glasses will disguise you for long. Jack was spotted but managed to evade the police and book a passage on a ship to Auckland.

This wire service news item appeared in most national papers, including the *Singleton Argus*, on 15 January 1926:

DE GARIS ARRESTED

DENIES HIS IDENTITY

As the *Maheno* was off the heads at Auckland on Tuesday morning, the vessel was boarded by uniformed and plain clothes policemen, and an officer of the vessel pointed out the man whose arrest was desired . . .

Before the steamer reached the wharf he was taken off in the police launch and then conveyed to the police station in a motor car . . . On the second day out, after advice had been received from the Sydney police that De Garis was believed to be on board, a steward found in his cabin a pair of pyjamas which bore the name of De Garis.

According to the De Garis legend, Jack sold a block of land to the detective on the return trip to Australia, but I can find no written evidence of that.

Jack's friends put pressure on Northcott to withdraw the charges and eventually that occurred. The amounts owing were huge by 1926 standards: £250,000 was owed to landowners who had sold land to the company; shareholders were owed £150,000; the bank £10,000; and normal business creditors, £6000.

Jack had a small victory in May, when a charge of fraud and false representation brought against him in Western Australia by a settler at Kendenup was found not proven in the Supreme Court.

He threw himself into selling real estate and took out leases on land around Mornington and Hastings where he hoped to find oil. He made valiant attempts to pay back money but the task was herculean. He did on several occasions walk into creditors' offices and hand over cash to people to whom he was in debt. On one occasion he handed £1000 to an old friend to whom he owed much more. The friend later remarked that he felt so sorry for Jack that he would have been satisfied with sixpence.

With personal debts totalling more than £40,000 and little chance of ever paying back more than a few token amounts, Jack left the family home in Hawthorn on the morning of 17 August 1926 and made his way to the house at Mornington.

Before leaving he called a plumber named Scott and made an appointment for him to call at the Mornington address at noon. When the plumber arrived, he found a note pinned to the door that told him instructions were under the doormat. There he found a sheet of paper that read:

> Sorry to drag you into this, but you are a plumber, and a plumber is needed. There may be danger to anyone else. The gas must be cut off outside the house. The kitchen is closed and full of gas, and you will find me there. The gas must be cut off and the door opened carefully before entering. No matches must be used. You had better ring the police, also my wife at Haw. 2839. Poor girl, she has no idea . . . Please see parcels under mat reach destination.
> C.J. De Garis.

The Melbourne *Argus* reported the subsequent events:

> After reading the message Mr. Scott summoned Constable R.F. Mason and a doctor, and together they entered the house. De Garis was found lying face downwards on a table which had been drawn close to a gas stove in the kitchen, which was full of gas. His mouth was over a gas jet, which had been turned on, and the doors and windows of the room had been closed so that no gas should escape.
>
> . . . It is understood that the body will be brought to Melbourne today, and the burial will take place in Melbourne.

The *Argus* then gave a long obituary in which it praised Jack as 'one of the most remarkable Australian business men of recent years'. Jack, the *Argus* said, was known as 'journalist, aviator, publicist, land salesman, company promoter, playwright, publisher, and in many other activities' whose 'enterprise and imagination several times carried him beyond the safe limits of finance, with the result that many of his ventures ended in considerable financial loss to himself and investors'.

Jack De Garis was aged 41 years and 9 months at his death.

In that short time he had achieved more than most of us could dream of in ten lifetimes. The name 'Sunraysia' is still used and recognised Australia-wide today.

In his eulogy at Jack's funeral, Reverend Charles Tregear said:

> Today we are laying to rest the body of no ordinary man. I will alter that, and say he was a most extraordinary man, a man with brains, wonderful vision, courage and business ability. But behind it all he was a kindly and good man.

PART TWO
THE ROGUES

'Rogue: A dishonest person . . . a cheat.'

Webster's New International Dictionary, 1929 edition

'Has he not a rogue's face? A hanging look to me . . . without the benefit o' the clergy.'

William Congreve, *Love for Love*, 1695, Act 2 Scene 7

6

JAMES HARDY VAUX—
SERIAL OFFENDER

'*. . . your roguery will very soon be found out.*'

Outcasts of Fortune

In September 1815, in the 'Coal River' convict settlement in the penal
colony of New South Wales, James Hardy Vaux found time to sit and
write the story of his life.

In the preface to this at times remarkably honest autobiography,
Vaux refers to himself as 'an outcast of Fortune'. Indeed, Coal River,
which became Newcastle, was the last resort. At that time in our history
it was the worst place to which those convicts who were habitual
offenders and recidivists could be sent. There they would labour at
digging and hauling coal until they either behaved well enough to
return to the 'normal' convict colony at Sydney Cove, or died in the
mines. It was the last step before hanging.

It can be argued that many of the 162,000 or more convicts transported to the colonies on the Australian continent were 'outcasts of
fortune', or 'victims of circumstance'. More generally, it is true to say
that many were born into an unfair society blighted by poverty, the

class system, the disenfranchisement of the landless population caused by the enclosure acts, the lack of any real social justice or equality in Britain and, later, the horrors of the Industrial Revolution.

Faced with the problem of massive unemployment after the Seven Years' War ended in 1763, the British parliament decided to steal the 'common' from the 'commoners' by passing the *1773 Enclosure Act*. This meant that 'common' land was now 'enclosed' and taken by those owning the rest of the land. When the unemployed masses could no longer grow crops and graze animals to feed themselves, there was a predictable increase in the crime rate. Veterans returning from the war, having helped their nation win a crushing victory and gain vast overseas territories, were denied any reward for their efforts. Unless they had twenty years military service and had been seriously wounded, they could be hanged if they resorted to begging.

During the period in British politics known as the 'Whig Oligarchy' (1714–1783), the parliament's answer to these social problems was to enact laws that became known as the 'Black Acts' or 'The Bloody Code'. There were 222 crimes for which the penalty was death by hanging. Due to the slightly more humane attitudes of many magistrates, judges and juries, however, more than 70 per cent of those sentenced to death had their sentences commuted to imprisonment or 'transportation'.

There are many examples of convicts for whom transportation was ultimately a godsend. Many 'victims of circumstance', born into a poverty trap of illiteracy and hopelessness—with no chance of an education, land ownership, self-determination or advancement in life—broke the law, came to Australia as convicts, served their time, took their chances and succeeded. James Squire, a gypsy from the most despised and lowest class of the British population, became a constable, successful businessman and Sydney's most respected citizen and philanthropist. His funeral in 1821 was the largest in Sydney's history to that point and his grandson would become a premier of New South Wales.

There are thousands of similar stories. People born into the worst imaginable circumstances who became convicted criminals, were transported, served their time then built decent lives and triumphed through hard work and resourcefulness when given a chance.

James Hardy Vaux, however, was *not* one of them.

In fact, quite the opposite was true in his case.

A Privileged Childhood

Although Vaux's writings contain a constant theme of blaming bad luck, external circumstances and the actions of others for the unhappy situations in which he constantly found himself—mostly in prison as the result of a seemingly endless series of crimes—his background was by no means one of struggle against poverty.

Judged by the social circumstances of the time, we might even say he had a comfortable, almost privileged, childhood and far more opportunities to succeed than any of the other 161,999 convicts transported to the Australian colonies.

Vaux's great-great-grandmother, Dorothy Hartopp, was the daughter of the baronet Sir Thomas Hartopp.

Sitting in the Coal River penal colony, quill in hand, in 1816, attempting to remember his family's genealogy, Vaux thought the ancestral home of the Hartopps was either 'Ragby, or Ragley Castle'. He was close, but no cigar. It was actually Rotherby Castle, in Leicestershire.

He remembered, quite accurately, that Dorothy married into a very well-to-do county family named Yonge and, two generations later, Vaux's grandmother, also Dorothy Yonge, married James Lowe, a very respectable court attorney of the King's Bench, with 'an extensive private practice'. James Lowe was also the deputy warden in charge of all the legal affairs of the Fleet Prison in London, which was a permanent and profitable tenure.

Vaux's mother, Sophia, was the only child of the marriage. According to her son she was 'brought up with the most affectionate tenderness, and well educated'. In 1781, however, when she was 27, Sophia married a 29-year-old named Hardy Vaux, against her parents' wishes.

Hardy Vaux was described by his son as being from a 'family much less respectable' than his mother's family, being employed 'in no higher situation than that of butler and house-steward to Mr. Sumner, a member of parliament, whose estate was situated near Guilford, in Surrey'.

Now, being the butler and house steward of an estate was a respectable position of trust, requiring literacy, numeracy, good manners and the ability to manage staff. A desirable position for a lower-middle-class man with basic education.

James Hardy Vaux, however, certainly appears to have felt, along with his maternal grandparents, that his mother married 'beneath herself' when she chose a man from 'below stairs' as her partner in life. His attitude towards his parents will be more clearly understood when I tell you that, when he was three years old, young James left his parents' home permanently and went to live with his mother's parents. In his narrative, detailing his life until 1815, he refers to this couple as his 'parents' due to the fact that, 'it is from them only I ever experienced parental affection'.

So, the subject of this story, far from being one of the impoverished, dispossessed victims of the British class system, was actually a beneficiary of all the advantages and privileges that system provided. His maternal grandparents had retired in very comfortable circumstances and he lived from the age of three until he was nine under the guidance of his grandfather, James Lowe, in Shifnal, Shropshire:

> In this neat little town, surrounded by the relatives of my grandmother, and many friends of his own, my grandfather having served his clerkship in the county, this worthy and truly virtuous couple enjoyed, for several years, uninterrupted happiness, their only care being centred in the education and indulgence of their grandson, of whom they every day became more extravagantly fond.

Apparently he was a voracious reader as a child on quite specific topics, two of which were maritime history and horseracing. These two subjects would each play a part in his later life, not necessarily to his advantage.

At age nine James and his grandparents moved, briefly, to London and joined his parents and his two younger sisters, who were now living in Holborn, where his father had gone into retail business as a hosier and hatter. The reunion was short but happy and his parents were, at that time, living comfortably enough to place their two surviving daughters (two other daughters and another son having died in infancy) in a boarding school in Berkshire.

James, however, tells us he was sent, at his grandfather's expense, to:

> . . . a respectable boarding-school at Stockwell, in Surrey . . . during which time I acquired a tolerable knowledge of the classics, and became as perfect in the French language as I could do without residing in

France. It was a custom at this school to allow of no English being spoken, except in the hours devoted to instruction, by which means our progress in French was much facilitated. The scholars had free access to a well-selected library, by which means I gratified my passion for reading, which increased with my years.

While young James spent three years at boarding school, the family situation deteriorated in London. His father's business failed and his maternal grandparents moved into their own accommodation due to family arguments. James was taken from school and once more lived with his maternal grandparents, who he says could not bear to be separated from their indulged grandson.

Hardy Vaux next set up in a new business as a chandler and candle-maker. This business also failed, as did several subsequent ventures, and the family were 'considerably impoverished' according to James's narrative, although they apparently managed to 'keep up appearances' until his father died in 1805, some fifteen years after James had permanently left their household to go to boarding school in Surrey.

In the meantime James continued to live with his grandparents, briefly in London and then in Cambridgeshire where they took a furnished house and he attended a local school run by a clergyman friend of his grandfather. By the time James was fourteen, they had returned to Shifnal in Shropshire where our hero became the inseparable companion of the son of a very wealthy family named Moultrie.

The two lads were such good friends that, when the time came for young master Moultrie to leave for Oxford, the Moultrie family made the incredibly generous offer of sending James with him—and paying his university fees for three years. James's family were thrilled and excited. His grandparents and several maiden aunts, from whom he was due to inherit considerable sums, encouraged him to accept the offer.

James, however, had been indulged to such a degree that he could not bear the thought of being separated from his grandparents and, against all their advice, pleaded with them to refuse the offer. It was the first of many poor decisions he would make, and probably the worst decision of his entire life.

The refusal caused social discomfort to his family and probably cost him the inheritance he would otherwise have received from several aunts, who were mortified at the thought of having to live with the embarrassment of their family's rejection of such a magnanimous gesture.

He also declined his grandfather's offer to set him up in the legal profession. Instead he was offered a place as apprentice with the Liverpool firm of Swan and Parker, who were linen-drapers with an international export business. Again, this was a generous offer, made this time by a relative who had paid a considerable sum for his own son to have the position. When poor health prevented the cousin from taking the apprenticeship, the position was given to James.

His grandparents paid to have him outfitted as a young gentleman should be and, aged fourteen and free from any sense of responsibility or respect for his family's generosity and kindness, James took the coach to Liverpool.

There he tells us he made a very good impression—for about one month!

> For the first month of my probation, I behaved extremely well, and by my quickness and assiduity, gained the good opinion of my employers, who wrote of me in the most favourable terms.

Decline and Fall

What followed, however, was four months of complete irresponsibility and a rapid decline into debauchery. An older apprentice took James to pubs and brothels and he contracted venereal disease. He started lying about being late making deliveries and became addicted to gambling at the local cock fights, soon lost all his allowance money, and started stealing the petty cash and falsifying accounts. As he lived on the premises it became easy to steal money and goods, and he was soon doing it daily.

After several confrontations with Mr Parker, a letter was sent to James's grandfather stating that his 'conduct rendered me unfit to be received into their house; therefore, desiring I might be recalled without delay'.

Although Mr Parker noted that James's 'smartness and activity are really wonderful' and his cleverness in thieving meant that 'it was not in his power to charge me with any direct criminality', Mr Parker concluded that the 'continued excesses of my conduct, left but too much room for unfavourable conjectures'. Swan and Parker was a large and successful company and obviously wished to remain so; employees like James Hardy Vaux were a liability they did not need.

Back home, with the family's substantial apprenticeship investment (some £100) now forfeited, James claims he 'could not help blushing at the consciousness of my own unworthiness; but the blind partiality of my dear parents, induced them to believe me less culpable than I really was; and to listen readily to any thing I had to offer in palliation of my errors'.

Having developed a taste for the freedom of living away from the family, he now persuaded his grandfather to arrange his return to London: 'My grandfather had of course many acquaintances in London, of his own profession, to several of whom he furnished me with letters of recommendation.'

Funded by his doting grandfather, who again called in family favours to get James a position in a cousin's legal office as a copying clerk, in the hope that he would advance in the legal profession by application to the law (and nepotism), our young gentleman was now back in London. There was no reunion with his parents, however, as James tells us he was:

> ... determined on becoming master of my own conduct; and accordingly took a neat private lodging, and regulated my mode of life conformably to the state of my finances. I breakfasted at home, dined at a tavern or genteel eating-house, and in the evening took my tea and read the papers at a coffee-house: after which I sometimes passed the night in reading at home, but most commonly went to one of the theatres at half-price, where I gratified my violent passion for the drama, which at once improved my understanding and amused my mind.

Of course, this was a lifestyle well beyond the scope of his meagre pay as a legal clerk and the situation worsened when some of the habits gained in his five months in Liverpool reappeared:

> About three months after my arrival in town, I began to grow less regular in my manner of life; my expenses increased; and I became

negligent of the office hours. I had contracted an intimacy with several young persons of both sexes, which unavoidably engaged me in a course of expensive dissipation, to which my means were inadequate. Though I occasionally derived small supplies from my grandfather, yet as he had no idea of the extent of my expenditure.

Commitment to a legal career lasted three months. Realising he could earn more in a job with less future prospects, James took a position as a clerk in a warehouse. Encouraged by his dissolute friends, he moved lodgings owing back rent, bought expensive clothes on credit and never paid for them. As he was still under 21, he knew he could not be arrested for non-payment of a debt, so he always made sure he had a bill for the clothing and other goods he purchased on credit.

After almost a year he returned to a position of legal clerk and then, realising his skill in copying and writing legal documents was well above average, he quit the firm he was with and started freelancing as a copy writer for various legal firms, buying his own paper and working in his own time.

It was around this time that James Hardy Vaux first encountered the 'flash language' that was to fascinate him and lead to his most notable achievement some twenty years later, in 1819, when *A Vocabulary of the Flash Language,* that he had compiled in 1812, was published in London. After long hours copy writing documents, he tells us:

> I frequently resorted to the Blue Lion, in Gray's-Inn-Lane, a house noted for selling fine ale, and crowded every night with a motley assemblage of visiters [sic], among whom were many thieves, sharpers and other desperate characters, with their doxies. I was introduced to this house (from which hundreds of young persons may date their ruin) by a fellow-clerk, who appeared to have a personal intimacy with most of these obnoxious persons; however, though I listened eagerly to their conversation, (part of which was then unintelligible to me), and fancied them people of uncommon spirit, I was not yet sufficiently depraved to cultivate their acquaintance; but sat with a pipe in my mouth, enveloped in smoke, ruminating like a philosopher on the various characters who tread the great stage of life.

It was in the Blue Lion that he met the character who was to be his partner in crime in the next phase of his 'career'. His new companion was of a similar age and had served on a British warship, spent all his wages, and intended to head for Portsmouth to seek work. The two set out on foot but made it no further than Kingston-on-Thames, which was then a village some 12 miles (20 kilometres) southwest of London, before they ran out of money and lodged in an inn with insufficient funds to pay the tab.

Finding themselves in the invidious position of either abscond-ing without their possessions, which were held by the landlady of the inn, or finding money quickly, James made use of a scam known as the 'letter racket'. He wrote a beautiful letter, with forged references, explaining that he was trying to get to Portsmouth to join the navy and serve his nation. He then took the letter to various retail businesses and offices, appealing to their patriotism and soliciting either money or testimonials supporting the venture.

This proved to be hugely profitable until a local magistrate heard about the activity and became suspicious. James was arrested but talked the magistrate around to discharging him on the condition he returned to London and never again appeared in Kingston. He was even given half a crown to return to London.

Finding that his travelling companion had departed for Ports-mouth by coach, James returned to London for one night and then immediately took the coach back to Kingston and repeated the scam in other parts of the town. He then proceeded to Portsmouth, visiting every town on the way to work the scam.

James found work as a clerk in Portsmouth but was dismissed for mocking a fellow employee, a Dutchman, and spilling hot tea on him. He returned to London, working the letter scam a few times on the way, and arrived back some £10 richer, two months after he had departed.

Back in London, in 1798, he survived by various scams such as buying clothes on credit and selling them without ever paying for them and 'bilking', moving lodgings secretly after getting well in arrears with his rent.

One night in a tavern he met a kindly stranger, a ship's warrant officer, who took a liking to him and offered to introduce him to a captain in order to procure a recommendation that he be accepted into the navy as a midshipman. James jumped at the opportunity and immediately wrote to his grandfather, again imploring him to call in favours and recommend him to the captain.

Having turned on the charm and been accepted by the captain, James again sought help from his long-suffering grandfather, who paid out a substantial amount of money to have his grandson outfitted as a midshipman, with a sea chest, uniforms, clothing, books, mess money and all the accoutrements required for the position.

Midshipman James Hardy Vaux served on the frigate HMS *Astræa* on the North Sea Station for a year and a half. He did not enjoy the hard work on deck and his fellow midshipmen mocked him for reading books, but he excelled at navigation and soon avoided the hard work by becoming the captain's clerk. This position gave him a comfortable private cabin, an easy life with no duties above deck, and every hope of being promoted to a naval ship's purser in the future.

In the spring of 1799 the *Astræa* was docked in London, awaiting a cargo of coins to be taken to Hamburg. Vaux was on leave and made his way to the theatre where he picked up a young prostitute with whom he became infatuated. Having spent his entire leave in her apartment, he returned to his ship for several days and then went ashore on day leave to meet her and never returned, deserting both the ship, the position of trust he had gained, and all his worldly possessions, including those purchased for him at great expense by his grandfather.

Left with a few clothes he had taken ashore, a family gold watch and £20, James attempted to set up home with his lover. She, apparently, was the daughter of a respectable tradesman. She had eloped from boarding school at the age of fifteen with an officer in the dragoons who had seduced her and subsequently abandoned her six months later.

Having purchased a suit of plain clothes and spent money on theatres and other amusements, Vaux was forced to pawn his watch. One night, having attended the opera and sent the maid for a plate of refreshments from the local tavern, he was no doubt pondering how to pay the rent when, at 2 a.m.:

> ... the door of our apartment was burst rudely open, and three persons entered, at the sight of whom, my unfortunate girl fainted in my

arms . . . One of the three persons, a respectable looking elderly gentleman . . . I soon conjectured to be her unhappy father . . . The other two immediately called the landlady of the house, by whose assistance they recovered the poor girl from her swoon; which having accomplished, they instantly hurried her down stairs, the old gentleman darting an angry look at me, and left me so stupified [sic] with grief and surprise, that I had not power to follow . . . It appeared that the young lady had been seen with me the preceding night at the opera-house, by a friend of her family, who knowing of her elopement, had officiously followed us home, and then immediately given information to her father, who applying instantly to Sir William Ford, the Bow-Street magistrate, that gentleman had detached . . . two of his principal officers . . . to assist him in the recovery of his lost child . . . The woman added that on learning from her, the life his daughter had led for some months prior to her acquaintance with me, and that I was not her original seducer, he had declined the idea of apprehending me.

Having lost his ship, his naval career, his belongings and his lover, Vaux was now also homeless and:

. . . the wearing apparel of my late companion being claimed by the landlady for some arrears of rent . . . I engaged a small apartment for myself in a more centrical situation; and, to supply my immediate wants, deposited one article after another at the pawnbroker's, till I had no longer any thing left to deposit.

A Life of Crime
Vaux briefly joined a small gang of billiard players who made a living scamming innocent gentlemen by gambling on games in the local billiard parlour, having duped the victims into thinking they were merely average players seeking some sport.

When the supply of gullible gentlemen became scarce, Vaux answered an ad for a clerk, placed by a London legal firm on behalf of a client. He made his usual good impression on the advertiser, who informed him that the position, at £1 per week, was at Bury St Edmunds, in Suffolk, some 80 miles from London.

The legal gentleman who conducted the interview was completely taken in by Vaux's lies and appearance and wrote a letter of introduction to his client, a wealthy landowner called Mr Dalton, who was also a partner in the legal firm. Vaux, of course, steamed open the seal and read the letter, which said, in part: 'I have every reason to believe him an expert clerk, and do not doubt but he will prove an acquisition.'

In his memoir, Vaux admits that he had no other intention than to rob his new employer of as much as he could, in as short a time as possible. He travelled to Bury and began working as Mr Dalton's clerk. Using his new employer's good name, he purchased clothing and a gold watch on credit and told his landlady that he would pay her at the end of the quarter. He then intercepted some of Mr Dalton's letters containing money and also a trunk of valuable clothing being sent to be altered. He left his own trunk, filled with bricks, in his room, and absconded to London owing two months' rent.

Having pulled off a very successful series of thefts and frauds in Bury St Edmunds, Vaux lived happily for several months in London and then took a job as a legal clerk in an office not far from the one in which he had been interviewed for the position with Mr Dalton.

One day his employer, a Mr Preston, called him into his office and locked the door. Vaux then noticed that Mr Dalton was standing in the room, the swindler having been recognised by a clerk from the nearby office.

Mr Dalton's chief objective was the return of the items and the stolen money. Vaux would possibly have been hanged for crimes including fraud, interfering with the mail, and stealing money, valuable clothing and a watch, but he was never charged. A respectable member of the legal profession named Presland, a relative of Vaux's grandfather who was also an acquaintance of Mr Dalton, was contacted and, with the collusion of the constable involved, he guaranteed the restitution of the losses to Mr Dalton.

Vaux was kept in custody at the constable's house for three days while pawn shops all over London were visited, items redeemed and restitution made for losses. In spite of the callousness and deviousness of his crimes, he managed to appear contrite and once again, his family bore the financial burden of his misdemeanours. Having recompensed Mr Dalton, paid off the constable and salvaged a little of the family's reputation, Mr Presland gave Vaux £5 and advised him to leave London and seek an honest living in the country. By this time, however, seeking an honest living was never an option for James Hardy Vaux.

At least he felt sufficient shame and guilt to prevent himself from returning to Shifnal to face his grandparents. In fact, of course, he never left London and, in spite of crocodile tears and false promises to Presland, had never intended to.

Vaux's next crime showed an amazing amount of ingenuity.

He saw an ad for a clerk and shop assistant to help with a retailer of fancy dress, who also rented masquerade clothing. The position involved living on the premises and the owner, therefore, required excellent recent references of diligence and trustworthiness. As a deserter from the king's navy, and knowing he could not possibly get a decent reference from acquaintances in the legal profession, Vaux needed to use his initiative and criminal cunning. He presented himself, as usual, as a charming and educated young man and told his prospective employer that his previous position was with a retailer named Drake in Portsmouth, who had recently retired.

Vaux assured the shop owner that 'Mr Drake' would provide a reference and gave him a non-existent address in Portsmouth. He then sought out the guard on the Portsmouth mail coach, bought him a few drinks and told him his name was Drake and he thought there would be undelivered mail for him at Portsmouth Post Office.

In exchange for a small amount of money the guard obliged, picked up the letter and brought it back to London. Vaux was then able to answer the letter, as 'Mr Drake', in a slightly different style of hand-writing and highly recommend himself for the position, for which he was naturally accepted. He then cunningly gave the letter to the man who drove the Portsmouth coach, rather than the guard, to post, to avoid either of the men suspecting foul play.

The position required Vaux to live on the premises and 'to attend the shop, to make out bills of parcels, keep a set of books, and occasion-ally to carry out light packages'. This provided plenty of opportunity to systematically steal lace, ribbons, garments and cash. Vaux also delivered goods, collected the money and issued receipts, then told his employer the deliveries were given on credit.

After ten weeks he 'did a runner' and pawned everything he'd stolen.

Two weeks later, he rather stupidly returned to buy some hand-kerchiefs from a pawn shop where he had previously pawned a rather expensive lady's riding outfit he'd failed to deliver. There he was rather suspiciously delayed by the shop owner until he became worried and attempted to leave the shop, only to find his recent employer and a constable blocking the doorway. Vaux was arrested and taken to the Covent Garden watch house.

Next morning he appeared before the magistrate at Bow Street and was almost freed. His recent employer having foolishly returned 'exhibit A' (the riding outfit) to the rightful owner the previous day, there was no evidence. Just as the case was being dismissed, however, Vaux's ex-employer announced he was having the prisoner charged with fraud, and he was re-arrested and spent a week in Coldbath Fields Prison. At the hearing he was committed to trial and spent ten weeks in Clerkenwell Prison awaiting the quarter sessions. There he learned a lot from fellow inmates and was fascinated by the use of the 'flash language'—the criminal slang that was a kind of code to enable them to talk freely among themselves.

The first good news in quite a while came when Vaux was told he was being tried at the Middlesex quarter sessions and not at the Old Bailey. This meant his crime was considered a 'misdemeanour'. At the trial he pleaded his innocence and made a good enough impression to cast doubt into the minds of the jury and the magistrate, who summed up as follows:

> Gentlemen, I am sorry, for the ends of public justice, that there is but too much reason in what the prisoner has advanced; but he is a very young man, and I sincerely hope that if he this day escapes the correc-tion of the law, he will never again transgress in a similar way . . . the case is not made out, and you must acquit the prisoner.

Vaux was disgusted to learn that the 'friend' with whom he had left his belongings had disappeared. It's amusing to read a callous pro-fessional thief's outrage at having been robbed: 'I had the mortification to find that this supposed friend had treacherously converted all my little property to his own use.'

During his time awaiting trial he had met many professional criminals and soon after he was released he bumped into one named Bromley on the street who took him to a pub called The Swan where petty crimes were planned. There were a few familiar faces there and Vaux and his new friend, Bromley, soon began working together and with others at shoplifting, pickpocketing, smash and grab, and robbing delivery men. They also travelled outside London running the 'letter racket'.

Needless to say their luck ran out, and on 17 August 1800 they were caught stealing a silk handkerchief. Bromley took it from a man's pocket in a crowd and handed it to Vaux. The act was seen by a constable and his brother, and Vaux and Bromley were arrested. In his memoir Vaux insists he never took the handkerchief but was moving away when arrested. Whatever the truth, the two had been observed acting suspiciously together in the crowd, a handkerchief was stolen—and they had committed many other similar crimes.

Vaux now appealed to his father and mother for help. They apparently believed he was innocent and gave character references and stood by him through the trial. The transcript of which he remembered by heart, it ended:

> Bromley called four witnesses, and Vaux two witnesses, who gave them a good character.
> Bromley's defence.—'I picked the handkerchief up in the crowd.'
> Vaux's defence.—'I am innocent.'
> Of stealing the handkerchief value eleven pence. Bromley, Guilty (age 20) Vaux, Guilty (age 18)

The handkerchief was actually valued by the court at 2 shillings. Vaux reminds us that the jury, were, however, allowed to place a value on goods stolen, 'in order to reduce the offence to a simple felony, by finding the value of the property under one shilling'. The difference of one penny meant that the death penalty did not apply.

The two convicted felons were hopeful that, at sentencing, they would receive only a fine but, a few days later, all those found guilty at the sessions of non-capital crimes were assembled in the courtroom and sentenced, *en masse,* to seven years transportation to New South Wales.

Interestingly, his father managed to pay (or bribe) the gaoler to keep James at Newgate Prison and not on the hulks, until he was embarked on the Thames on the convict transport *Minorca*. The same gaoler arranged for a certain amount of luggage and possessions, provided by his family, to be taken on board. Vaux might have been better off on the hulks. In Newgate he was close to death from 'gaol fever', a contagious disease caused by overcrowding, for three weeks.

Now, dear readers, I wonder how many of you are shocked at this point in the narrative to realise that all the crimes, betrayals of trust, frauds, thefts, lies, desertions, immoral indulgences and selfish acts that have been listed in this account of the life of James Hardy Vaux so far occurred before his nineteenth birthday. It has also, perhaps, occurred to you that James Hardy Vaux hasn't even reached New South Wales, and the worst is yet to come!

Transported

On the voyage to New South Wales, Vaux managed to become the captain's clerk. This entailed writing neat copies of the ship's log and captain's journal, and led to the captain agreeing to recommend him for a clerk's position in the colony and deliver a letter, written by Vaux extolling his own virtues and talents, to the governor's office. Vaux was well qualified for this position, it was one he had held on the HMS *Astræa*.

The story of our hero's first spell as a convict in New South Wales is all about his ever-changing relationship with the governor of the day, Governor King. Reading between the lines of his sometimes honest, but often self-indulgent, autobiography, I get a sense of Philip Gidley King's character and the workings of his mind in regard to Vaux.

The *Minorca* arrived in Sydney Cove on 15 December 1801. The letter of self-recommendation having been forwarded to the commissary, Vaux was called before a panel including the governor for a brief interview on his arrival. It is clear from Vaux's own account of the meeting that King saw through the pretended innocence and exaggerated good manners, but also recognised that Vaux might have some valuable skills that were scarce in a penal settlement that desperately needed an efficient bureaucracy.

Having made it plain to Vaux that he did not believe his claims, the governor gave a clear indication that the prisoner was to be given an opportunity to prove himself. Vaux's recollection of the conversation's conclusion is:

Governor: 'Well, Mr. Vaux, I shall send you to a place, where your roguery will very soon be found out.'

Vaux: 'I hope not, your Excellency; I trust you will have . . .'

Governor. (Interrupting): 'Well, I hope so too, Mr. Vaux; I hope so too, I hope so too, Sir; but mind—I only give you a caution; take care of yourself.'

Governor King then scribbled out a note, handed it to Vaux and dismissed him. As he handed the indecipherable note to his guard, Vaux recalls that he clearly saw the initials 'PGK' and realised that the governor's signature was rather easy to forge.

With that, Vaux was assigned as clerk to a storekeeper in the Hawkesbury district. The governor made regular enquiries about his behaviour and received excellent reports. There were requests for him to be sent to Sydney to work in the governor's office, but the store-keeper, Mr Baker, pleaded to keep him employed, saying that he could not manage without him.

Vaux lasted three years with Mr Baker, before being called upon to join the clerical staff at Government House. That was the longest period of time, since he was fourteen, that the now 22-year-old James Hardy Vaux had managed to live without resorting to criminal activity. It wasn't to last much longer.

It was a turbulent time in the colony. Governor King had to deal with the rebellious New South Wales Corps and the convict uprising at Castle Hill in March 1804, while trying to make use of emancipated ex-convicts, and those still serving their time, to help fill necessary positions in an expanding settlement. There was a real need for educated men who could read and write well and add up. Documents needed to be copied by hand, in neat handwriting—carbon paper was not invented until 1806 and was not in common use for decades after that time.

So, after three years of a quiet, apparently crime-free life, Vaux was recalled to Sydney, given a small brick house to live in, supplied with food and clothing from the government stores, and put to work in a position of trust in the governor's office.

The result was inevitable.

Given the opportunity, once again, to live beyond his means through debt and bad company, Vaux was soon looking for ways to steal and cheat. He began forging King's initials on forms to requisition stores and, with the help of several other clerks, removing the goods from the stores and selling them around Sydney Town.

Within months the crimes were detected and all the evidence pointed to James Hardy Vaux as the chief perpetrator. The governor gave him several chances to confess, to no avail. Then, exasperated at Vaux's denials and refusal to cooperate, the governor called Dr John Harris to escort Vaux to the prison to be flogged until he explained the fraud. It was necessary for a surgeon to attend floggings due to the brutal physical nature of the punishment and the possibility of arteries being opened.

Faced with the immediate threat of extreme physical punishment, Vaux tells us:

As there was already sufficient and incontrovertible proof of guilt against me. I, therefore, determined to acknowledge my errors, and submit my fate to the Governor's pleasure. Of this intention I acquainted Mr. Harris, who immediately stayed the proceedings about to take place, and supplying me with pen and paper, desired me to write my declaration, which he would himself convey to the Governor. In the letter I hastily composed, I informed his Excellency, that feelings of remorse and regret for my ill conduct, rather than a fear of punishment, had induced me to confess to him that I was guilty of the charge brought against me on the present occasion, and with shame I acknowledged having repeatedly transgressed in a similar manner, in order to defray the expenses of the unbecoming course of life I had imprudently fallen into.

Next day he was placed in leg irons and appointed to the 'road gang':

I was in consequence set to work at mending the public-roads, &c. &c., and as I had never before used a heavier tool than a goose-quill, I found this penance to bear hard upon me, and repented me of the evil which had brought me to this woeful condition.

After only one month on the road gang, Vaux was one of a group of convicts sent to do farm labouring at the Castle Hill settlement. Again he was forced into manual labour but managed to cajole the superintendent to allow him a regular Friday evening pass to Parramatta, 8 miles away. From there he walked the 16 miles to Sydney, where he regularly stayed illegally until he walked back to Castle Hill on Sunday evenings. Naturally he was eventually caught and given 50 lashes.

Vaux served as a farm labourer for ten months until the clerk to the superintendent of the Castle Hill settlement, an ex-convict who had served out his ticket of leave, returned to Britain. There was no one else as qualified as Vaux, and he was given the position.

Not only did he manage to stay out of trouble for the rest of his time in the colony, he made rapid advancement, by being seconded to help the Parramatta magistrate, the Reverend Samuel Marsden, and conduct the 'muster' (census) of the Parramatta settlement, as part of the first muster of the British population in the colony of New South Wales.

The census showed the total population of the colony to be a mere 7126 in 1806, eighteen years after its foundation. There were 1400 adult females and only 360 were officially married. Of the 1800 'children' (aged under nineteen), half were illegitimate.

With a population that small, it is easy to see how Vaux found it difficult to avoid detection while practising the sort of frauds and criminal schemes that had worked so well for him in Britain. London had a population of more than one million in 1801.

Vaux impressed Marsden with his knowledge of legal matters and his undoubted skill as a clerk, to such an extent that he became the clerk of the magistrates court at Parramatta and was given a very comfortable dwelling.

At the same time Governor King was preparing to leave the colony, having resigned due to poor health and having failed to prevent the officers of the New South Wales Corps from running the colony as they pleased. As the governor lived mostly at Parramatta, Vaux became King's secretary as well as the clerk of the magistrate's court and spent time sorting out King's papers both before and after William Bligh arrived in the colony to take over as governor in August 1806.

As both King and Marsden were returning to Britain on HMS *Buffalo*, Vaux was invited to travel with them and perform the duties of clerk as well as tutoring their children. The *Buffalo* was due to sail in August 1806 but King suffered a nervous breakdown and his health was too poor to travel, so the departure was delayed until February 1807.

As King held the rank of 'post captain' he was technically in command of the *Buffalo*, while Captain Houston ran the vessel. So Vaux's duties included keeping the ship's log and King's journal and acting as the ex-governor's secretary, writing letters etc. He also did some clerical work for Marsden as well as tutoring King's twelve-year-old daughter and two of Marsden's children.

Home Again

The voyage of HMS *Buffalo* could have been the making of James Hardy Vaux as a respectable, trustworthy and valued gentleman in a lucrative 'white-collar' profession. Predictably, however, it concluded with him sinking to a position about as low as it was possible to go on the vessel.

The voyage was long. Delayed by filthy weather attempting to round Cape Horn, a prolonged stay for repairs in Brazil, and the fact that the ship was leaking badly and required constant pumping day and night to stay afloat, the *Buffalo* finally reached Portsmouth nine months later in November 1807.

Much had changed during the voyage.

The *Buffalo* had not been properly provisioned and the food was poor quality. Mrs King restricted Vaux's alcohol rations and the relationship between Vaux and the ex-governor deteriorated as the voyage went on. After the lengthy stay in Rio for repairs, the ship began leaking again almost immediately they put to sea on 12 August 1807.

Sometime in September Vaux was ordered to take his turn at the pumps. He objected and appealed to King, as captain of the vessel, to excuse him from this extra duty, pointing out that, his sentence having now expired, he was a free man and considered himself a passenger on the ship as he was now neither an indentured convict nor a crew member, and was still engaged each day in clerical duties.

At this point King, according to Vaux: 'worked himself up into a violent rage, the consequence of which was (as usual with him,) a torrent of abuse; and as I knew by experience that it was in vain to attempt pacifying him, when in this mood, I quitted the cabin'.

The result of this was that King gave Vaux the choice of signing on as a crew member or being impressed into the service, and so Vaux joined the ship's crew, which meant not being free to leave the ship, or the navy, when they reached England. When Vaux asked again to be exempted from pumping, King gave him the choice of continuing to work as his clerk and man the pumps at night when required, or 'to do my duty before the mast entirely, and keep my watch in common with the rest of the crew'. Vaux then replied that:

> I should prefer doing my duty on deck. To this he assenting, I made my bow and withdrew. Here ended my functions in the clerical capacity with Captain King. From this day I never wrote a line for him; and thus was I rewarded for my past services.

Vaux accuses his employer of betrayal, reminding us that King had written a general pardon for him before leaving Sydney which included the words, 'taking into consideration the good conduct of James Vaux, and to enable him to serve as my clerk on board His Majesty's ship *Buffalo*'.

What Vaux neglects to mention is that he was given a free passage home and obviously exasperated his master with behaviour that Philip Gidley King (a sick man recovering from a nervous breakdown who was to die within ten months of reaching England) considered to be insolent and ungrateful.

When the ship reached Portsmouth, Vaux waited a few days and had his possessions taken ashore by a woman who visited the ships selling food and doing washing for the sailors who didn't have shore leave. He then deserted, picked up his belongings and took the coach to London. He visited his mother and sisters and learned that his father and grandmother had died during his absence.

Fearing that he would be sought by impress officers as a deserter, he travelled to Shropshire and spent two weeks with his grandfather, who had been reduced to living on the charity of the family who had offered to educate his grandson a decade earlier. Much of his grandparents' wealth had been spent trying to establish their errant grandson in an honest position and buying him out of trouble.

A letter from his mother reported no visits from naval men or constables and he made his way back to London, where his grandfather had again arranged a position for him, as a clerk in the Crown Offices. He broke his journey at Birmingham and enjoyed three days spending the money his grandfather had given him in bars and brothels, before taking the coach to London.

At a coach stop outside London, he stole a parcel from under the seat while the coach was unattended and added it to his bundle, which the coachman handed to him when he left the coach at the first London stop. The stolen parcel contained a quantity of nails and a letter with £47 and 9 shillings in bank notes and coin.

The position at the Crown Offices paid £1 a week and Vaux soon quit and took a job as a proofreader for a printer for £2 a week. This lasted only until he met his old accomplice Bromley, who had served his time on the hulks. Vaux then quickly returned to pickpocketing and shoplifting, using Bromley (who 'had neither the appearance nor the manners of a gentleman') as his accomplice to keep watch and carry away stolen goods.

On 21 July 1808, at St Paul's, Covent Garden, Vaux married Mary Ann Thomas, a nineteen-year-old prostitute. She was, according to his memoirs, 'well and tenderly brought up', but had been seduced and abandoned and declined into prostitution. She was five or six months pregnant when they married.

In October of that same year, Vaux was accused of picking a pocket in the Drury Lane Theatre and set upon by a group of gentlemen as he left. They had sent for a constable when a fellow 'gentleman thief' stepped in and saved the situation by bluff. The trauma resulting from the event and near miss caused Mary Ann to give birth prematurely to a baby boy, who died eight hours later.

In November Vaux stole an expensive snuff box by cutting a gentleman's pocket at a crowded political meeting. He left it to be filled at a shop attached to the meeting hall and was arrested when he went to collect it. He was committed to trial and sent to Clerkenwell Prison awaiting the assizes. The contents of his pockets were confiscated and advertised as stolen property.

Vaux prepared his own defence and hired a seasoned attorney to argue the case—that he found the snuff box near the hall. There was enough doubt to acquit him on lack of evidence, plus the fact that none of the items in his pockets, which included a knife and a pair of scissors, were claimed as stolen property.

In February 1809 he was not so lucky. He had met two brothers, professional shoplifters, in prison while waiting to be tried for stealing the snuff box, and they had given him a list of shops that were prime targets for theft. Once released Vaux, using the alias of James Lowe (his grandfather's name), stole from most of the shops on the list and, posing as a wealthy customer, made a hit on a jeweller's shop in Piccadilly and shoplifted several valuable items.

By now there was a reward posted for his capture and pawnbrokers were no longer to be trusted. Vaux was almost caught several times and finally lingered too long in a tavern frequented by thieves and was arrested by two constables, who had obviously been tipped off by an informant for the reward.

There was a mountain of evidence against him and James Hardy Vaux was found guilty and sentenced to death at the Old Bailey.

Vaux then spent eleven weeks in prison, often as cell mate to prisoners who were hanged while he remained waiting for his fate to be announced. Several of these men he read to and comforted in the period between the announcement of their death and the actual hanging, which was often as long as a week.

One morning he and another prisoner, named Cook, were summonsed to the cell door and the announcements were made. Cook was informed by the turnkey that 'the result was unfavourable', then he announced that Vaux had been 'respited'.

The sentence was commuted to transportation for life but Vaux then spent a year on the hulk of the *Retribution*, on the Thames at Woolwich, of which he wrote:

If I were to attempt a full description of the miseries endured in these ships, I could fill a volume; but I shall sum up all by stating, that besides robbery from each other, which is as common as cursing and swearing, I witnessed among the prisoners themselves, during the twelvemonth I remained with them, one deliberate murder, for which the perpetrator was executed at Maidstone, and one suicide; and that unnatural crimes are openly committed.

Transported Again

On 15 June 1810, aged 28, Vaux went aboard the transport *Indian*, which reached Sydney in December that year. He was assigned as a labourer to a Hawkesbury settler who, according to Vaux, treated him so badly that, after five weeks, he feigned illness and spent a month in the hospital in Sydney. As his master did not provision him during his stay in hospital, he was free of him and was appointed to the 'town gang', which did labouring tasks around the city. Within a few weeks, he was made deputy-overseer of the gang.

Vaux was once again living a relatively comfortable life in Sydney Town, as a lodger with a respectable family, when his luck took another turn for the worse.

On the voyage out, he had befriended a convict named Edwards who was then assigned to Judge Advocate Jeffery Bent. Edwards was caught stealing from Bent by breaking into his bureau and Vaux was arrested for receiving stolen goods. At the trial Edwards implicated Vaux as having proposed the thefts and the *modus operandi*. Both were sentenced, in 1811, to hard labour at the 'Coal River' colony, at Newcastle.

In 1812, during his time there, Vaux compiled the famous slang dictionary for the use of magistrates, *A Vocabulary of the Flash Language*.

In January 1814, after returning to Sydney, he applied for clerical positions but was refused any and forced to remain on the town gang as a labourer.

He was offered the opportunity of hiding away aboard the *Earl Spencer*, an East Indiaman leaving Sydney. The ship was searched and more than twenty would-be escapees were apprehended on board. Vaux almost escaped detection and was among the last of the hideaways detected. The men caught were given 50 lashes and Vaux recalls:

> The day after the corporal punishment had been inflicted, twenty-three of our number were ordered to return to the respective employments in Sydney, from which they had severally absconded, and myself and three others were sentenced by the Governor to be sent to the coal-river for one year . . . I was accordingly embarked with eleven other prisoners, and a second time landed at Newcastle, from whence I had been absent nearly twelve months. On my arrival, it happened that the store-keeper of that settlement was in want of a clerk, and he, applying

to the commandant for me, I was appointed to that situation, in which I still continue.

It was at this point that Vaux wrote *Memoirs of the First Thirty-Two Years of The Life of James Hardy Vaux, A Swindler and Pickpocket; Now Transported for the Second Time, and For Life, to New South Wales*, from which this account of his life is mostly taken. But his story does not end there.

The two works came to the attention of Barron Field, who replaced Jeffery Bent as judge of the Supreme Court of Civil Judicature in New South Wales, in 1816. Field was an established author of a legal book and also a would-be poet, and he published his collected verse, *First Fruits of Australian Poetry*, in 1819.

Field arranged to have Vaux's writings published in London in 1819 and Vaux received £33, 18 shillings and 8 pence in royalties. The *Memoirs* were republished by John Hunt in 1827 and reprinted in 1829 and 1830. As the first full-length autobiography written in Australia, the book provides a fascinating picture of criminal life in London and the penal and convict systems. *A Vocabulary of the Flash Language* is a valuable glossary of London criminal slang circa 1800, and was the first dictionary compiled in Australia.

On 3 August 1818 at Newcastle, Vaux had married a 35-year-old supposedly widowed washerwoman named Frances Sharkey, a former Irish convict one year younger than Vaux. The following month he was allowed to return to Sydney as a clerk. In January 1820 he received a conditional pardon and became a clerk in the Colonial Secretary's office.

In 1823, for some reason hard to fathom, James Hardy Vaux converted to Catholicism and told Father John Therry that he was still supporting his 'wife' Frances Sharkey, although they were no longer living together and had both still been married when they tied the knot in 1818.

At the end of 1826 the new governor, Ralph Darling, dismissed Vaux in accordance with his policy of not employing convicts and ex-convicts as clerks. The following year Vaux wrote a letter to *The Australian* newspaper complaining about 'unfair dismissal', although Darling's directive was a general one, not a personal one.

In April 1827, at St John's Parramatta, Vaux married his housekeeper, Eleanor Bateman, another Irish ex-convict. A second edition of his autobiography was published that year and, possibly using the money from the royalties, Vaux broke the terms of his pardon by leaving the colony and sailing to Dublin, possibly via Batavia and London on a vessel named *Comet,* or via Rio and Liverpool on the *Midas.*

Transported Yet Again

Inevitably, in August 1830 in Dublin, Vaux was convicted once more, this time under the alias of another family name, James Young (or Yonge), for passing forged bank notes. He pleaded guilty and, with the cooperation of the bank concerned (Vaux having written them an eloquent grovelling letter), his death sentence was commuted to transportation for seven years. On his arrival at Sydney in the *Waterloo* in May 1831 he was recognised and his previous life sentence was revived.

The *Sydney Gazette* of 27 October 1831 published a short article poking fun at Vaux and his time in Britain. The article claims that he was spotted in London and chased by the renowned ex-convict turned detective, Israel Chapman. The article also states that Vaux was abandoned as being untrustworthy by his family and old criminal friends in Britain and found no friends in Ireland. It also claims that Vaux's first wife, Mary Ann, was deceased and ends by noting that his epitaph will probably not be an accurate account of his character, though the litany of crimes in his autobiography will be:

> ... when he slumbers beneath the turf, the record of his actions, in the volumes he has published, will speak more for the man, while living, than the brightest epitaph that could adorn his urn.

The *Gazette* wrongly states that he is being sent to the Moreton Bay convict colony, while records show he was sent to Port Macquarie penal settlement. There he served out the seven-year sentence handed down in Dublin, but not the reinstated life sentence.

Back in Sydney in 1838, he worked as a clerk for a wine merchant in George Street.

There is no happy ending to his story. There is no witty anecdote to round off the deplorable and lamentable life of James Hardy Vaux.

The ending of this tale is, indeed, the most sordid and disgusting episode of the entire saga.

The *Sydney Gazette* reported on 23 May 1831:

James Hardy Vaux.—This celebrated member of the 'Felonry,' whose autobiography is to be found in the published collection of the lives of distinguished and celebrated persons, appeared on summons at the Police Office, yesterday, charged with attempting to commit a criminal assault on a little girl of about eight years of age. The evidence gone into against him appeared very conclusive, and the impression of guilt was further heightened by the fact that he had called upon the prosecuting parties, and endeavoured to prevail upon them not to appear against him. He was remanded in custody for further examination, but was allowed bail; himself to be bound in £80, and two sureties in £40 each. Vaux was latterly a clerk in the employment of Mr. Wood, of George-street, wine merchant.

The case came to court in August, before Mr Justice Willis and a Special Jury, and the *Gazette* reported:

Supreme Court.—Criminal Side. TUESDAY. AUGUST 6.

. . . James Hardy Vaux was indicted for an indecent assault on Ann Arundel, a child eight years of age at Sydney, on the 13th of May last. The particulars of the case appeared in this journal at the time. Guilty—Two years imprisonment with hard labour, and afterwards to find sureties to be of good behaviour.

The *Sydney Herald* of 9 August 1839 added:

The prisoner, who is the notorious author of 'The autobiography of a swindler and thief,' decoyed the child of a neighbour into a dark room, under pretence of giving her some sweetmeats and a penny, and there behaved very indecently. The jury found a verdict of guilty. In passing sentence, His Honor lamented that he could only pass a sentence which he felt to be altogether inadequate.

In 1815, Vaux had summed up his own decline and fall by stating that he had, by:

> ... my own vicious conduct, and partly (perhaps,) from the malignity of my fate, have forfeited all hope of attaining that respectable rank in society, to which, in the happy days of youthful innocence, I had every reason to look forward with confidence.

The 'malignity of my fate' suggests that bad luck played a part in his descent into crime and debauchery. He seems to find it terribly unfair that, whenever he had a few passing thoughts about leading a decent life, some temptation came his way. I'm inclined to think that the 'malignity' was in his nature, rather than his 'fate'. By his own admission, he committed many more crimes than he was ever caught or punished for. Every time he was tempted he gave into temptation. Every time he was trusted, he abused the trust. Eventually, he could not even be trusted to be alone with his neighbours' eight-year-old daughter.

There is nothing good to say about James Hardy Vaux. He is the antithesis of those transported convicts who rose from poverty and illiteracy to some level of respect and achievement worthy of admiration. He was given every opportunity to lead a decent and respectable life, and, time and again, he callously and selfishly declined to do so. He is the only convict known to have been transported three times to New South Wales for three separate crimes.

He is remembered for his slang dictionary and has even been credited with contributing to creating our 'Aussie language'.

I think such claims are nonsense. He merely made a list of the criminal phrases he knew and explained them, he never invented any of them and there is nothing 'Australian' about them. The dictionary is a list of the jargon used by London criminals during Vaux's lifetime.

The *Sydney Gazette* was quite right when it claimed, in 1831, that his self-confessed criminal actions would be his true epitaph, because there is no known grave or epitaph. He disappears from the pages of history when he walks out of prison in 1841, aged 59. There is not one skerrick of evidence about where he went and what he did. Surely if he stayed in New South Wales or returned to London there would be some hint in census records, death notices or court records—or even anecdotal evidence. Did he change his name? Did he head to some Pacific Island or some remote corner of the British Empire and live as an expat, or was he lost at sea?

One branch of the family tree lists his death date as 1851 with a question mark, but there is no evidence of him existing anywhere after 1841. He has no monument or known resting place to be remembered by, and he doesn't really deserve one.

What he did leave us is a fascinating and articulate autobiography that is a window into the criminal world of late Georgian London and the struggling fledgling penal colony of New South Wales. It is also a sometimes disarmingly honest glimpse into the callous, conniving, self-centred mind of a man whose 'continued excesses' of conduct (as his first employer noted when Vaux was just fifteen) leave 'too much room for unfavourable conjectures'.

7

ARTHUR ORTON—
THE WAPPING LIAR

'Goodbye, Mr Castro.'

The Butcher's Son

Arthur Orton was born in the East End of London in the dockside suburb of Wapping in 1834, the eighth child in a family of twelve. His father was a butcher who supplied meat and other products to ships and bred Shetland ponies. As a child Arthur was already quite 'stout' and would be known in his youth as 'Fatty', 'Fatboy' and 'Bullocky'.

When he was six Arthur survived a fire, which burned through shops and houses in Wapping for over a day and killed three people. This evidently left the plump little boy traumatised with a condition that made him twitch. It was misdiagnosed as St Vitus dance and he was treated with cold baths.

As sailing seemed to 'cure' the condition, he was apprenticed as a cabin boy aboard a ship called the *Ocean* and went to sea just after his fourteenth birthday. By the time the *Ocean* arrived in Valparaíso, in Chile, six months later, the chubby fourteen-year-old had had enough of a sailor's life and he deserted and made his way inland to a village called Melipilla, where he was taken in by a family named Castro.

Although he arrived in the village dressed in rags and penniless, Arthur told everyone his father was Queen Victoria's butcher and the young lad lived, apparently happily, as a member of the Castro family for eighteen months, in which time he learned to rope and ride and work with cattle. These skills would come in handy later, during his life in Australia.

Evidently the villagers had a whip round and collected enough to pay for his passage back home in June 1851; perhaps they had heard enough stories about Queen Victoria's butcher—Arthur's greatest skill in life was telling stories.

Back in Wapping, aged sixteen, he worked as a butcher with his father for less than two years before heading off, with a consignment of Shetland ponies, to seek his fortune in far-off Van Diemen's Land. He stayed back home long enough to acquire a girlfriend, fifteen-year-old Mary Ann Loder, and, no doubt, tell her lots of stories about his life as a Chilean cowboy.

From the far-flung colony, he wrote long, sentimental and quite articulate letters to Mary Ann, which were full of rather rudimentary spellings and signed with a strange symbol—of a crescent and stars. He told her Hobart was dreadful and he was heading for the gold-rushes in Victoria. He seemed very excited about news of the battle at Eureka Stockade.

Arthur seemed always to attract trouble. He went to work for a butcher in Hobart and was charged with selling diseased meat. He was acquitted but his employer took the rap, and Arthur moved on.

He borrowed money from an old family friend, an ex-convict named Euphemia Jury, who was related to one of Arthur's sisters by marriage and was now the wife of a publican in Hobart. Arthur borrowed £15 from Euphemia to set up a butcher's stall in Hobart's new meat market and wrote to her promising to soon repay the loan, along with some other money he had inadvertently taken 'by mistake' at the same time as he was given the loan.

Failing to repay debts was second only to story-telling in Arthur Orton's list of personal character traits and, after the market stall failed, the money was never repaid.

Instead, Arthur departed the colony sometime in 1856. He'd arrived in 'Van Diemen's Land' but he actually left 'Tasmania'—the colony having changed its name on 1 January 1856 in order to leave behind the awful history of brutality, genocide and lawlessness associated with the name 'Van Diemen's Land'.

The name lived on, however, in the 'Vandemonian trail', a well-worn migration path that led from Tasmania via Port Albert to Gippsland, and on to the goldrushes in the Victorian High Country and then on to Beechworth and Mansfield, and thence to the developing grazing districts of the Riverina.

Port Albert became the gateway to Gippsland, a fertile area developed as a cattle-raising district. Many ex-convicts, sons of convicts, ex-bushrangers, gold seekers and other 'Vandemonians' made their way along this trail to the cattle grazing country and goldfields of Victoria during the boom years of the 1850s. Melbourne's population increased 1700 per cent in ten years, to half a million by 1860.

Arthur worked at horse-breaking and made his way from Port Albert to Boisdale, 65 miles (105 kilometres) away, where he was taken in and employed by the Foster family, who owned cattle properties in the district. Mrs Foster was kind to Arthur and gave him medicine for sore throats and lent him books. In 1857 he took the lonely job of stockman, living in a hut at the Fosters' highland property 55 miles away, at Dargo.

Mrs Foster sent him books to read and he apparently gained some romantic notions and ideas from the novels he read. One was a romantic novel about class struggle and ambition in Ireland, written in 1829 by Gerald Griffin and titled *The Rivals*.

One day two guests arrived at the stockman's hut and stayed overnight. One was Harry Clare, a prospector believed to have a stash of money hidden somewhere. The other was another 'Vandemonian' named Tom Toke. The men were apparently prospecting together. Toke was later charged with Clare's murder and was found in possession of his watch, horse and quite a lot of money. As Clare's body was never found, Toke was later acquitted. In the meantime, however, Orton deserted his post as stockman and returned to Boisdale and went to work at a hotel livery stable in town.

Not only did he 'repay' the Fosters' kindness by leaving their cattle unguarded, he sued them for unpaid wages. When the case came before the court in Sale, he was awarded £10 of the £160 he'd claimed.

It has been suggested that Orton deserted his post rather than be called as a witness in the murder trial. However, he did not leave the district but worked at various stables breaking in and trading horses. He also told people his real name was De Costello and his family were Spanish nobility.

In May 1859 he was listed in the Victorian Police Gazette as 'Arthur Ortin', wanted for stealing a chestnut mare. The mare was later found wandering in the bush near Port Albert, not long after the paddle steamer *Shandon* left for Melbourne. Three days after the *Shandon* had berthed in Melbourne a man known only as Arthur, apparently a native of Chile, gained employment with a butcher named McManus at the Reedy Creek goldfields near Kilmore on the Sydney Road. He worked there for six months and then did casual work around the town. In November 1859, after some horses went missing and a reward was posted for information about them, Arthur disappeared. The horses were found nearby.

'Arthur from Chile' was never seen again in Australia, nor was Arthur Ortin, or Arthur Orton.

The Wagga Wagga Butcher

Tom Castro, full name Tomas de Castro, was a butcher in Wagga Wagga, where he had set up a shop in a slab hut behind a hotel in 1864.

He had previously worked for quite a while riding the mail run from the village of Boree to Narrandera. This mail run was an extension of the mail run from Hay, part of a network of mail runs and coach services operated by James Gormly.

Previous to that Castro had worked in Hay as a butcher and delivery-man for about six months, before leaving hurriedly after a courtship that failed to end in marriage when an unpaid debt evidently forced Tom's departure for Wagga Wagga.

Previous to living in Hay, Tom had been employed at Deniliquin, at John Burrows' butchery, for eighteen months. At Deniliquin he boasted of being the heir to a fortune, but was in court over an unpaid promissory note for the purchase of a mare named 'Goldie'.

Castro had made his way to Deniliquin from Bendigo where he had briefly worked as a bullock driver. He had arrived in that town in early January 1860; just a few weeks after 'Arthur from Chile' disappeared from Kilmore.

In Wagga Wagga in April 1863, Tom Castro sold Goldie for £20, after racing her unsuccessfully. He worked in various capacities and spent some time prospecting at Tumut, before establishing his own butchery.

Tom was noted for using a large American-style saddle and boasting about his horsemanship, although poor Goldie had been unshod for some time when he went to race her at Wagga Wagga and needed a good few inches taken off her overgrown hooves; he had to borrow money to shoe her for the race. Tom was laughed at by local horsemen and was several times thrown off while attempting to break in horses. While recovering from one fall, he met Mary Ann Bryant, an illiterate, pregnant servant girl recently arrived in town from Goulburn.

The couple set up home in a windowless hut near Tom's shop. After Mary Ann had given birth to the daughter she was carrying when they met, the couple were married in January 1865, in a private ceremony by a Wesleyan minister. Tom signed 'Tom Castro'—son of 'a Chilean merchant'—and Mary Ann made a cross.

The business struggled along. Tom loved gambling and drinking and one of his best mates was Dick Slate, a reasonably well-educated native of Hampshire, who might have talked about the Tichborne family. Dick disappeared from town after a local farmer had been assaulted and robbed one night. At some point after chatting to Dick Slate, Tom carved the initials RCT on a flask and a tree.

Tom spent much of his time visiting the local library and reading novels by Captain Marryat, Gerald Griffin and others, many with plots about missing heirs and lost fortunes. His favourite novelist was Mary Elizabeth Braddon, a prolific author of 80 novels including the hugely popular *Lady Audley's Secret*, which involved upper-class secrets, class discrimination, bigamy and adventures on the Australian goldfields.

After reading one of Mary Elizabeth Braddon's novels entitled *Aurora Floyd*, Tom paraphrased a passage from the novel in his pocket notebook: 'Some men has plenty money and no brains. And some men has plenty brains and no money. Surely men with plenty money and no brains were made for men with plenty brains and no money.'

The notebook contained a few other interesting things, as we shall find out later.

Tom had been involved in a court case to do with stolen cattle. He had helped a man named Allen to take the cattle across the Murrumbidgee River and Allen had sold two of them to Tom. Again, someone else took the rap; Allen got five years, and Tom got off. During the court case he met local solicitor, William Gibbes, who was also involved in acting against Tom on behalf of a client to whom Tom owed money.

Castro and Gibbes discussed the possibility of Tom's bankruptcy and other things. In the course of these conversations, Tom claimed to 'own property in England', which could solve his debt problems. In August 1865 Gibbes read notices that were placed in Australian newspapers seeking information about the possible whereabouts of Sir Roger Tichborne, who was believed to have drowned in 1854, but was rumoured to have survived. Gibbes immediately went to see Tom Castro.

This is the advertisement as it appeared in Australian newspapers.

Public Notices.

A HANDSOME REWARD will be given to any person who can furnish such information as will discover the fate of ROGER CHARLES TICHBORNE. He sailed from the port of Rio Janeiro on the 20th April, 1854, in the ship La Bella, and has never been heard of since, but a report reached England to the effect that a portion of the crew and passengers was picked up by a vessel bound to Australia (Melbourne, it is believed); it is not known whether the said Roger Charles Tichborne was amongst the drowned or saved. He would at the present time be about 32 years of age, is of a delicate constitution, rather tall, with very light brown hair and blue eyes. Mr. Tichborne is the son of Sir James Tichborne, Bart. (now deceased), and is heir to all his estates. The advertiser is instructed to state that a most liberal reward will be given for any information that may definitely point out his fate. Gentlemen in a position to refer to the shipping reports may be able to find some record of the saving of the shipwrecked persons from La Bella, and a very careful search, if with a successful result, will amply repay any one who will take the trouble to investigate the matter. All replies to be addressed to Mr. Arthur Cubitt, Missing Friends' office, Bridge-street, Sydney, New South Wales.

Now even the less devious among you will realise that advertising that there is good money in the form of a 'most liberal reward' to be had for 'any' information is likely to attract certain types of individuals to concoct 'information'.

The reply that came, via Mr Cubitt, from the office of solicitor William Gibbes in November 1865 was, however, totally beyond Lady Tichborne's wildest hopes. Apparently a client of Mr Gibbes had informed the solicitor that he not only had 'information' concerning Roger Charles Tichborne, he was in fact (you guessed it) Sir Roger Charles Tichborne *himself*!

The Real Sir Roger

Born in Paris in 1829, the real Roger Charles Tichborne was brought up in France and his first language was French. His mother, Henriette, was the illegitimate child of a French duke's daughter and an upper-class Englishman who had apparently seduced her while he was in Paris under civil arrest during the Napoleonic Wars.

Henriette was raised in an atmosphere of luxury and privilege, but was somewhat of an embarrassment to all concerned. Still unmarried at age twenty, her father suggested a marriage of convenience to James Tichborne, a son of his old mate Henry Tichborne. All three Englishmen had been 'internees' in Paris during the war and James was a rather unattractive chap, unmarried at age 47. It seemed a good solution to various problems.

Roger's parents' marriage was not a happy one; they lost two daughters in infancy and lived apart after the birth of a second son, Alfred, when Roger was ten. Roger was not sent to live in England until he was fifteen. French was his native tongue and he spoke English with a strong French accent. Totally spoiled by his mother, his father sent him to Stonyhurst Jesuit College for two years then bought him a commission in the 6th Dragoon Guards Regiment, based in Dublin.

Roger was teased and bullied at Stonyhurst and while in the Dragoons, for his slight build, narrow chest and French accent. His nicknames were 'Froggy' and 'Frenchy' but, more commonly, 'Smallcock'. Roger had a small and 'inverted' penis, which made him a figure of fun in the officers' quarters and must have made his life hell at school. I'm not telling you this out of mere prurient interest, it is really important later on—honestly.

While on leave Roger often stayed with his uncle, Edward Doughty, the 9th Baron Tichborne, and developed a very strong relationship with his cousin, Katherine Doughty. Katherine's parents liked their nephew but thought the idea of first cousins marrying was not wise and the liaison was banned (despite the fact that Queen Victoria was at that time happily married to her first cousin and busy producing a series of nine children).

The Tichborne family was Roman Catholic and first-cousin marriage was frowned upon in the Catholic Church. There is some evidence that Roger asked the family to request a papal dispensation but the idea was also vetoed by his aunt and uncle. It is believed the cousins kept meeting in secret, although forbidden to do so.

It was soon after this that Roger, having spent three years in the regiment, sold his commission and headed to South America. In doing so he escaped his obsessive and neurotic mother, the disappointment of a failed romance, a banned marriage, and bullying at school and in the army.

A servant named John Moore was sent along as his 'minder' and when they arrived in Valparaíso, in Chile, they found letters waiting— informing them that Edward Doughty had passed away, in 1853, and, because his uncle had no sons, his father was now the 10th Baron Tichborne, which meant that Roger was the heir to the title, family fortune and estates. It was a very lucrative inheritance including large land-holdings in Hampshire and real estate in London.

Roger spent ten months travelling in South America before paying off John Moore in Santiago. The servant wrote to Roger's father complaining about his treatment at the hands of the young 'gentleman'. A lazy and rather inept traveller, Roger hunted and fished, sent specimens home and attempted taxidermy on an albatross, managing to impale his eyelid with a fish hook in the process. After crossing the Andes and arriving in Buenos Aires, Roger took a passage to New York via Jamaica on a ship called the *Bella*.

The *Bella* was lost at sea. An empty lifeboat and wreckage was found drifting off the Brazilian coast and Roger was presumed to have perished; he was officially declared dead in 1855. His younger brother, Alfred, inherited the Tichborne title in 1862, when their father died. Alfred died only four years later, aged just 27, and a son, born four months after his death, became the 12th Baron Tichborne at birth in 1866.

The Dowager Lady Tichborne never recovered from the loss of her adored older son and had now lost Alfred as well. Having grown up as an unwanted illegitimate child, suffered through an unhappy marriage, borne four children and now lost them all, she was not a very happy or mentally stable woman.

Henriette is often portrayed in the Tichborne saga as 'deranged by grief' at Roger's disappearance. What many chroniclers miss is evidence that she was a 'deranged', neurotic and difficult woman well before her son's disappearance.

While in South America, Roger had written to the family's business manager, his friend Vincent Gosford, saying how wonderful it was to be away from his mother and commenting: 'I am very sorry my mother's character is so disagreeable, it must make Tichborne a kind of hell for my father and everyone in the house.'

In a later letter, giving instructions in the event of his father's death (James Tichborne was past 70 when he became the 10th Baronet), Roger had told Gosford to ensure his mother was looked after but insisted that she could not live at Tichborne when he became baronet as it would be 'quite impossible' for him to 'put up with her character'.

It seems Henriette wasn't just a deluded old lady saddened by grief who wanted her son to be alive. She was disliked by the Tichborne family and was impossible to live with. She hated England and the English and was, quite possibly, barking mad.

She decided to spend considerable amounts of money advertising for any news of her long-lost and much-adored older son. She visited Portsmouth Harbour and enquired about any news of survivors of the *Bella* or ships in the vicinity of the wreck. Apparently, in exchange for payment, she was told there was a rumour that some passengers and crew survived the wreck and were picked up by a ship heading to Melbourne.

She then paid for the advertisement in Australian newspapers.

The Claimant

Although 'the claimant', as Arthur Orton/Tom Castro was to become known, was physically much larger than Sir Roger, had a different build, lighter hair, totally differently shaped ears, was often unwashed and spoke no French, these discrepancies did not appear to bother Lady Tichborne.

She was rather at odds with the family into which she had married and obsessively refused to believe Roger had drowned. She was so desperate to find him that she sent for Castro, who arrived in London in December 1866. But quite a few things occurred in the intervening year.

Tom Castro, William Gibbes and Mr Cubitt made a plan. Tom's identity was to be kept secret until some things were sorted out between them. Gibbes had Tom write a will as Sir Roger Tichborne before he would proceed with advancing him money and taking the claim further.

After an exchange of letters between Cubitt, Gibbes and the Dowager Lady Tichborne, the reward of £250 was claimed and various increasingly larger amounts of money were forthcoming for the claimant's travel and living expenses from Wagga Wagga to Goulburn and then on to Sydney and finally by ship to London.

The claimant and his wife, along with her daughter, Annie, and their new daughter, Mary Agnes Teresa, travelled to Goulburn and stayed with Mary Ann's family. There they remarried in a Catholic church with the claimant signing as Roger Charles Tichborne. Mary Ann used her usual cross.

In the meantime a strange coincidence became apparent; two ex-Tichborne employees were living in Sydney. One was an Irish gardener named Guilfoyle, who met the claimant and seemed to accept his *bona fides*. The other was a much more important character in the plot, a black gentleman of West Indian descent, Andrew Bogle, who had served the Doughty family for many years and was living on a pension of £50 a year, provided by Lady Doughty, Edward's widow.

Bogle, who had a certain affection for Roger Tichborne as a lad and admitted that he had long hoped that he had survived, was convinced almost immediately that the claimant was Sir Roger. When they met, the claimant asked, 'Is that you, Bogle?'

Now, it may occur to the more cynical of you that a well-dressed black man appearing in the claimant's hotel in Sydney might be rather obviously assumed to be the man in question. Bogle, however, was chuffed and delighted to be recognised and, apparently, replied in the affirmative, adding 'How stout you've got!'

The colony was abuzz with the news that a long-lost nobleman was among them and, with the typical sycophantic vigour of the times in the Australian colonies, the claimant was accepted as genuine and fawned over and doted upon.

This gave his 'team', consisting of the solicitor Gibbes and Bogle and others, the chance to begin raising money and organising financial backing in order that the claimant could travel to Britain and claim his inheritance.

Credit and loans and bills for expenses were all to be paid back in full when the claimant received the vast estates and wealth that he obviously seemed to deserve. This pattern would remain as his template for the entire period of his 'claim'—the best food, wine and alcohol, cigars, accommodation, clothing and transport—all on credit.

Sydney bankers and wealthy 'friends' were enticed into 'investing' in the venture. Later, in Britain, there were actually 'Tichborne Bonds' that sold in the hundreds of thousands. They were to be redeemable, with a dividend, when the title was finally claimed.

The Castro family (minus Annie who remained in Goulburn), Bogle and his son, a secretary with the wonderful name of Truth Butts, and a nursemaid left Sydney on the SS *Rakia* and arrived in London via Panama on Christmas Day. The claimant visited the Tichborne estates in Hampshire and amazingly convinced some he met of the truth of his claim, while the Tichborne family's former solicitor, Edward Hopkins, became an ally.

Several weeks later, having secured the aid of a London solicitor, John Holmes, and delayed the inevitable as long as possible, the claimant travelled to France to meet Henriette.

The meeting was held in a darkened room as the claimant was either feigning illness or was so nervous that he was genuinely ill. The bereaved mother claimed to recognise her son in the darkened room and, after her acceptance, settled him and his family in England with a handsome allowance. She wrote to her daughter-in-law, Teresa: 'I have fully recognised him—as it is really him—and I cannot conceive those who knew him very well will not recognise him.'

This was not what Teresa, Alfred's widow, wished to hear. It meant the end of the £1000 a year she received as mother of the 12th Baronet, Alfred's son, Henry, born four months after his father's death.

Holmes had Lady Tichborne sign a document at the British Embassy in Paris, acknowledging the claimant as her son Roger, but Roger's old tutor in Paris, Father Chatillon, was brave enough to go against the wealthy old woman's wishes—and declared the claimant was an imposter.

Lady Doughty had declared the claimant an imposter as soon as she had been shown the first photograph to arrive from Australia. Lady Tichborne had looked at the same photo and declared it was Roger.

Thanks to detectives the family sent to follow the claimant, and investigate in Australia, they came to believe that 'Tom Castro' from Wagga Wagga was, in fact, London-born Arthur Orton. Foolishly, the claimant had even visited Wapping as soon as he arrived back in London, on Boxing Day 1866, and made enquiries about Orton's family and Mary Ann Loder at the local pub, where the suspicious owner had asked his visitor if he was actually Arthur Orton.

The claimant travelled in an expensive carriage and ate and drank only the best food and wine and smoked the best cigars. He quickly gathered a coterie of sycophantic supporters who revelled in his generosity. He dined often with his supporters and eventually weighed a few ounces under 27 stone (170 kilograms).

Those who opposed his claim to be Sir Roger mostly had no financial interest in it being true, but obviously some had much to lose. The Tichborne family invested heavily in disproving the claim, eventually spending about £100,000 to fight it.

Katherine Doughty, now Lady Radcliffe and mother of a large family, never believed the claim. She met the claimant twice in very guarded and chaperoned situations. On the second occasion, she cleverly took an aunt and a female cousin, wearing veils, to meet the claimant.

The real Sir Roger should have known them by their voices, general demeanour and childhood memories. The claimant failed to identify them and panicked, saying, 'Too many veils!'

When the ladies attempted to converse in French, Sir Roger's native tongue, about shared experiences, the claimant again panicked and cried out, 'Non, non.'

The ladies then rose, and Sir Roger's cousin, Carolyn Nangle, terminated the brief visit with the words, 'Goodbye, Mr Castro!'

In July 1867, the illiterate Mary Ann Castro, now styling herself as 'Lady Tichborne', had given birth to a boy. This potential heir to the title was named Roger Charles Doughty.

On 31 July the first steps in the legal battle were taken. The claimant's team made a claim in Chancery, the equity court, to freeze the money being collected from rents on Tichborne estates and other sources of income, until the rightful title could be determined. The family turned to Jack Whicher, 'the prince of detectives' and one of the founders of Scotland Yard, who had successfully solved several famous puzzling cases. He soon uncovered evidence of the claimant's Boxing Day visit to Wapping, along with evidence that he had contacted the Orton family and was paying them to deny that he was Arthur.

Seven months after the Chancery lodgement, the saga took a sudden turn. Just before noon on 12 March 1868, the Dowager Lady Tichborne was found dead by a servant. At the funeral Orton and Bogle displaced Henriette's two half-brothers, Alfred Seymour and Lord Arundell, as chief mourners.

The *Pall Mall Gazette* reported that two respected members of the upper class had been 'extruded by the Australian claimant, a large and corpulent man, supported by a Jamaican negro'.

The 'Tichborne Affair' quickly escalated into class warfare, with xenophobic overtones on one side and claims of unfair privilege and elitist snobbery on the other! Many working-class people, along with some liberal-thinking, anti-establishment figures and newspapermen, liked the idea of a common man taking on the privileged snobs.

The whole affair was spinning out of control as the newspapers devoted millions of columns of small print to reporting the most minute details. The public took sides, as people do in such cases. Readers struggling to understand how this happened in Victorian England might cast their minds back to the way sensations like the Lindy Chamberlain and Schapelle Corby cases polarised the nation and were grist to the mill of the media, rumour mongers, cartoonists, comedians, social philosophers, social reformers and politicians. Imagine something a thousand times more sensational and popular—and you have the 'Tichborne Affair'.

There were plays and pantomimes about the case, souvenir miniature dolls, posters, cards, handkerchiefs, books, cartoons. The claimant was bigger news and more 'popular' as a public figure than the royal family. Music hall songs and skits about him were written and performed all across the nation and a comic miniature version of him, 'Little Tich', became one of the most popular variety acts of the time.

Commissions of Enquiry were established by Chancery in South America and Australia and both sides had detectives and investigators active on those continents. The claimant finally agreed to go to South America and be part of the investigations. He sailed to Argentina via Portugal and stayed many weeks in Buenos Aires, but declined to travel overland to Chile for fear of bandits. (This proved to be a very wise decision. Bandits attacked the coach he was booked to travel on and all on board were murdered.)

The claimant's reluctance to travel to Chile and face the commission, however, disgusted some of his most powerful supporters and several, including the solicitor Holmes, changed their minds and declared the claimant to be a fraud. With Commissions of Enquiry gathering evidence, things were looking grim and the claimant was forced to go to court.

Tichborne v. Lushington

The first trial lasted almost a year, from 11 May 1871 to 5 March 1872. *Tichborne v. Lushington* was a civil trial to establish Orton's claim to the Tichborne inheritance. The estate had been leased to Colonel Lushington who had allowed the claimant to visit and was merely the 'name' taken to court as he had legal ownership of the estate at the time and, if the claimant's right to the estate could be established, his identity would be proven.

Nearly a hundred people spoke in the claimant's defence; most of them by now had a pecuniary interest in proving that the claimant was Sir Roger Tichborne.

The Evidence *For* 'the Claimant'

The claimant's case was built on several factors including that he seemed to be able to recall fragments of information from the personal life of Roger Tichborne.

He was acknowledged by Lady Tichborne and Mr Ballantine, appearing for the claimant, described the dowager as: 'An extremely beautiful woman of strong good sense, a perfect woman of the world and perfectly able to form a sound judgement.'

In addition, Sir Roger's former servant, John Moore, bewildered by the claimant's ability to recall incidents in South America, said he now believed he was Sir Roger.

To account for the rather vast difference in appearance and manner, Sir Roger had, it was claimed, been physically and psychologically altered by his ordeal at sea and had forgotten his native tongue. His personality had been altered by his low and impoverished later life.

The claimant swore under oath that a mysterious letter, left by Roger with the family's solicitor and estate manager in 1852, contained instructions to be followed in the event of Katherine Doughty being pregnant. In other words, the claimant claimed to have 'deflowered' his cousin. When asked did he mean he had seduced his cousin, he replied, 'I most solemnly swear to my God I did.'

The Evidence *Against* 'the Claimant'

On the other hand, there was considerable evidence against the claimant, the most obvious being that the claimant could not speak French and the physical differences between the two men. This included the fact that Sir Roger had been tattooed as a youth and the claimant had no tattoos.

Clearly, Lady Tichborne was far from being a person 'of sound judgement'. John Moore somewhat undermined Ballantine's claim that the dowager was of sound mind when he agreed that he had once said of her: 'She would believe anything . . . if they sent over an Egyptian mummy and ticketed it "Roger Tichborne" she would acknowledge it as her son.'

It was also argued that the claimant had obviously been 'coached' by those with a vested interest.

The claimant had written a will in Wagga Wagga, as Sir Roger Tichborne, in which he bequeathed property that the family had never owned and put his mother's name as Hannah Frances—right initials, wrong names. (The claimant countered that he wrote the will knowing it to be untrue and would be deemed false, but he wrote it so Gibbes would forward him money.)

A detective sent to Australia by the Tichborne family returned with a pocket notebook once owned by Tom Castro. It contained the paraphrased quote from the novel previously mentioned, various attempts at signing Sir Roger Tichborne's name in different ways and with different spellings, the name and address of Mary Ann Loder in Wapping and the moon and crescent symbol. It also contained the note: 'I, Thomas Castro do hereby certify that my name is not Thomas Castro at all. Therefore, those that say it don't know anythink [sic] about it—R.T.C.'

Lady Radcliffe (née Katherine Doughty) was called as a witness and, when asked if there was any truth in the claimant's evidence, she replied, 'Certainly not. Not one single word.'

This was the absolute hiatus of the class warfare element of the case. Either the claimant had impugned the honour of a titled, respected, married lady and proved himself to be no gentleman at all—or the upper classes were no better than the common immoral working-class folk, fornicating outside of wedlock and then lying to protect their privilege! It appeared to be a 'no win' for the claimant. Either way he was certainly 'no gentleman'. Support for the claimant disappeared in certain quarters but was polarised even more in the press and with the public.

The Verdict

On 5 March 1872 the jury informed the judge they had heard enough and they found against the claimant.

Orton was arrested the same day on charges of perjury. Deeply in debt in spite of thousands of bonds being sold at £65 each to support his case, loans and gifts of money, as well as that provided by the late Lady Tichborne, he did not have the bail money, set at a staggering £10,000.

The claimant's trail of debt and promised unpaid wages to servants, plus legal bills, hotel bills, extended credit etc., led all the way back to Wagga Wagga. Nothing had been paid for since the claim began. From a cell in Newgate Prison, Orton appealed to 'every British soul ... willing to defend the weak against the strong' to donate money for his bail.

Amazing as it may seem, the money was raised. Half was donated by a member of parliament and staunch 'claimant supporter', Guildford Onslow. The affair was now a political *cause célèbre*. The resultant perjury trial, *Regina v. Castro*, was the longest in British history until 1996.

Regina v. Castro

While on bail Orton attended rallies and gave demonstrations of pigeon shooting, at which he was rather good. A typical event would see him compete against the local pigeon-shooting champion and then attend a rally at which various public figures and local dignitaries gave speeches in favour of his claim.

Defending 'Castro' (who continued to be known as 'Sir Roger' by most of Britain) was an interesting fellow, Dr Edward Kenealy, who had an axe to grind. He hated Catholics and campaigned endlessly against Roman Catholicism. The Tichborne family were famously Catholic, perhaps the wealthiest and oldest Catholic family in Britain. (One of the family had been hanged, drawn and quartered for his role in the religiously inspired plot against Elizabeth I.)

Kenealy's opening address lasted for a month.

The court held commissions in various towns in Australia and South America and witnesses came from around the globe to testify. Witness after witness swore that the claimant was Arthur Orton: including Mary Ann Loder and others from Wapping, the wife of Tomas de Castro from Melipilla, Euphemia Jury from Hobart, and the now widowed and remarried ex–Mrs Foster from Boisdale (who added that there was no 'Tom Castro' in the employ of the Fosters, ever—just Arthur Orton).

The old evidence was trawled over. Lady Radcliffe testified, when asked about the claim of seduction, that 'Roger would never have thought of such a thing'. Vincent Gosford, the Tichborne estate manager, said the letter left by Roger in 1852, and written in his presence, contained matters relating to property and a sworn promise by Roger to build a church should he be allowed to marry Katherine upon his return from South America, nothing more.

In a desperate attempt to prove the case for the defence, Kenealy used two pieces of sensational so-called 'evidence'. He produced a witness who claimed he had been on the ship *Osprey* that rescued Sir Roger, and he asked the claimant to show the jury his penis.

Kenealy claimed that the defendant had an inverted penis, which was a rare enough deformity to prove he was Sir Roger 'Smallcock' Tichborne. He made this claim after the court had been cleared of women and children, and the jury (all male in those days, of course) dutifully trooped into the barristers' robing room where the claimant dropped his daks and gave them a good look.

The defendant's penis did, indeed, appear to be 'inverted'. Whether this proved that he was Sir Roger, or was merely due to the fact that he weighed 27 stone and the presence of a stomach that size in any male can cause the penis to disappear, we'll never know. A doctor, who Kenealy claimed would testify that the claimant had the same condition, declined to appear for the defence.

The second piece of evidence involved a wait for a seafaring witness to arrive 'from overseas'. The claimant took advantage of the break to continue his fundraising tour, talking about his adventures in South America and Australia to huge and enthusiastic sell-out audiences in theatres around the country.

The seafaring witness was a certain 'Jean Luie', alleged steward of the *Osprey*, who told a story about a deranged Englishman saved from a drifting lifeboat.

It all was going well for the defence until the prosecution produced a witness named Mrs Lundgren. She testified that 'Jean Luie' was, in fact, her husband Carl, a convicted liar, thief and con-artist now bigamously married to another woman and recently released from prison. He had never been on a ship called the *Osprey*.

With his star witness back in prison on multiple charges of bigamy and perjury, Kenealy's case collapsed. 'The claimant' was convicted and became simply 'Arthur Orton', sentenced to two terms of the maximum penalty of seven years for perjury.

Arthur's End

The case was over but the Tichborne phenomenon would continue for another 30 years. Edward Kenealy started a newspaper, *The Englishman*, which attacked the judges and those he saw as the political enemies of the claimant. The attacks led to him being struck off as a barrister in 1874.

In 1875 Kenealy was elected to parliament at a by-election in the working-class seat of Stoke-on-Trent. Prime Minister Benjamin Disraeli had to change parliamentary procedure when Kenealy took his seat in the Commons, as no other member would officially 'introduce him'. Kenealy moved a motion to have the Tichborne case examined by a royal commission. The vote was lost 433 votes to 3. He lost his seat at the general election in 1880 and died the following year.

Arthur Orton served ten years in prison, getting out in 1884. He immediately went on the theatre circuit aided by his eldest daughter, Mary Agnes Teresa, now calling herself Agnes. She had been well educated at boarding school at the expense of the claimant's supporters and was a capable young woman who spoke several languages. The 'act' consisted of telling his story with photos to prove he was Sir Roger, telling of his life in prison and attacking those who had 'cheated' him out of his rightful inheritance.

For a while, support for his cause was rekindled, more pigeon shooting and a wave of public curiosity brought in the money, but gradually 'Sir Roger' became a curiosity rather than a working-class *cause célèbre*. He began touring with a travelling show called *Captain Transfield's Circus* but interest waned and the tour was cancelled. Then an eleven-year-old sensation, known as 'Young Nimrod', started beating the claimant, and everybody else, at pigeon shooting.

Around this time Orton met 'Nellie Rosamund', a popular male impersonator, dancer and singer whose real name was Rosina Enevers. The two became soul mates and lovers and toured together. Nellie's big hit was 'The La-di-dah Brigade', a song poking fun at the gentry. Rosina became pregnant and Agnes quit in disgust at her father's 'immorality'.

The couple visited New York in 1886 and a daughter was born there, only to die, supposedly from cholera, three weeks later. The death certificate listed her parents as Sir Roger and Lady Tichborne.

Orton and Rosina would go on to have four children, all of whom died in infancy, at least one, perhaps all, of congenital syphilis.

Of course they could not have been legally married as Orton had never divorced Mary Ann Bryant/Castro/Tichborne, who had continued to call herself Lady Tichborne while the claimant was in prison. During that time she gave birth to a further four children to various fathers, to add to the four she'd produced with the claimant and the one she'd been carrying when they first met, who had been left behind in Goulburn.

A court legally relieved Orton of any responsibility for his wife when presented with the evidence of Mary Ann's adultery and drunkenness. He had attempted to care for her but she continually pawned whatever was provided for her. She ended her life in the workhouse.

The other three children from the claimant's marriage to Mary Ann changed their names and disappeared from the story. Only Agnes stayed loyal and claimed her father was Sir Roger Tichborne until her death in 1926.

Orton and Rosina returned to London in 1871. They tried to run a tobacconist shop which failed. 'Sir Roger' appeared in pubs as a curiosity and they lived together in poverty until 1895, when a series titled 'The Claimant's Confession' appeared in several issues of the magazine *People*.

In a sworn affidavit, Orton admitted he was Arthur Orton from Wapping and told how he, Dick Slate and Gibbes concocted the fraud in Wagga Wagga, based on Slate's knowledge of the Tichbornes and the advertisement seeking information about Sir Roger.

He further claimed his intention was to get as much money as possible in advance and desert his wife and child once the ship reached Panama. This fits in perfectly with a claim by the girl hired as Agnes's nursemaid (oddly also named Rosina) that the claimant had unsuccessfully attempted to seduce her and get her to run off with him when the ship reached South America.

Orton admitted that it all changed when he reached Sydney and found that Guilfoyle and Bogle amazingly accepted him as Sir Roger, the deception took on a life of its own and he went along for the ride: 'The story really built itself . . . and in that way it grew so large that I really could not get out of it.'

The confession was made for payment and the claimant soon withdrew the confession and returned to the claim that he was 'Sir Roger'.

Having wasted away in poverty to a mere 18 stone (114 kilograms), the claimant died in bed beside Rosina of heart failure at about 5 a.m., very appropriately on April Fool's Day 1898.

Some reports erroneously say that the claimant's 'tombstone' was inscribed 'Sir Roger Charles Doughty Tichborne'. This is quite wrong, although the cemetery records do show that name for a person buried in a pauper's grave. It's the name Rosina gave the police surgeon when Orton died and thus it's the name under which he was buried and it is possibly inscribed on the coffin.

There was no tombstone.

8
KATE LEIGH—THE QUEEN OF CRIME

'She'd hit you with an iron bar as soon as look at you.'

The Girl from Dubbo

The woman we remember as Kate Leigh was born Catherine Mary Josephine Beahan in the central western New South Wales town of Dubbo, in 1881. Her parents were Timothy and Charlotte Beahan (née Smith), both Australian-born of Irish Catholic descent, but more about that later.

Dubbo, gazetted as a village in 1849, took its name from a property established by squatters in 1828. It became a municipality, with a population of 850, in 1872 and, in 1881, the same year that Kate was born, the railway arrived and the population grew steadily from that point.

Timothy made and repaired shoes and trained racehorses, while Charlotte attempted to raise their eleven kids who survived infancy. Catherine, always known as 'Kathleen' and nicknamed 'Bonny', was the ninth. She was a pretty, bright-eyed, petite girl who only ever grew to 152 centimetres, just short of 5 feet.

With her mother occupied with raising two kids younger than her, Kate wagged school, roamed the streets and became what would later be termed 'delinquent'. Kate's face had a distinctive feature when she smiled, a gap between her two front teeth. This is considered an attractive feature in many parts of the world and, way back in the 14th century, in *The Wife of Bath's Tale*, Geoffrey Chaucer told us it was considered to be a sign of lasciviousness and sexiness in a woman. In Kate's case, it seems, Chaucer was right.

Kate's father evidently made some effort to control his daughter by beating her, depriving her of food and locking her up. Apparently she turned to her mother for sympathy and defied her father's efforts to control her. Kate was picked up by police while she was wandering the streets when she was fifteen. Charged with being a 'neglected child' and having no apparent means of support, she was remanded for a week and, evidently after police consulted with her parents, who said they could not control their daughter, she was sent to the 'Industrial School for Girls' at Parramatta.

This institution had originally been the 'Female Factory', where convict women were housed during the era of transportation. In 1864 it became a reform school for wayward girls, who lived there until their eighteenth birthday. There, the girls were kept 'off the streets' and taught domestic skills and, hopefully, some measure of self-discipline.

Back home in Dubbo, Kate's father, Timothy, had his own problems. In June 1897 he was arrested for breaking into the local department store with two other men. They were acquitted three months later. Kate's mother, Charlotte, would fall foul of the law seven years later in 1904, when she was convicted of stealing shoes, which some may find a rather unusual crime for the wife of a shoemaker. Kate's older brother, Joseph, was charged, in his teenage years, with stealing and 'lewdness' and eventually, in 1900, was sentenced to two years hard labour for stealing sheepskins. In 1898 her younger brother Jack was implicated in a case that involved the theft of a gun.

One positive thing the Industrial School for Girls gave Kate was a love of cooking, something she enjoyed all her life. Self-discipline, however, was one thing the school failed to instil. Kate was released into the community in 1899 and became an unmarried mother in 1900. She chose to keep her daughter, Eileen, and struggled on, surviving as a waitress, shop assistant and factory worker in the seedy suburb of Surry Hills, where she would live the greater part of her long life.

In February 1901, Kate served fourteen days in Biloela Gaol, the women's prison on Cockatoo Island, for 'vagrancy'. Biloela had originally been a convict prison and then, until 1880, the notorious home for young female offenders, as well as orphans and neglected girls. After the New South Wales government set up a system of fostering for orphans and abandoned children, Biloela became the remand centre and prison for women.

Vagrancy was the 'crime' of having no provable means of support, which normally implied prostitution or living with criminals. At some point after leaving the Industrial School, Kate met a petty criminal named James Lee, who she married in May 1902.

James was born in Tumut, in southern New South Wales, and was described as 'half caste Chinese' in prison records. It is assumed by most of Kate's biographers that James Lee was the father of Eileen, but her birth certificate reads 'father unknown'. Two months after their wedding the couple were charged with breaking and entering the house of a Chinese man, Willie Ping. They were acquitted, but the judge raised doubts about Kate's evidence, her relationship with Mr Ping, and her role in the event. The judge suspected it was a case of 'gingering' where a prostitute or her pimp steals from their client, or the pimp poses as an outraged husband and attacks and robs the client.

In 1903, Kate was back living with her family in Dubbo, where she was accused of soliciting, and indeed practising, as a prostitute in the yard of a neighbour. The resultant row with her father evidently saw her 'thrown out' of the house, but a subsequent reconciliation led to the family taking the neighbour to court for slander. The case was not proved.

By 1905 Kate was back in Sydney with her husband who was charged with assaulting and robbing their landlord, publican Pat Lynch, who said he'd accompanied the couple upstairs to look at the wallpaper. In a sensational attempt to 'help' her husband, Kate claimed that her husband found her in bed with Lynch, having sex in lieu of the rent, because they were broke. Her husband corroborated Kate's story and claimed Lynch got out of bed and assaulted him.

The truth seems irrelevant, but it was possibly another attempt at the 'gingering game'. Nevertheless, the judge had both Kate and James Lee charged with perjury. Several months later, on appeal, there being so many versions of the event that the truth seemed impossible to fathom, both were found not guilty of perjury. James was convicted of stealing in 1906 and, in 1907, was sentenced to twelve months hard labour in Bathurst Gaol for larceny.

James and Kate Lee were, more than likely, involved in prostitution and dealing opium, which was big business in Sydney at the time. There was a very strong racist feeling and the opium dens in the Haymarket area in Sydney added to the anti-Chinese sentiment. The *Police Offences Amendment Act* finally banned the smoking of opium in 1908. By then James had become an opium addict and he and Kate were most likely selling opium during the years they lived together. Around 1902 they changed the spelling of their Chinese surname to the more European 'Leigh'.

By 1910, James Lee was well and truly off the scene and out of Kate's life when she was convicted and fined for using 'insulting language' but, in May 1913, she made headlines as a heroine. Kate had sold the lease on a cafe she ran to a couple named Kiely and was helping them as a waitress, when the incident occurred:

THE BRAVERY OF A WOMAN. EXCITING AFFRAY IN A SYDNEY CAFE.

A FRANTIC CHINAMAN WITH A KNIFE. PROPRIETOR OF THE CAFE STABBED.

SYDNEY, MONDAY.

A fierce struggle in which the bravery of a woman was revealed, occurred in the Senatorial Cafe, Elizabeth Street, on Saturday night. About 7.15 o'clock, according to the story of the Europeans concerned, a Chinese entered the restaurant and asked for some tea. Miss Kate Leigh, who has just transferred the business to Mr. and Mrs. Edward Kiely, said it was too late to get any.

When Kate refused to serve the customer, he flew into a rage and the new owner's wife asked Kate to give him some tea. He then said he didn't want any tea and threatened Kate with a knife. Mr Kiely intervened and was stabbed. Mrs Kiely ran out the back and grabbed a hatchet and gave it to Kate, who held off the enraged man and attacked him with a chair, her feet, fists and the hatchet until help arrived:

> Some young men came on to the scene, but the Chinese still fought with demoniacal fury. The knife was wrenched from the hand of the Chinese just as some constables arrived and arrested him. Miss Leigh escaped without a scratch. Kiely was taken to the hospital, suffering from deep wounds in the abdomen and back. Several stitches were inserted and an operation performed, and the patient showed a slight improvement late last night. The Chinese, who states that his name is Ah Sock, and that he is 34 years of age, has been charged with assault occasioning actual bodily harm.
>
> *Barrier Miner,* 19 May 1913

By now Kate was a 'known criminal' with convictions for insulting language, indecent language and keeping a house frequented by prostitutes, for which she was placed on a twelve-month good behaviour bond, after spending time in Long Bay prison on remand. By the end of 1913, she was living with a well-known criminal, Samuel 'Jewey' Freeman, in the worst part of Surry Hills, a slum known as 'Frog Hollow'.

On 10 June, Freeman and his 'sidekick', Ernest 'Shiner' Ryan, made headlines, and history, by stealing half of the payroll of the Eveleigh Railway Workshops as it was being delivered to the entry gates at Redfern. It was the first time in Australian criminal history that robbers had used a getaway car. The 'cab driver', who had delivered the payroll and attempted to follow the fleeing robbers, told the judge he couldn't keep up with the car, as his horse was too slow.

Ryan and Freeman were caught, found guilty and sentenced to ten years. Hilariously Ryan had sent his share of the money to a 'trusted friend' in Melbourne and, when he reached Melbourne, having evaded police by travelling disguised as a woman, his friend had vanished, with the money, to Tasmania. Ryan was arrested in Melbourne and Freeman was caught boarding the Melbourne train at Strathfield. Only £600 of the £3300 was ever recovered, hidden in the chimney of the Melbourne house where Ryan was arrested.

Several days before the Eveleigh heist, Freeman had attempted to rob the Oxford Street Post Office and had shot and wounded the night watchman. Freeman was charged with shooting with intent to kill and the case was heard immediately after he was sentenced for the Eveleigh robbery. Kate attempted to give Freeman an alibi, stating that they were at a skating rink during the day (which was, on investigation, found to be closed at the time) and, later that day, they were in bed together.

In their book, *Gangland Sydney*, James Morton and Susanna Lobez point out how outrageously shocking it was for a woman to admit such a thing in 1914, so surely such a confession made the alibi believable. Even the *Sydney Morning Herald* was flabbergasted, as Morton and Lobez point out:

> . . . the *Sydney Morning Herald* was taken in.

> 'Her admission, made in public and on oath, a woman's confession of her own lack of virtue, would have gone far to swing the scales in favour of Freeman. It seemed unbelievable that a woman would publicly parade her shame unless the facts were correct.'

> But, as she would prove time and again, Leigh was not simply a woman . . .
>
> Morton and Lobez, Gangland Sydney, p. 19

Chief Justice, Sir William Cullen, however, was not 'taken in'. The *Sydney Morning Herald* reported, on 1 April 1915:

CENTRAL CRIMINAL COURT.

(BEFORE THE CHIEF JUSTICE, SIR WILLIAM CULLEN AND A JURY OF FOUR.)

MR. R.J. BROWNING, CROWN PROSECUTOR.

FIVE YEARS FOR PERJURY.

Kate Lee, aged 34, who has been convicted of perjury in connection with the trial of Samuel Freeman . . . on a charge of shooting with intent to murder, in connection with a burglary at the Oxford-street

Post-office, was called up for sentence. Mr. Gannon, K.C. instructed by Mr. E.R. Abigail, represented the prisoner, and asked for leniency. Detective Soutar stated that the woman had been for years the associate of very bad characters. She always appeared to be very ready to help criminals who got into trouble.

The Chief Justice said it was no pleasure to him to inflict heavy sentences. But there was only too good reason to suppose that the art of perjury and subornation of perjury was being carried out to a length which sometimes threatened very seriously the administration of Justice in this State. There was a difference between falsely swearing a man into gaol, and falsely swearing a man out of gaol. But anyone who falsely swore to the innocence of a guilty person, at once threw suspicion on someone else. It would be an enormous thing if the law allowed it to be thought that such a crime would be treated leniently. 'You might as well have no laws at all,' his Honor continued, 'If you allow the decision of trials to be obtained on manufactured evidence . . . The perjury in this particular case was a very insidious thing.

'. . . It is impossible for me to say that the Jury put a wrong construction on the evidence, which was altogether too strong for me to think that deliberate perjury was not committed.'

His Honor sentenced the woman to five years' penal servitude.

So Kate Leigh went to prison and served more than four years of the sentence in the State Reformatory for Women at Long Bay. Built in 1909 the Long Bay Reformatory was designed especially for women as a reasonably civilised institution with 280 cells, bathrooms and toilets in every hall, and a huge modern kitchen and workrooms. It was a far cry from the primitive Biloela prison for women on Cockatoo Island, where Kate had spent two weeks back in 1901 for 'vagrancy'.

While Kate did her time in Long Bay, working in the kitchen, her fourteen-year-old daughter, Eileen, was sent to a convent. This appears to have had minimal effect on Eileen, as the *Truth* newspaper would name her the 'third worst woman in Sydney' in 1930, as she followed her mother into a life of crime.

While Kate was busy cooking in Long Bay prison, World War I occurred and the world changed forever. Some of the changes would immeasurably benefit her criminal career.

Six O'clock Closing

It was during World War I that an event occurred that led to the citizens of New South Wales being denied legal access to alcohol after 6 p.m. for four decades. This helped create a post-war crime wave in Sydney that lasted until World War II. Kate would be the most successful of the criminals who rode that wave.

Added to this was the odd fact that one word in two pieces of legislation, passed in 1902 and 1908, meant that the two 'master criminals' who led Sydney's crime empires during this period were not 'masters' at all. Both were mistresses, or more correctly, 'madames', who, unlike many of their male henchmen, would outlive the era of crime they helped create. One was the famous London-born prostitute Matilda Twiss, better known as Tilly Devine. The other was the subject of this story, the very experienced criminal and former gaol-bird, Kate Leigh.

Kate emerged from prison aged 38 and soon realised that post-war Sydney was perfectly set up for a new lucrative criminal activity, one that would fit in well with those she already knew how to operate, prostitution and drugs. The new 'pot of gold' was 'sly grog'.

Until 1916 the closing time for pubs throughout Australia was 11 p.m. The Temperance League and various women's groups had been lobbying for a change in licensing laws for decades. The temperance movement began in the 1820s and gathered momentum with the founding of the Salvation Army in 1864. By the 1870s rallies, marches and meetings commonly called for various levels of alcohol restriction, from stricter licensing laws and earlier closing times, to complete prohibition. By the 1890s, popular slogans like 'Lips that touch liquor will never touch mine' and 'Girls—wait for a temperance man' encouraged women to marry teetotallers.

With the outbreak of war in 1914 churches and temperance groups called for a reduction in drinking and leisure activities as part of the war effort. Laws applying to liquor trading were, of course, a state matter. The first state to vote for six o'clock closing was South Australia, at a referendum held in conjunction with a state election on 27 March 1915.

A deputation from the Temperance League addressed South Australia's state parliament and it was agreed to put the question to a referendum. The Temperance League campaigned for a six o'clock vote with the slogan, 'Lock up the liquor—not the man'. Given a choice of voting for every hour from 6 p.m. to 11 p.m., 56 per cent voted for 6 p.m. and 34 per cent for 11 p.m.

The situation in New South Wales was quite different.

In December 1913 the Holman Labor Government went to the polls with a policy of leaving the pub closing time at 11 p.m., and won the election. Two and a half years later, at a referendum in June 1916, the public attitude had changed—significantly. Given the same choice as South Australians, 63 per cent voted to close pubs at 6 p.m. and 35 per cent voted for 9 p.m. Less than half a per cent voted for 11 p.m. closing.

There was a fairly obvious reason for the turnaround in attitude.

In late November 1915, there had been a drunken rampage by around 1500 military trainees who were based at the army training camp at Casula, near Liverpool. For several days from Friday 26 November, thousands of soldiers hit the streets of Liverpool and spread to the city, taking over hotels and carousing drunkenly in an openly lawless manner.

The Liverpool Council and the NSW Police Department had long been warning the army about the discipline problems at the Casula camp. In the midst of World War I the army, however, had other priorities. But on Valentine's' Day, 14 February 1916, the police and council's worst fears came true.

An estimated seven thousand Australian trainee soldiers mutinied at Casula, defied orders, marched into Liverpool, took over the town and wrecked the hotels. Many then took the trains into Sydney and terrorised the city until ten o'clock at night.

All pubs were targets. Men simply invaded and took over the bars. Those publicans who tried to close their doors had them smashed open. Queen Victoria Markets, Regent Street Police Station, Grace Brothers Store, the *Evening News* offices and the Manly ferry wharf at Circular Quay were all attacked during the afternoon. The sheer weight of numbers meant that police were powerless to stop the rioting.

Eventually, a series of emergency measures brought the anarchy to an end: all 'train services from Liverpool were cancelled from 4 p.m., all hotels in the city of Sydney, Redfern, Glebe, Paddington and Newtown were closed by 8 p.m. and the premier, William Holman, called a crisis cabinet meeting. The police used state government cars to rush to trouble spots and called in 500 reinforcements from the suburbs, while the army mobilised 1500 regular soldiers at Victoria Barracks. At the peak of the drama a battle occurred at Central Railway Station between the rioters and the police in which seven men were shot and one man was killed.'

After the riot, hundreds of soldiers were sent to prison, 37 men were found guilty of various offences in civil courts, 280 were court-martialled and 'dismissed with ignominy' from the Australian Imperial Force (AIF), and the system of housing and training army recruits was overhauled. Then the community demanded their say, and six o'clock closing was enforced.

Four months after the day of the riot, the people of New South Wales overwhelmingly voted to close all pubs at 6 p.m. Hooliganism and public safety concerns produced a vote for 6 p.m. closing that was significantly larger than the vote in the supposedly 'wowser' state of South Australia. The New South Wales liquor industry and hoteliers campaigned heavily for a 9 p.m. compromise, but it was a lost cause. Victoria and Tasmania followed suit and introduced six o'clock closing before the end of 1916, but Western Australia and Queensland held out and never introduced it.

Sly Grog Empire

Six o'clock closing was a godsend for Kate Leigh. It marked the beginning of the 'sly grog' racket in New South Wales and heralded in the era of crime empires in Sydney. Restricting legal access to alcohol was an open invitation for criminals to provide it, and then use the profits to help build empires in prostitution, drugs, stealing, handling stolen goods and standover rackets. That's exactly what Kate Leigh did, and she did it very well.

She bought a house at 104 Riley Street, in East Sydney, and set up the back room as a 'sly grog shop'. As business grew she started renting other houses and soon had half a dozen establishments operating around the Surry Hills area. These were known as 'Hills Hotels' and the layout was always pretty much the same.

Kate favoured larger terraces with two entrances. Often there was a 'legitimate' business—fruit shop, general store or just a rented room— at the front and a spacious 'lounge', which was the illegal pub, at the back of the dwelling. There was always a second door, at the back or the side but sometimes at the front (i.e. 'next door') where patrons could exit as the police attempted to get through the front door. At the height of the sly grog era, Kate had twenty or more of these establishments operating. By the late 1920s, as well as the house in Riley Street, she owned houses in Lansdowne Street and Devonshire Street, and owned or rented other places around Surry Hills and nearby suburbs like Darlinghurst, Kensington and Ultimo.

Kate's liquor—beer, wine and spirits—was always good quality, unlike many sly grog establishments, and her illegal pubs were always tastefully furnished with lounges and radios. The key word was 'Mum'. Patrons would knock on the door and ask, 'Is Mum in?' Men looking for an illegal drinking place would ask in shops, 'Do you know where Mum lives?' Kate herself became known as 'Mum'. Witnesses giving evidence would say things like, 'Mum wasn't there at the time,' or, 'Mum was there but she never sold me any drink,' or, 'Some bloke hit me outside in the yard, it wasn't Mum.'

Kate always needed strong 'henchmen', standover men who could protect her and her customers from the other criminals who preyed on those running illegal operations. These men also made sure the customers, as well as being protected, took no liberties and showed the respect due to Kate and her 'gang'. In 1922 Kate finally divorced James Lee and married one of these men, Edward 'Teddy' Barry, a labourer and petty criminal with experience at running sly grog operations. Kate always claimed she never operated as a street prostitute (a very shaky claim at best) but she had quite openly been a gangster's 'girl'. After ruining her reputation lying to protect James Lee, and her five-year gaol sentence for attempting to protect 'Jewey' Freeman, she was determined never to play second fiddle to a man again, but she did need protection night and day.

The marriage to Edward Barry helped Kate to get her sly grog empire established, but once that was accomplished he didn't last long. He was out of the picture by the mid-1920s and moved to Western Australia and remarried. He had changed wives but evidently not his habits when he was charged with frequenting a brothel in Fremantle in 1928. Although Kate had no use for him once she had set up her empire and he had skedaddled to Western Australia, she felt kindly enough towards him to give him a room in her house many years later, when he returned penniless to Sydney. He died in Kate's house in 1948 and she attended his funeral, wearing her new silver fox fur stole.

Kate would not remarry until she was 68, but she liked to keep a man around and several of her standover men shared her bed over the intervening years. Hard man Henry 'Jack' Baker would be her protector and partner for fifteen of those years.

One claim that Kate made *was* evidently genuine. She never drank. Once, a constable, giving evidence against Kate for violently assaulting a man, claimed she had been drunk at the time. Before Kate could explode in a fit of rage, the magistrate hearing the case interrupted and told the constable that he knew that Kate Leigh never drank alcohol.

Kate's sly grog operations lasted into the 1950s, but were at their peak in the late '20s and through the '30s. By the 1940s it was getting harder to operate as freely. Several things were making life tough for 'sly groggers', and for criminals generally, as we shall see later.

The 'Snow Queen'—Prostitution and Cocaine

It may surprise some readers to realise that, in the 1920s, it was calculated that there were 5000 drug addicts in the Kings Cross area of Sydney.

Marijuana, opium and cocaine were all freely available. But it was cocaine that was the most popular and it was available from pharmacies, as it was not a banned drug until 1926. Before 1926 it was common for street prostitutes to buy 'snow' from street dealers who bought or stole the drug from pharmacies, mixed it with boric, or boracic, acid and sold it hit by hit to the 'working girls'. Once the drug was illegal the 'big criminals' moved in, importing the cocaine or working with corrupt pharmacists and managing the distribution networks. The two biggest cocaine dealers in Sydney were Kate Leigh and Tilly Devine's husband, Jim Devine.

The connection between cocaine and prostitution was simple. The girls could work more easily when 'coked up' and, as cocaine is a stimulant, they could also work longer. Girls working in brothels were often paid in cocaine once they were addicted. It is estimated that 75 per cent of Sydney's prostitutes in the 1920s and '30s were cocaine addicts. Prolonged use of cocaine cut with toxic substances like boracic acid and detergent caused their faces to deform and turn white and slowly destroyed their internal organs, as well as causing all the usual long-term effects of cocaine addiction.

Kate Leigh used her illegal 'sly grog' activities, and her famous small-time 'charitable acts', to cover the fact that she was Sydney's 'Snow Queen', luring middle-class as well as working-class girls into prostitution by introducing them to cocaine at 'parties'. Her sworn enemy, Tilly Devine, wrote to the *Truth* newspaper claiming Kate was a 'white slaver' and 'dope pusher', which she was. Tilly failed to mention that, in conjunction with her husband, she ran a not dissimilar operation.

It may seem odd to some readers that the two 'master criminals' during Sydney's crime wave from the 1920s to 1940s were female. This is partly explained by a small legal quirk in the New South Wales legislation regarding vagrancy and prostitution.

Stewart Smith, in the *Regulation of Prostitution Briefing Paper 21/99*, NSW Parliament Library, explained the history of the legislation:

> In 1908, legislation was passed in NSW that made 'soliciting by women' an offence for the first time. This was in order to 'meet what has been found to be an obvious difficulty in the way of the police in maintaining order and decency in the public streets.'
>
> Under the now repealed Vagrancy Act 1902, 'whosoever being a common prostitute, solicits or importunes for immoral purposes any person who is in any public street, thoroughfare, or place' would have been liable to imprisonment with hard labour for a term not exceeding six months.
>
> In addition, it was an offence under the Vagrancy Act 1902 for a **male person** to knowingly live wholly or in part on the earnings of prostitution. Amendments passed in 1908 created the further offence of running a brothel so that:
>
>> If any person, being the owner, occupier, or agent of any house, room, or place, or being a manager or assistant in the management thereof, induces or suffers any female whom **he** knows to be a common prostitute to be in that house, room, or place for the purpose of prostitution, **he** shall be liable to a penalty not exceeding twenty pounds, or, in the discretion of the justices, to be imprisoned for any term not exceeding six months.

The words 'male person' and 'he' meant, quite simply, that women were immune from many of the laws concerning prostitution, including running a brothel, although they could be prosecuted for soliciting and for some fringe elements of the 'world's oldest profession'.

Although both Tilly Devine and Kate Leigh were involved in prostitution, sly grog, drugs, petty theft and handling stolen goods, Tilly's mainstay was prostitution while Kate's was sly grog and cocaine. Tilly, who was a working prostitute in London before coming to Sydney as a war bride in 1920, was running eighteen brothels by 1930 and was still operating one successfully in 1968.

The heart of Tilly's empire was Woolloomooloo, but it took in Darlinghurst and Kings Cross—and her prostitution organisation was three-tiered. There were classy bordellos where the most attractive girls worked as 'call girls' for the professional businessmen, police, overseas visitors and politicians. Then there was a string of well-run tenement brothels along Palmer Street for the less wealthy customers, with lounges and private rooms, where the professional or part-time working-class prostitutes and housewives needing extra cash could work in safety. For the sailors from the nearby docks, the older prostitutes, known as the 'boat crew', were able to use Tilly's rooms on a 'casual' basis. Legislation that drove prostitutes off the streets was welcomed by Tilly, it made her brothels safe havens where girls could work unmolested, but they paid a high price, with Tilly taking half their earnings.

Kate's territory was Surry Hills and nearby suburbs, and she employed a similar prostitution system but on a smaller scale, using cocaine to keep both the classier prostitutes and the street girls working. Kate always boasted that she was never a working prostitute and was never convicted for running a brothel.

Gang Wars

Until 1926 there were three big 'crime gangs' operating in Sydney's inner suburbs. Kate's gang based in Surry Hills, Tilly's mob in Woolloomooloo, and Phil 'The Jew' Jeffs' gang, which specialised in illegal gambling, drugs and sly grog around Kings Cross. The three tolerated each other.

In November 1926 a Melbourne standover man named Norman Bruhn arrived and upset the status quo by attempting to muscle in on the other three. His attempt to break into the lucrative Sydney crime scene lasted almost exactly eight months, until he was shot dead, probably by a gunman associated with the Devines named Frank Green.

Once the balance of power was upset, things changed. Jeffs started selling adulterated cocaine and was attacked in the street by a gang possibly connected to Kate's gang. After the street brawl he was taken to the Darlinghurst Police Station, released at 3 a.m. and returned to his home in Kensington. As he slept, two men broke into the house and shot him twice as he lay sleeping. Thinking he was dying he identified the men to police. When he unexpectedly recovered, however, he refused to name his attackers in court and retired to Woy Woy on the Central Coast for a while and invested in real estate, before returning to run his clubs in Kings Cross. Jeffs was never a major player in the gang wars that followed his close call.

This left the gangs run by Kate Leigh and Tilly Devine to go to war for supremacy in the Sydney crime market.

After several skirmishes, the war broke out into shootings. In July 1929, a fight between two prostitutes led to a fist fight between one of Kate's gang, Greg 'The Gunman' Gaffney, and the Devines' gunman Frank Green. Green was living in the Devines' house at Maroubra and protecting Tilly's brothels with standover tactics. He was also robbing other illegal gambling and sly grog haunts at gunpoint.

Two days later Gaffney ambushed and shot Green, who was treated at Sydney Hospital, then picked up by Jim Devine and Tilly's bodyguard Sid McDonald and driven to the house at Maroubra. Gaffney, with another gang member, Bernard Dalton, and Wally Tomlinson, Kate's lover at the time, attacked the Devines' house at midnight. In the gunfight outside the house Jim Devine shot Gaffney and Tomlinson. Gaffney died a few hours later after promising Devine he would not name him as his murderer when the police arrived. Tomlinson, shot in the arm, escaped with Dalton. In court Jim Devine claimed he fired to frighten off the attackers and he was found not guilty of murder, as he was protecting his home and the lives of those in it.

With Kate Leigh having a brief 'holiday' in Long Bay for 'keeping a house frequented by thieves', the Devines decided to make an all-out attack with rocks and bottles on Kate's gang in Kellett Street,

Kings Cross. During the attack they grabbed Kate's chauffeur Bruce Higgs and slashed his face to ribbons with razors.

Frank Green was determined to finish the business with Kate's gang. He and Jim Devine found Tomlinson, Dalton and others of the gang drinking in the Strand Hotel, on the corner of Crown and William streets near Kings Cross. Green entered the bar alone and openly challenged them. He then waited outside with Jim Devine. When Dalton and Tomlinson left the hotel at closing time, Green shot Dalton through the heart. As Tomlinson bent over his dying friend, Green shot him in the same arm, his left, where Jim Devine had shot him at Maroubra. Tomlinson taunted Green, saying, 'Have another go,' and Green stood over him and shot him in the stomach. Green and Devine then fled the scene.

Assuming he was mortally wounded, Tomlinson named Green and Devine to police. Jim Devine was picked up the next day and, a month later, Green was tracked down in a shack near Cronulla and arrested. Miraculously, Tomlinson pulled through and nervously testified against Green at the hearing, but claimed Jim Devine was not present at the shooting.

There was so much contradictory evidence at Green's trial that the jury could not make a decision and a retrial was ordered. Meanwhile, the Devines had a contract out on Tomlinson for giving evidence against Green. A friend of Green's, John 'Snowy' Prendergast, along with his brother and two others, made two attempts to find Tomlinson in Kate's house. After they broke in and smashed up the place on 20 March, Kate told the police and bought a rifle. Five nights later, they returned and fired shots at the house from the street.

The next morning the four men broke into the house carrying pistols and Snowy Prendergast attempted to climb the stairs to the bedroom. Kate was standing in her nightgown on the stairs holding the rifle. She warned Prendergast to leave and, when he advanced, pistol in hand, she shot him in the stomach. He staggered into the back lane and died. When the police arrived, Kate told them, 'They broke up all my furniture . . . This is one of them. I shot him.'

She was acquitted of a charge of murder, the judge finding her action 'justifiable homicide', on the grounds of self-defence.

Green was acquitted at the second trial. The judge said he found it hard to convict under the circumstances, due to conflicting evidence given by witnesses, and suggested that the gangs find better ways to sort out their differences. Green later fell out with the Devines, did several stints in prison for consorting, and died in Paddington aged 54 in 1956.

Tomlinson was out of Kate's life by 1932 and lived to the reasonably old age of 68.

Big Bill and the Consorting Law

The violence that had erupted between the various Sydney gangs in the 1920s led to the licensing of handguns in 1926. Being caught with an unlicensed gun meant prison, so the gangs switched to using razors. The *1930 Crimes Amendment Act* made 'unlawful possession of a razor' punishable by six months in prison *and flogging*! Also in 1930 the *Vagrancy Act*, amended in 1929, came into force and it included harsh penalties for 'consorting'.

The consorting laws were a stroke of genius. They gave police the power to lock up anyone for six months, just for being seen in the company of known criminals on six occasions. The police didn't have to prove anything, they only had to know, or suspect, that one of the group was a criminal. In its first two years of operation, the Consorting Squad made 265 arrests and secured 179 convictions.

Consorting laws didn't stop crime, but they stopped gangs from forming or operating as a group and broke up the continuity of leadership and planning among professional criminals. They were also an excellent tool for pressuring criminals into informing on one another, as they could be used as a kind of blackmail. Rival gangs were always loath to 'shelf' (give evidence or inform against) members of enemy gangs. It was considered the worst crime in the criminal world and was often punished by murder, but when threatened with a prison term for consorting, many criminals risked it.

William MacKay, a policeman from Glasgow who came to Australia in 1910, proved to be effective at enforcing the new laws as a superintendent. His first task as a New South Wales policeman had been to keep an eye on the 'Wobblies', supporters of the IWW (International

Workers of the World) who were active during World War I, and restrict their 'subversive' activities. He proved to be very good at that and was appointed by Labor Premier Jack Lang to harass and manage the New Guard, the right-wing vigilante group who claimed to be helping police protect Australia from unionism. MacKay changed public opinion by treating the organisation as criminals, dealt harshly with their demonstrations and destroyed their credibility.

MacKay's officers successfully infiltrated both right-wing and left-wing extremist groups like the New Guard, the All for Australia League and the Communist Party. He collected information which led to the Communist Party being declared an unlawful association under the *Crimes Act* in 1932.

As detective inspector in charge of the Criminal Investigation Branch between 1928 and 1933 MacKay, aided by the consorting laws and laws banning handguns and 'concealed weapons', ended the 'razor wars' between Kate's gang and several other gangs, most notably the one led by Kate's sworn enemy, Tilly Devine.

During that period MacKay also slowly controlled Kate Leigh by putting her illegal pubs under surveillance and harassing her customers, forcing her to close her 'sly grog shops' one by one. She was sentenced to two years in Long Bay in 1930 for consorting and possession of cocaine. She served one year and paid a £260 fine in lieu of the second year.

In 1936 MacKay became Commissioner of Police and reached some sort of agreement with Kate Leigh and Tilly Devine. The killing and cocaine dealing was to stop and the sly grog and prostitution rackets would be tolerated if well run. The consorting laws helped rein in the gangs and both Kate and Tilly served time and agreed to leave Sydney for extended periods rather than serve more time.

Tolerating 'sly grog' meant Kate had opposition from nightclubs operated by Phil Jeffs at Kings Cross, and fancy restaurants like Romano's. In 1947 private clubs were able to legally serve alcohol after hours. Although Kate was still operating in the early 1950s, her sly grog empire had crumbled away to just one or two operations. In 1955 the people of New South Wales voted to allow pubs to trade until 10 p.m. Kate commented that, 'the bloom has gone off the grog'.

End Game

After the departure of Wally Tomlinson, Kate lived on and off for fifteen years with her protector and business partner Jack Baker.

From 1936, Bill MacKay cracked down on violence and drugs, but turned a blind eye to well-run brothels and nightclubs serving alcohol after 6 p.m. Tilly Devine's brothels and Kate Leigh's 'hotels' operated under a shady 'tolerated by police with a mild level of policing to satisfy the law and the wowsers' kind of arrangement. Legend has it that MacKay called Kate Leigh and Tilly Devine to a meeting and told them to stop the killing, the gang war violence, the thieving and the drug pushing or he'd lock them both up for twenty years.

Kate continued her sly grog business and was raided occasionally and fined and gaoled a few times. In 1950 one of the strangest events in Kate's life occurred. At the age of 68 she married Ernest 'Shiner' Ryan, in Fremantle, Western Australia. He had gone to prison for the Eveleigh Workshop robbery in 1914 and spent 37 years of his life behind bars for that and subsequent crimes. Evidently the two had been lovers before Kate became Samuel 'Jewey' Freeman's 'girl' and had never forgotten one another.

Ryan and Kate had exchanged 'love letters' during the last years he spent in Fremantle Prison and he evidently 'went straight' after his release in 1940 and was a much-loved figure who made kids' toys and chatted to everyone around Fremantle. Kate flew to Fremantle to marry him in 1950 and he moved to Sydney with her. The marriage lasted six months before he moved back to Fremantle.

Ryan didn't want to live in Sydney and Kate wouldn't move to Fremantle. Ryan lived another four years on the pension and was forced to pay Kate most of it as support. She sent his shirts and underpants to a Perth newspaper with a note asking them to deliver them to him as she didn't know where he was—and she thought they might. After his death she placed a sentimental little verse in the newspapers to mark the anniversary of his passing every year. They never divorced.

There was a sentimental side to Kate, as well as the callous, brutal one. The press treated her differently from Tilly Devine and often mentioned her good deeds and charitable acts. She was often witty in court and appeared 'homely' and typically Australian when compared to Tilly, who never lost her South London accent or her vicious vindictive nature, quick temper and tendency to swear like a wharfie.

The ex-policewoman interviewed by Larry Writer in *Razor*, known by the alias 'Maggie Baker', summed up the two women this way: 'Tilly was a spiteful person. Tilly would lie. Kate never lied. If you found her out she'd admit it. Tilly never admitted anything.'

Kate blocked off Lansdowne Street every Christmas for over twenty years and put on a massive party for local kids, at times catering for more than 300 of them. It was said that most of the toys she gave the kids as gifts had been stolen, but the locals didn't seem to mind. She paid for the funerals and hospital bills for Surry Hills people who were in trouble or struggling financially. Jack Baker's grandson, Hal Baker, adored Kate and told how she gave his grandfather money to buy Shetland ponies for the local kids to ride. She raised her nephew, William Beahan, who testified at her bankruptcy hearing in 1954 that she had never drank or smoked and loved kids. She is reputed to have hit her last husband, Ernie Ryan, over the head with a frying pan for swearing while there were children in the kitchen.

In 1947, private clubs were legally allowed to serve alcohol 'after hours' and nightclubs and restaurants could serve alcohol with food. Kate Leigh slowly lost her empire and as mentioned was declared bankrupt in 1954. Hit with a massive tax bill, she pleaded poverty but paid the money, claiming friends had 'helped her out'. In 1955 six o'clock closing ended, and that more or less ended Kate's criminal career.

Kate's last conviction, her 107th, came in 1954 when she was 73. A dissatisfied customer, who had been sold two bottles of 'wine' that turned out to be water, confronted Kate at her door and threatened to throw the bottles through her front window. The spritely senior citizen ducked back inside, reappeared with a rifle and said, 'Get going ya mug, or I'll blow your brains out.'

Charged with assault with a weapon, Kate was acquitted when police testified the rifle wasn't loaded, but she was convicted, once again, of selling sly grog.

There are many amusing anecdotal stories about Kate.

The retired policewoman, given the alias 'Maggie Baker' by Larry Writer in his book, recalled her first encounter with Tilly Devine, who grabbed her savagely and tried to prevent her walking her beat:

> Next thing, a woman wearing a great big black hat got off the tram. It was Kate Leigh, she came up to where Tilly was shaking me like a rag doll and, without a word, she king hit Tilly Devine and then sat on her in the street and said, 'Go and do what you gotta do, love. I'll be here when you come back.'

On some occasions, Kate's sense of humour was 'deadpan', while other times it verged on the surreal. On New Year's Eve 1942 a constable from Darlinghurst knocked on Kate's door in plain clothes and bought some liquor, which Jack Baker loaded into the waiting car. At the trial Kate kept a straight face when accused of selling sly grog: 'I've never had a sly grog business,' she protested, 'but I may have run a private hotel where liquor was sometimes sold.' She then claimed that Jack Baker was the boss of the establishment. When the judge asked 'if Jack was her lover', she exploded, 'Don't you dare talk to me like that, do you think I'd be sleeping with some big buck nigger?' The totally Caucasian Jack Baker, who everyone knew had been Kate's lover for over ten years, looked at the ceiling as the judge sent them both to Long Bay for six months and fined them £100.

On one of the last occasions that Kate's home was searched by police, in April 1953, she locked the chief of the vice squad, Detective Sergeant Ron Waldron, in her bedroom for some time and told him through the locked door, 'You might as well search it properly.' In court she said she'd only done it 'for a joke' and they were 'old friends'.

Kate was declared bankrupt after the tax department finished with her, her debts were calculated to be seven times the value of her assets. She continued to live in the upstairs room of her property at 212 Devonshire Street. Her nephew, William Beahan, ran a store in the downstairs shopfront room.

When Frank Green died in 1956, stabbed to death by his girlfriend while attacking her with a carving knife in a drunken rage, a reporter visited Kate to ask if she would attend the funeral. 'Hell, no,' she replied, but added that, if she knew where he was buried, she might 'dance on the bludger's grave'.

Kate died in St Vincent's Hospital aged 82 in 1964, after suffering a stroke. She was buried with full Catholic rights at Botany Cemetery, now known as Eastern Suburbs Memorial Park. Quite a few policemen attended her funeral, as did her once-hated enemy, Tilly Devine. They had formally 'made up' in 1947, and there is a photo of them hugging, but they never became friends. Tilly claimed she was at the funeral 'to have a stickybeak'.

Kate's grave is unmarked.

In 2015, her old home at 212 Devonshire Street sold for $1.7 million.

In an interview with author Larry Writer, retired Consorting Squad Superintendent, Ray Blissett, then in his 90s, said that Kate was 'the best informant the police ever had'. Commenting on her funeral, Blissett said:

> Jack Aldridge, one of the best detectives Sydney ever knew, read the lesson for Kate when she died. But he didn't tell the truth. He didn't tell what she was really like. She was an old bitch, she really was. She'd hit you with an iron bar as soon as look at you.

The Criminal Breed—The 'Convict Taint'

Kate Leigh served thirteen prison sentences in her lifetime and some biographers note that both of Kate's Australian-born parents were arrested and remanded for stealing, and that her mother was convicted and at least two of her siblings, Jack and Joseph, also had criminal records.

There is, however, one thing about all the biographies, articles and books on Kate Leigh that puzzles me. It is the fact that nobody has ever thought to explore Kate's ancestry, most writers simply commenting that her background was Irish Catholic.

Indeed, three of Kate's grandparents were Irish Catholic. The fourth, her mother's mother, Margaret Maynes/Smith, who was transported, convicted of manslaughter, in 1838, was Catholic, but was from Yorkshire.

Looking at Kate's family tree, we find that three of her four grandparents were convicted of crimes and transported as convicts to New South Wales, while the fourth, Esther Burn/Leavers/Beahan, was the daughter of two transported criminals. Esther married twice, both times to men transported as convicts.

On Kate's father's side, both her grandfather, Thomas Beahan, and his father, Patrick Beahan, were separately transported to New South Wales as convicts.

Kate's mother, Charlotte, was the daughter of two convicts transported for 'life', a sentence usually reserved for those originally sentenced to death. Charlotte's father, John Smith, an Irishman, was convicted at the Wiltshire Assizes in 1819 and arrived in 1820 on the convict transport *Coromandel*. Charlotte's mother, Margaret Maynes, arrived nineteen years later, in 1839, on the *Mary Anne*. Margaret was twenty years younger than John, who she married in May 1841. She had been convicted of manslaughter at the Yorkshire Assizes in July 1838.

Thomas Beahan, Kate's father's father, was convicted of robbing a warehouse and sentenced to seven years transportation. He arrived in the colony aged eighteen, on the convict ship *Medina*, in 1823. Thomas had grown up fatherless from age seven, as his father Patrick had been transported to New South Wales as a convicted criminal in 1812. Patrick was a free man when his son arrived in 1823 and was farming rented land at Windsor, northwest of Sydney. His son was assigned to him, as a convict labourer, and Patrick was granted land on the western edge of Sydney at Penrith.

Patrick applied to have his wife and daughter brought to New South Wales from Dublin and, thanks to the 'clemency of government', that was arranged and they arrived in 1826 on the first 'free immigrant ship' to the colony, the *Thames*. After fourteen years, the Beahan family were finally all together again, in sunny New South Wales.

In 1829, when he was 24, Thomas Beahan married a widow, Esther Leavers (née Burn). Esther was aged 25 and had five children, the oldest aged eleven. Her first husband, the ex-convict James Leavers, had died, aged 51, the previous year. Esther's parents were both convicted at County Carlow Assizes in 1809, probably of the same crime. They arrived, with seven-year-old Esther, in 1811, on the transport *Providence*.

Between 1830 and 1842, Thomas and Esther had six more children, to add to the five she already had when they married. In 1842 Thomas, who had received his 'certificate of freedom' in 1830, was convicted, with two others, of the armed robbery of a house in North Richmond and 'putting to fear' the residents.

Transportation to New South Wales had ended two years previously, but transportation to Van Diemen's Land was still occurring. After spending time on the prison hulk *Phoenix*, in Sydney Harbour, Thomas was transported from New South Wales to Van Diemen's Land and served eight years of a ten-year sentence, partly at Port Arthur and partly at the barracks in Hobart. He received a conditional pardon in 1848 and a full pardon in 1850 and returned to New South Wales.

Esther died in 1861, aged 57, but Thomas lived to 77 and died in 1883. It is an odd quirk of fate, and perhaps an omen, that Thomas Beahan lived the last years of his colourful life, and died, in Surry Hills, where his two-year-old granddaughter, Catherine ('Kathleen') Beahan, would, as Kate Leigh, establish her crime empire four decades later.

There was great pressure to end transportation when free settlers arrived in numbers and settled in Sydney in the 1830s and it finally ended to New South Wales in 1840. In the 19th century most people in New South Wales were keen not to be associated with convict ancestors and avoided any mention of what was known as 'the convict taint'. Sometime in the 20th century that changed. As the convict era faded further into the past, it became a more romantic notion to have a convict ancestor somewhere back in your family tree. It was something of which you could be proud.

Kate Leigh lived into the second half of the 20th century, when many Australians were attempting to find a convict somewhere back in the family tree. Kate would have struggled to find anyone in her family tree who *wasn't* a convict, or the child of one. Kate's DNA, inherited from her Australian-born parents, was 100 per cent convict origin. I am certainly not trying to say that criminality is in our DNA. I simply find it interesting that Kate's ancestry has not been explored.

Considering that Kate Leigh was known, in her lifetime, as 'Sydney's Queen of Crime' and 'The Worst Woman in Sydney', it's a very interesting family tree.

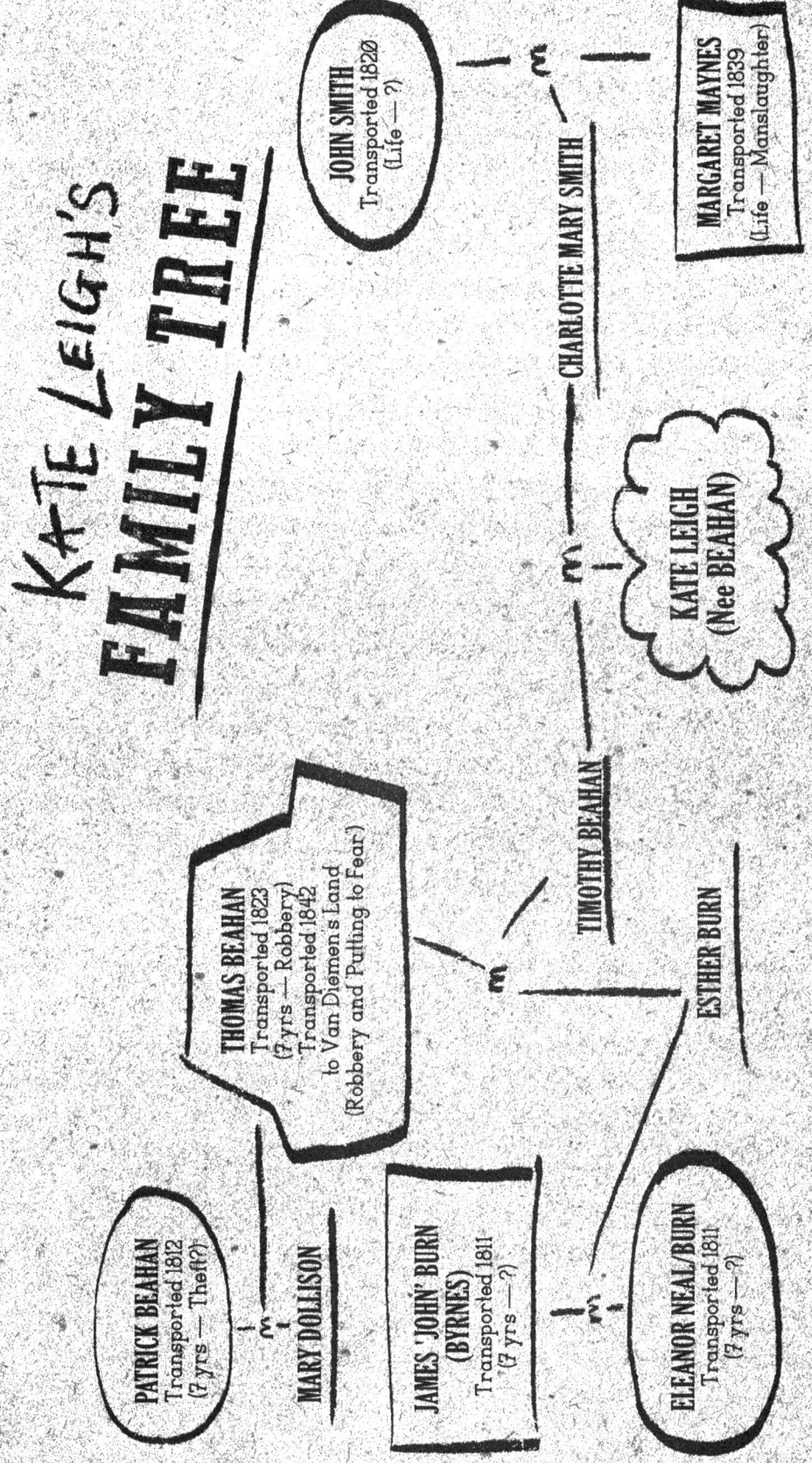

9

TOM SKEYHILL—THE FAKE HERO

'Life experience had taught him that it did not take much to manufacture credible truths from his lies.'

Tom Skeyhill and Me

I first became aware of Tom Skeyhill's verse sometime in 2003 or 2004, while researching and editing material for a collection of writings about the Gallipoli campaign called *Cobbers: Stories of Gallipoli 1915*.

The book, published in 2005, included factual accounts, verse and stories, written by soldiers and nurses who were there, as well as stories about the campaign and its emotional impact at home, by writers like William Blocksidge, E.C. Buley and the famous Steele Rudd, whose son fought at Gallipoli.

The contents of *Cobbers: Stories of Gallipoli 1915* was predominantly made up of extracts from long-out-of-print books, published between 1915 and 1930. These were written by high-ranking commanders, like General Birdwood and Colonel Beeston, officers who were professional authors, like Major Oliver Hogue and Captain Frederick Loch, and soldiers who published books of their experiences after the war, like Hector Cavill and Eric 'Haystack' Hanman.

At the Australian War Memorial in Canberra, I was given the very humbling privilege of looking through the original 150 submissions for the *ANZAC Book*, compiled and edited by official war historian Charles Bean. It was designed as a morale-boosting exercise for the men in the trenches at Anzac Cove, after the failed attempts to take control of the peninsula in August 1915 led to a stalemate. For the following four months, until the evacuation, there was little action and most casualties were from frostbite and disease.

Bean asked the men to submit verse, stories (both serious and humorous), as well as drawings and cartoons. There were prizes for the best offerings and the money raised from sales of the book went to the Army Corps. After the evacuation from Gallipoli, Bean spent several months editing and compiling the book, which was published in early 1916 and had sold more than 100,000 copies by September of that year.

In a private reading room at the Australian War Memorial, I was given two manila folders containing all 150 original submissions to peruse and use, including those that never made it into the *ANZAC Book*.

Cobbers: Stories of Gallipoli 1915 brought back to the public domain many long unavailable and forgotten writings about the campaign, and a few stories and poems that had never been published since they were written in the trenches in 1915.

Somewhere along the way during my research, I stumbled upon *Soldier Songs of ANZAC*, by Tom Skeyhill. I think it was one of the books suggested by the staff at the State Library of New South Wales' Mitchell Library, in response to my queries about writings from the Gallipoli campaign. They were also the people who arranged for me to have access to the War Memorial archive collection in Canberra— God bless 'em.

Skeyhill's verse was, of course, not among the submissions for the *ANZAC Book*, as he was no longer at Gallipoli when that morale-boosting literary exercise took place.

As a result of 'discovering' Skeyhill's work, I included some of his verse in an anthology I compiled in 2007, *The Book of Australian Popular Rhymed Verse*. I included four of his verses in a book called *The Best Gallipoli Yarns and Forgotten Stories* and wrote a piece on him, based on the biographical evidence I could find at the time. I called the piece, 'An Interesting Character'.

I also set the same four poems to music and used them in a dramatic musical presentation (a 'play for voices') called *We Were There: The Story of Gallipoli*, which was performed live quite a few times and released as a CD in 2014, in the lead-up to the centenary of Anzac Day in 2015.

In a presentation launching *The Book of Australian Popular Rhymed Verse*, as part of the 'spoken word' section of the Port Fairy Folk Festival in 2008, I talked about war poetry, mentioned Tom Skeyhill and recited two of his verses. After the launch I was approached by a member of the audience who said he enjoyed the presentation but warned me politely that many people in the district had no time for Tom Skeyhill. He suggested I might check a little more deeply into Tom's life and told me that Tom, as a teenager, had stolen money from the post office and absconded from his hometown of Hamilton.

Tom was born in Terang, 45 kilometres from the city of Warrnambool, which is 25 kilometres from the festival town of Port Fairy. His family moved to Hamilton, some 80 kilometres north of Port Fairy, when Tom was twelve. The advice given to me that day in 2008 was in the nature of, 'Jim, many people around these parts don't have much time for that bloke.'

I had always found audiences in that part of Western Victoria were extremely proud of the district's role in the Anzac story. A large percentage of the Light Horsemen who willingly left their horses in Egypt and went to fight as infantry at Gallipoli, when they heard about the losses at the landing, were Western Districts men. Scores of them died at the badly botched battle at The Nek on 7 August 1915.

I was perplexed to hear that Tom Skeyhill's reputation, as a respected war hero, verse writer and much acclaimed speaker, did not extend to the district in which he grew up.

When I found time, I went back to researching Tom through the National Library of Australia's search engine Trove, which enables us to read all the significant Australian newspapers and magazines ever published, from the time of first settlement in Sydney to 1956. I began to realise that, in my earlier writing about him, I had been repeating and reinforcing certain untruths and deliberate deceptions created by

Tom Skeyhill about himself. Consequently I began to revise my own opinion of Mr Skeyhill and did more research and further reading.

I soon discovered that someone else had been on the same trail. In 2010 Professor of Cultural Studies at Canberra University, Dr Jeff Brownrigg, wrote an exposé of Tom's life with the subtitle, *The Story of Tom Skeyhill, Master of Deception*. It is a very thorough, but at times confusing, account of the details of Tom's life. The book's title *Anzac Cove to Hollywood* (perhaps suggested by the publisher or a publicist) is rather odd, as Tom never had any connection with Hollywood. Nevertheless the book certainly helped to corroborate things I had found out—and told me much more that I hadn't been able to uncover.

In 2004, I had written:

> Tom Skeyhill was an interesting phenomenon. While at Gallipoli he wrote a large amount of rhymed verse that was popular at the time, but his fame was fleeting and his volumes of verse now long forgotten. Skeyhill fought as a regimental signaller of the 2nd Infantry Brigade and was blinded at the second battle of Krithia on 8 May 1915. He was hospitalised in Egypt and later at the Base Hospital in Melbourne. His patriotic stirring doggerel was published, both here and in New York, and he was something of a celebrity during and immediately after the war. Later he recovered his sight and lived into the 1930s.

I did manage to get a few things right. He is 'an interesting phenomenon', and he did write a lot of verse that was published during and after World War I. He was a signaller in the 2nd Brigade. He was also at the 2nd Battle of Krithia and spent time in hospitals, became a celebrity and was subsequently forgotten.

However, I got a few things wrong in 2004. He only wrote two or three poems at Gallipoli, as he was only there a fortnight. He didn't 'recover his sight' after the war, because he never lost it. He was not blinded at Krithia—he faked the whole thing to get out of the war, gain attention and sympathy, and make a lot of money.

The Fantasy of 'The Blind Soldier Poet'

On 25 May 1932, the *Sydney Morning Herald* published the following obituary of Tom Skeyhill, under the headline:

TOM SKEYHILL—End of Romantic Career:

The career of Mr. Tom Skeyhill, whose death is reported from New York, was, for its sheer romance, almost without parallel. From the most humble beginning, he eventually achieved fame throughout the English-speaking world as poet, lecturer, author, playwright, and philosopher. To most Australians, however, he will best be remembered as 'Signaller' Tom Skeyhill, the blind poet, who in 1917 toured Australia, lecturing on his experiences at the war, and delivering recruiting addresses.

A native of Victoria, he was working as a telephone attendant when the war broke out, and at the age of 19 years he enlisted, sailing from Australia with the first contingent. He filled in many hours on Gallipoli writing verse, not with the idea of turning it to profitable account, but merely to give expression to the inspiration as it seized him.

After the evacuation of Gallipoli he was transferred to France, and after having engaged in many stern fights he was wounded and he became practically blind. Not only was his sight diminished to such an extent that he could see only the faintest glimmer, but oftimes he suffered acute attacks of inflammation of the eyes which compelled him to spend days at a time in bed. Yet his great affliction left him undaunted. Even when in the grip of one of these attacks he would bravely leave his bed to fulfil a lecturing engagement. He continued to express himself feelingly in verse, and also showed that he was an orator of no mean order.

His commanding presence, and faculty for giving voice to vivid phrases caused him to be much sought after as a platform speaker. Immediately he became a national figure, but he did not allow the improvement in his financial position to diminish his interest in his late comrades, and it is estimated that the War Chest, Red Cross Society, and other patriotic organisations benefited to the extent of £10,000 as the result of his efforts.

His lecturing tours in the United States were even more successful than those which he had conducted in Australia. There, his services were eagerly availed of for the campaign in support of the famous Liberty Loan. He was credited with having raised 100,000,000 dollars on behalf of USA war funds, 25,000,000 dollars having been raised at a meeting which he addressed for 25 minutes at the Metropolitan Opera House, New York, on 9 October 1918.

His eyesight had suddenly been restored to him in May of that year. Following several days of pain in the back of his head, he underwent a slight operation on the vertebrae of the neck. Almost immediately he had an improvement in his eyesight, and in response to specialised treatment it gradually improved until finally he was able to write and use a typewriter.

After four years in America he returned to visit his parents at Hamilton (Victoria) in 1921, with a wide reputation as an orator, author, and philosopher. He had filled many roles during his absence from Australia, but, perhaps, his greatest achievement was that of exhaustively investigating conditions in Soviet Russia. He was commissioned by the American Affiliated Lecture Bureau to carry out this adventurous and, at that time, somewhat hazardous undertaking. Owing to the refusal of the Reds to allow him to enter the country, Mr. Skeyhill gained admission to Russia by sleighing across the frozen Gulf of Finland, and by using forged passports and a disguise.

Once across the border he was taken under the care of friends, and was enabled to visit the big cities and centres of political activity. Having seen Russian conditions free from the customary stage management that is provided for visitors to that country, Mr. Skeyhill declared that Russia offered a tragic lesson to the world, and he warned his fellow-Australians to resist to the utmost the teachings and influences of extremists, lest their own country might be afflicted with the ruin, chaos, and despair that were everywhere in evidence in Russia.

He returned to America, and his lectures for years afterwards commanded great attention in the United States. An honorary degree was conferred upon him by the University of Ohio. Still later, he turned his hand to writing stories and plays, but continued to find time to express himself in characteristic verse.

The problem with this obituary is that it is actually a fictional account of the life of a fictional character, one that Tom Skeyhill created over time by spinning a web of lies and creating a fantasy world of falsehoods around himself.

Versions of this pack of lies have appeared in articles about Tom Skeyhill in newspapers, websites and military writings, for more than one hundred years, purporting to be genuine accounts of his life.

Even his biography in the *Australian Dictionary of Biography* is riddled with false information. This is how the dictionary describes Tom's later life:

> He later wrote plays, including *Passing Shadows*, *Moon Madness* and the successful *The Unknown*, and a biography of Sergeant Alvin York, which was filmed in 1941. Skeyhill was killed in an air accident at Hyannis, Massachusetts, on 22 May 1932. He was survived by his wife Marie Adele, a New York actress, and by their daughter Joyce. Though he had lived in New York, he was buried with a military funeral at West Dennis, Massachusetts, where he had had a summer home.

There is no evidence to show that Tom ever wrote any plays, apart from the fact that he *said* he did. There is certainly no evidence that he wrote plays that were *performed* anywhere. If they had been, there would be evidence in newspapers and theatre magazines, but there isn't.

His biography of Alvin York was written in the first person and is full of embroidered information from York's diaries, to which Skeyhill added material, in his own swashbuckling style. It was not used as a basis for the film and York himself was reluctant to give Tom any credit, or give his estate any remuneration, when the film was produced in 1941.

Also, Tom was not 'killed in an air accident', as the dictionary states. The Melbourne *Herald* reported accurately, on Monday 23 May, the day after Tom died: 'New York, May 23, Mr Tom Skeyhill an Australian, died at Hyannis Massachusetts, as the result of injuries received in a forced landing in an aeroplane on Saturday.'

Tom survived the crash landing, along with the two others in the aircraft, which was attempting to land on his property at Hyannis Port. Tom had a broken femur and was driven to hospital in a private car by someone who had witnessed the accident. He died in hospital after a blood clot from the wound moved to his lungs. An emergency operation at midnight failed to save him and he died on the afternoon of the following day.

The autopsy, carried out in the hospital mortuary, concluded Tom's death was 'due to a pulmonary embolism following his broken left thigh'.

Also, Tom was not married to Marie Adele (sometimes 'Adels'), although the two had lived together for several years and had a daughter. Tom did not leave a will and his estate was administered by the Commonwealth of Massachusetts. An official notice appeared in local newspapers calling for parties interested in his property to declare their interest as the administrator could find no widow or heir in the records for the County of Barnstable, where Tom's property at West Dennis was situated.

Members of the Cape Cod American Legion arranged a military funeral for Tom and fired a salute as he was buried at West Dennis Cemetery. Not bad for a bloke who was on active service in a war zone for a total of thirteen days.

Tom's headstone reads:

Tom Skeyhill
1896–1932
Born in Australia
English Soldier in World War
Author Lecturer

It is rather fitting that Tom's carved epitaph is inaccurate—he was born in 1895 and was an Australian soldier.

The story of how he got away with so many deceptions for so long is, I think, the most interesting thing about him. The truth about Tom Skeyhill is that he was a pathological liar who distorted history and conned and misled many thousands of normal, decent, but extremely gullible, Americans and Australians. What is more, he did it all for his personal gain.

Early Days

Tom Skeyhill was born in 1895 in the Victorian town of Terang, where his father was the manager of the local aerated waters and cordial (soft drink) factory. On both sides, his grandparents were Irish migrants and his mother's father, Hugh Donnelly, was a pioneer of the Warrnambool district. Hugh was, evidently, a yarn-spinner or 'shanakee' in the Irish tradition, renowned for telling tales of the old days and the fabled 'mahogany ship' found and then lost again in the sand dunes between Warrnambool and Port Fairy.

In 1902, when Tom was seven, the family moved to Hamilton, 110 kilometres to the west, when his father, James, had purchased his own aerated waters factory. Tom, the oldest of the four Skeyhill children, attended St Mary's Convent School and was a promising student. He developed a love of poetry and began writing rhymed verse. He also demonstrated skill at debating and public speaking and, in his final year at school, became a member of the local Hibernian Society, where he developed his skills in oratory and debating.

In spite of the promises shown as a student, Tom, like most children in country towns in 1909, left school at thirteen. He secured a job as a telegram boy in the Hamilton Post Office. This is where the story gets interesting.

In early 1969, Melbourne *Age* journalist Michael Ryan travelled to Hamilton to research Tom Skeyhill's early life. He interviewed a number of locals who remembered Tom and did not think kindly about him. In the article that appeared in *The Age* on 10 March, under the headline 'Skeyhill—Man of Mystery', Ryan noted:

> Thomas Skeyhill walked under a shadow even before he first left Hamilton. From school he went to work in the Hamilton post office until it was found that he had absconded with some of the funds.
>
> He was found wandering in scrub near Portland and, in the meantime he had been struck deaf and dumb. Skeyhill's silence lasted until some sporty boys stuck a pin in him at the YMCA hall one night arousing a string of curses.

The inference is that Tom, having stolen money and absconded to the coastal town of Portland, some 90 kilometres away, then feigned dumbness and amnesia, in an attempt to explain or obscure the crime.

It is possible that Tom's charade was inspired by a story in the *Hamilton Spectator* in June 1911. A local boy, Duncan McGillvray, was lost in the bush while hunting and when discovered several days later, hungry and frightened, could barely mumble his name and had no explanation for what had happened during the time he was lost.

It seems that Tom returned to Hamilton, but at some point was sent to live with an aunt at Gembrook, east of Melbourne in the Dandenong Ranges. Why he left Hamilton we don't know, but it was possibly due to his unpopularity after the alleged theft from the post office.

We have no way of knowing how happy Tom was, living in a rural setting outside of Melbourne, some 350 kilometres from home. However, it seems he wanted a change of circumstances. The *Portland Guardian* reported, in 20 February 1914:

STRICKEN DUMB

A Melbourne wire dated Tuesday says: Stricken dumb by the shock of an accident to his hand Thomas Skeyhill, aged 19, whose parents live at Hamilton, is answering questions by gesture at the Melbourne hospital today. At Gembrook yesterday afternoon he was cutting eucalyptus leaves and was carrying an arm full of leaves when he slipped and fell upon a hook, severely cutting the first finger on his left hand. He walked alone to Gembrook station, about 8 miles, where the engine driver of the train tied a bandage around the finger. The lad could not speak and was conveyed by train to Melbourne. On the journey a Mrs Hornhill, of Armadale, took an interest in him, and on arrival at Flinders Street station, brought him in a cab to the Melbourne Hospital. Afterwards she accompanied the lad to the residence of his aunt Mrs E. Wright, at Myrtle Street South Yarra. Mrs Wright took the boy to the hospital again this morning. He is still unable to speak, but otherwise seems to be alright, and shows that he feels no pain. Dr Nance believes the case to be one of hystero-epilepsy. The victim of the strange accident is the son of Mr and Mrs J.P. Skeyhill, of Brown Street, Hamilton, and was formally employed at the local post office.

Tom was back home in Hamilton on Saturday 21 February, two days after the 'accident', and the *Hamilton Spectator* was able to report, on the following Monday:

STRANGE LOSS OF SPEECH

Mr. T. Skeyhill, who was stricken dumb on Tuesday by the shock of an accident to his hand, returned to Hamilton on Saturday. In the evening he visited Dr. Scott for the purpose of having his finger dressed. The doctor found that the injury was rapidly healing, but the young man had not yet recovered the power of speech. He has, however, been able to articulate three or four words on two occasions—once while in Melbourne and on Saturday—and Dr. Scott is of the opinion that he will soon be all right again.

Apparently Tom stayed with his parents for the next eight months and departed by train for the Broadmeadows training camp on 14 October to join the 8th Battalion as a signaller, after the outbreak of war in August.

Anzac Cove and Cape Helles
When the 8th Battalion left for Albany on 18 October, to join the ANZAC convoy, Tom stayed behind to complete his training, and was attached to a group who were to be reinforcements for the 7th Battalion. He sailed to Egypt on HMAT *Themistocles* in December and joined the ANZAC force near the pyramids at Mena Camp.

In March 1915, he was hospitalised with tonsillitis for a week but had recovered in time to rejoin the 8th Battalion when they embarked from the port of Alexandria for the island of Mudros, where they arrived on 17 April.

Eight days later they were part of the famous landing on Ari Burnu beach, on the Gallipoli Peninsula on the morning of 25 April 1915.

Tom spent ten days with the ANZAC force at what became known as 'Anzac Cove'. It was obviously a life-changing experience for all involved, including Tom. In between digging trenches and laying telephone wires as part of his job as a signaller, he found time to write some verse.

During the first week at Anzac Cove, Tom wrote the two poems that are arguably his best. For the first time his flowery romantic doggerel is replaced by some genuine feeling and observation, expressed in a truly 'Aussie' voice. Although the voice is rather overdone, and very derivative of the work of Australia's most popular verse writer at the time, C.J. Dennis, it is graphic, recognisably Australian and 'singable'.

His poem, 'Shrapnel', contains an odd and spooky premonition about the condition that would become known after the war as 'shell-shock' and many decades later as 'post-traumatic stress disorder'. The last two stanzas of 'Shrapnel' read:

It's always bloomin' shrapnel, wherever you may be,
Sittin' in your dug-out, or bathin' in the sea.
At Shrapnel Gully, Deadman's Gully, Courtney's Post and Quinn's,
At Pope's Hill and Johnson's Jolly . . . that deadly shrapnel spins.

I don't mind bombs and rifles, and I like a bayonet charge,
But I'm hangin' out the white flag when shrapnel is at large.
When I get back to Australia and I hear a whistlin' train,
It's the nearest pub, for shelter from that shrapnel once again!

Tom's parody of the popular song, 'My Little Grey Home in the West', is actually a rather good attempt at irony and expresses very well the stoic character of what would become known as 'digger humour'. It was called 'My Little Wet Home in the Trench'—here's one of the verses:

There's a Little Wet Home in the Trench,
Which the raindrops continually drench,
There's a dead Turk close by, with his toes to the sky,
Who causes a terrible stench.
There are snipers who keep on the go,
So we all keep our heads pretty low,
But with shells dropping there, there's no place can compare,
With My Little Wet Home in the Trench.

The ten days he spent at Anzac Cove were certainly the most important ten days of Tom's life. He was later able to use those experiences to extrapolate a web of lies, exaggerations and misinformation that would create a false persona, from which he was able to achieve undeserved fame and respect, and construct a successful and very lucrative career as a speaker.

On 5 May 1915, the 8th Battalion assembled at Brighton Beach just to the west of Anzac Cove to embark for Cape Helles in order to reinforce the British 29th Division.

On the morning of 25 April, the British had landed at Cape Helles, under a heavy artillery barrage from the Turkish defences above them on the ridges, by running the troopship *River Clyde* onto the beach. The British suffered massive losses (2000 men) in attempting to land and establish a foothold. On 28 April they attempted to take the village of Krithia by charging across open country at the well-defended ridges that protected it.

Major-General Hunter-Weston was the officer in charge and he tragically bungled the whole affair, throwing 14,000 Allied infantrymen in wave after wave at Turkish machine guns and a 300-metre-high ridge. In the carnage that followed what became known as the First Battle of Krithia, another 2000 British troops were lost, along with 1000 Frenchmen.

After reinforcements arrived on 5 May, Hunter-Weston, devoid of any new ideas, common sense or respect for the lives of the men he commanded, attempted to do the whole thing over again, in what became the Second Battle of Krithia.

From 6 to 8 May, Hunter-Weston used exactly the same failed tactics and achieved the same result, a military debacle and a crushing defeat. This time, however, the Allied casualties were 6500 men. Historian Les Carlyon wrote that Hunter-Weston 'seemed without imagination . . . He threw away troops the way lesser men threw away socks.'

In one hour, at the Second Battle of Krithia, 1000 Australians died. There is a photograph taken after the battle of the survivors of D Company 7th Battalion, still standing and able to fight. D Company would have contained 200 to 250 men when the Anzacs landed on 25 April. In the photo, taken after the Second Battle of Krithia on 8 May, there are exactly 27 men.

It was on 8 May, in the midst of the carnage and chaos that was the Second Battle of Krithia, that Tom Skeyhill, waiting in the trenches as the 8th Battalion took part in the battle, claimed that a high-explosive shell landed at his feet, exploded and blinded him.

Having been 'stricken dumb' twice in his life—the second time just fifteen months earlier as a result of the trauma of cutting a finger—Tom was now, in the midst of battle, 'stricken blind'.

There were no witnesses to the event. Tom had his eyes bandaged by another Victorian, F.W. Arnold, who survived the battle and became head teacher at Corryong Primary School after the war. Arnold then guided Tom from the battlefield to a field hospital. In later years Tom evidently told of being rescued from 'no man's land' eleven hours after he was 'wounded'.

Tom had no visible wounds or bleeding. His bandages were removed at the field hospital and small shrapnel fragments were suspected as the cause of his blindness, but none were subsequently found. Four days later Tom was on the hospital ship *Braemer Castle*. There was apparently no further medical examination of his eyes until he reached the General Field Hospital at Heliopolis, in Egypt, on 15 May. This is hardly surprising as the *Braemer Castle* carried 850 wounded men and two doctors.

Tom's admission record at the hospital gave his age as 22 and his problem as 'Shrap. eyes'. Doctors could find no damage, however, and soon ruled out shrapnel, and suspected damage from the concussion of an extremely close explosion. It seems odd that, if this was the case, Tom's ears were fine and there were no wounds or burns.

Tom was discharged from hospital on 27 July but was exempt from duty due to his blindness. He remained in Egypt until 16 September 1915, resting and creating and dictating verse to a friend. During this time he wrote some of his most popular verses, 'The Sniper', 'Red Cross Nurse' and 'The Holding of the Line'. These came to the notice of Colonel James McCay, who was also in the hospital at Heliopolis recovering from being badly wounded in the leg at Cape Helles.

McCay became interested in Tom. He could see the usefulness of his verses as a way to boost morale among the troops still fighting and as a recruiting tool. Back home, after being wounded and repatriated, McCay would become involved in recruiting, write the introduction to Tom's first book of verse, and make opportunities for Tom to speak in support of the war effort.

Tom's poems were published in the English-language Egyptian newspapers. The *Egyptian Mail* published a small 'supplement' booklet of the poems and some were printed in British and Australian newspapers.

Tom arrived home on the troopship *Beltana* on 10 October 1915. His first volume of collected verse, *Soldier Songs of Anzac*, was published by George Robertson on 3 December 1915; it was well into its third edition by mid-1916.

According to Jeff Brownrigg, Tom was discharged from the Australian Imperial Force (AIF) on 28 September 1915 in Melbourne (on another page Brownrigg lists it as 29 September 1915), which would mean he was discharged while aboard the *Beltana*. The Australian War Memorial records show Tom not being discharged until a year later, 28 September *1916*.

On arriving home Tom spent some weeks in the Repatriation Hospital at Heidelberg and, at some stage in November 1915, appeared in his uniform to speak and perform his verse and songs at Melbourne's Tivoli Theatre.

'Eloquent, Thrilling, Awe-Inspiring'

Tom very quickly 'got his act together' and, by January 1916, was touring the theatres of Victoria with a very polished show.

The colour poster for the 28 January performance in Albury tells us that:

Under Vice-Regal Patronage
SIGNALLER TOM SKEYHILL
(The Blind Soldier Poet)
Author of 'Soldiers Songs from ANZAC'
In his graphic and thrilling war story
WITH THE ANZACS AT THE DARDANELLES
A true and accurate account of the part played by the Australians in
THE LANDING AT THE DARDANELLES

. . . will be:

Describing all the fierce fights for ANZAC and Cape Helles

The poster goes on to tell us that this will be:

> Eloquent thrilling awe-inspiring and illustrated with over 200 maps,
> plans, diagrams and actual photographs taken on the spot and
> in the thick of the fighting.

We are also informed that tickets are 2 shillings or 1 shilling and that
Private Bobby Pearce is the business manager of the enterprise. Pearce
also had a reasonable tenor voice and sang several patriotic songs in
the show.

Bobby Pearce was a good match for Tom Skeyhill. A grazier's son
from a property near Tallangatta in northeastern Victoria, he was
four years older than Tom and had enlisted (occupation 'farmer') as
a private in the 4th Battalion in Sydney at the start of the war. The
publicity material for the theatre shows stated that Pearce had returned
from Gallipoli with four bullet wounds in his abdomen. Army records,
however, tell a different story.

According to official wartime medical documents, Pearce's injuries
consisted of a scalded foot caused by a shrapnel wound on 8 May at
Gallipoli, and a hernia. His main problem was the hernia, apparently
sustained while jumping from the boat on landing on the morning
of 25 April. Pearce had undergone several hernia and appendectomy
operations before enlisting. These had caused him ongoing trouble
before the war and required two further operations, the last just
six months before he enlisted.

A 'Medical Report on an Invalid' form, dated 15 June 1915 in Egypt,
states that his disability was caused by 'adhesions following general
peritonitis' and gives the cause of the problem as: 'Peritonitis and appen-
dicitis painful attacks at intervals. Increased after injury at Gallipoli.'

The form says the origin of the disability was, however, Australia.

Nevertheless, on 25 June, the army medical board declared Pearce
unfit for active service and eligible for a war pension. He left Alexandria
on the troopship *Ballarat* on 5 July 1915 and arrived in Melbourne on
6 August. He was officially discharged from the AIF on 10 November
1915 and became Tom's manager sometime in December.

For the next two years Tom Skeyhill and Bobby Pearce toured
constantly. Tom's books were bestsellers and the shows were well
received everywhere they were performed.

The immediate popularity of Tom's shows and books ran parallel to a renewed campaign to encourage the enlistment of recruits into the AIF. The campaign began in November 1915 and was a success at first. By the middle of 1916, however, enlistment began to fall again. The AIF lost 27,000 men in the major battles in the Somme Valley in July 1916 and the British requested another 35,000 Australian troops to replace them.

As recruitment slowed Prime Minister Billy Hughes called for a referendum to introduce compulsory conscription. The campaigning for the referendum caused a bitter debate that split the population into two camps. There were rallies, protests and marches leading up to the referendum on 28 October 1916. The proposal was defeated, to the surprise of most pundits, when 51.6 per cent of the 2.3 million voters voted 'no' to conscription.

With the support of military men like Major-General James McCay, and many civil dignitaries, Tom became a useful tool for those leading the recruiting drive and, later, the campaign for a 'Yes' vote at the conscription referendum. Having cleverly 'conned' his way out of the war by feigning blindness, Tom had no qualms about encouraging other young men to enlist, serve and die in the war. Some of his poems, like 'Me Brother Wot Stayed at 'Ome', attempt to shame others into enlisting:

I'm sick of fightin' Turkeys
Out on my bloomin' own,
When I thinks of 'im in 'Stralia –
Me Brother Wot Stayed at 'Ome.

Given the mood of the time, the loss of Australian lives on faraway battlefields and the passions aroused by the referendum debate, we can easily imagine the effect of Tom's sentimental verses, recited movingly by the author, wearing his army uniform, 'blindman's glasses', and effectively stage-lit at the end of his 'act':

The blue sea seems a-sighing,
In the morning air so clear,
As though grieving o'er the fallen,
Who never knew a fear . . .

Sleep on! Dear fallen comrades!
You'll ne'er be forgotten by
The boys who fought beside you
And the boys who saw you die.

The two former privates were able to benefit from Tom's involvement in the recruitment drive, the 'Vote Yes' campaign and his fundraising appearances for the war effort and the Red Cross. Visits to towns and cities around Australia would involve a public meeting with Tom sharing the platform with local military and civil dignitaries to appeal for recruits, speak in favour of a 'Yes' vote, and raise money. Tom appeared with former prime minister Alfred Deakin in Melbourne and New South Wales Premier William Holman in Yass. After a public daytime rally, or perhaps the next night, following an evening rally, Tom and Bobby would stage their show, sell Tom's books and pocket the proceeds.

This *modus operandi* continued for almost two years, by which time the show had visited many towns and cities on two occasions. The novelty of two veterans of Gallipoli singing and reciting about, and explaining, a campaign that had occurred at the start of the war was losing its impact.

Then, on 6 April 1917, the United States joined the war. It would be many months, however, before they recruited and mobilised men and manufactured equipment to make an impact on the war in Europe. Tom saw an opportunity to repeat his success, using a similar approach in a much larger marketplace. He packed his bags and headed to Hawaii in December 1917.

Home of the Brave, Land of the Gullible

Tom's timing was perfect. He arrived in the US in the midst of a fundraising campaign to support the American efforts in World War I. The situation was not unlike the ones he had used in Australia to promote himself and make a lot of money while being seen as a war hero supporting the war effort by appearing at fundraising events, encouraging recruitment and speaking in favour of the 'Yes' vote for the conscription referendum. The population of the United States was, however, 113 million, compared to Australia's 5 million. Tom was now in the land of opportunity.

He found himself an American agent who made the right contacts. He arrived in Hawaii, where the first two shows made him $2000, at a time when the average annual salary in Australia was £200 a year. In San Francisco he made valuable contacts through helping to raise money for the war effort and appeared at an event with President Woodrow Wilson. That led to appearances in New York. Tom appeared with former President Teddy Roosevelt at a fundraising event at Carnegie Hall and later claimed that Roosevelt said of him: 'You are the finest soldier speaker in the world . . . I am prouder to be on stage with you than any other man I know.'

There is no record of this, apart from Tom's much-repeated account, but Tom was now a master at making a 'bit part' in such events appear to be the leading role in his publicity. Tom also claimed to have drawn a crowd that blocked traffic on 5th Avenue when he spoke from the balcony of the Millionaires' Club building, and set a fundraising record at the Metropolitan Opera House when his 23-minute performance resulted in $23 million being pledged for the war effort.

Just who else appeared at the 'Met' that night to help raise the money, I don't know and there is no photo of the 5th Avenue crowd. There is, however, a photo of Tom addressing a massive crowd in Times Square, and he was described in the popular *Literary Digest* magazine as: 'a young Crusader, a Knight of the Holy Grail . . . the sort of man worth reading about carefully'.

I have to smile reading those words, because reading about Tom 'carefully' enough to discover the truth is something that is not easy to do, as I have found out. Almost everything written about Tom, from the time he returned home in 1915 from Gallipoli, was written, related or interpreted in prose by Tom himself. Reading carefully between the lines and sorting out the fiction and the distortions from the facts is no easy task.

Often the only thing to do is explore the background to the events Tom claims are true and try to see how he managed to connect people, events and half-truths to make a thing appear credible—and then published it in his publicity repeatedly until, as time passed, it was accepted without question.

The story of how he 'recovered his sight' is a good example of this.

From as early as August or September 1915, Tom was hinting that his 'blindness' might not be permanent. The *Hamilton Spectator* published an article containing news collected from letters sent home by local men serving overseas, on 4 October 1915. One letter from a Private MacDonald mentioned that he had seen Tom in Egypt and that his eyesight was a little better. Tom was already amending his 'story' by declaring that he could occasionally make out shapes and colours.

By late 1917, Tom was, no doubt, finding his 'blind act' rather restricting. He was constantly required to have a minder, to keep up the charade, and was keen to manage his own affairs now that he was established as a 'famous speaker'. Being blind had been a drawcard but being 'miraculously cured' would be even better.

The story he told of how it happened changed over the years. After his death his mother related it this way:

> Dr Riley Moore of Washington, assisted by other doctors, had Tom on the massaging table for 18 hours, and by constant massaging of the vertebrae brought about a condition which released the optic nerve and his sight was restored. All over America the operation was recognised as a wonderful one.

Tom's other versions of the story often mention that he was introduced to Dr Moore, of the Smithsonian Institution, by his good friend Theodore Roosevelt.

The cleverness of Tom's concoction is only uncovered by tedious research. Roosevelt's connection with the Smithsonian Institution is well documented. He went on a Smithsonian-sponsored trip to Kenya collecting natural history specimens not long after his presidential term ended, and he was known to be a great supporter of the institution.

But just who was Dr Moore?

Well, Dr Riley Dunning Moore was an aide to Aleš Hrdlička, the man who first proposed the theory that the ancestors of Native Americans migrated from Asia across the Bering Strait. Hrdlička founded the Department of Physical Anthropology at the US National Museum (now the Smithsonian Institution National Museum of

Natural History) in 1903. Moore worked for Hrdlička collecting specimens, mostly bones, and as an aide, from 1912 until 1918. Hrdlička was dissatisfied with Moore's work and wrote to a colleague that he would like to find 'a better prepared man' for the position. Moore resigned on 20 June 1918 and set up in private practice as an osteopath.

Tom claimed to have had his sight restored 'by March 1918'.

The tenuous implied connections—Roosevelt, Smithsonian, bones, Riley Moore, osteopathy, vertebrae, manipulation, nerves, optics—all seem to make sense in retrospective publicity. Actual details? Well, we know Tom met Roosevelt once and we know Roosevelt was connected to a museum at which Moore was an aide to a famous anthropologist.

Dr Moore and a team of 'other doctors' working eighteen hours massaging Tom in some sort of clinic at least six months before Moore quit his ancillary position at a museum? I leave the reader to judge.

There are many more of these types of concoctions during Tom's fifteen years living in the United States, so I will simply summarise the most obvious examples.

A Catalogue of Chautauqua Concoctions

The hugely popular Chautauqua speaking circuit was the brainchild of Reverend John Vincent and a businessman, Lewis Miller. In 1904 on the shores of Chautauqua Lake, in western New York State, the two men started a program that was designed to educate and inspire Sunday school teachers. Lectures on topics as diverse as current affairs, history, self-improvement and literature were conducted in tents along the shores of the lake.

Middle America was thirsty for knowledge and the concept quickly blossomed and became a huge and extremely lucrative business. There were rival agencies and circuits quickly developed all around the US. The Redpath Circuit Chautauqua Bureau, which had been established in 1904 was, by the mid-1920s, the largest in the country and had venues operating in 10,000 towns and cities across 45 of the 48 American states.

By 1919 Tom was managing himself and working on several speaker circuits, including the Redpath Circuit Chautauqua Bureau and the Affiliated Lyceum and Chautauqua Bureau. In 1923 he signed up to perform on the Redpath organisation's major circuits. This meant that he could repeat the same 'lecture' day after day for an entire season, moving from town to town.

Tom's first lectures on the circuits consisted of versions of the performance he had given for two years back in Australia, modified to suit American tastes. He also modified his appearance, having extensive dental work done to give him a truly 'American smile' and adding a smart US Army–style collar and tie to his Australian uniform. Later he replaced the hatband on his slouch hat with a striped 'big game hunter'–style one, making him look like a precursor to Stewart Granger's character in 1950s African adventure movies.

He soon realised that middle-class American audiences had little knowledge of Australia or the war in Europe and never thought to challenge the veracity of what the famous 'war hero', poet and military expert told them.

Tom's 'War Lecture Tour' performance was still being presented at times on the Redpath circuit in 1927, when Tom would sometimes deliver two or three lectures over several days at large Chautauqua gatherings. Here is the print version of part of a lecture given at Michigan City on 20 August 1927. Tom is describing the landing at Anzac Cove:

> Hardly had the first man jumped from the boat into the water to rush to the shore when from the tops of the cliffs hell broke loose. From the ambush the Turks unseen, poured a white hot stream of death into the massed ranks of the attackers. Before we could get off the boats we lost 20,000 men and the sea became red before we knew we were hit.

Now, the truth is that the entire ANZAC force at Gallipoli during the campaign numbered no more than 25,000. Combined Australian and New Zealand men killed in the ten-month-long campaign totalled 10,539. Estimated Allied dead on the peninsula during the ten days Tom spent at Anzac Cove were about 2300.

The more Tom 'got away with', the more outrageous his claims became. Once he realised how gullible audiences were and his, often fake, credentials were established, he abandoned the truth entirely. The solid reputation of the Chautauqua circuits, and the assumed honesty of those who spoke on them, also helped his audiences accept what he said without question.

It seems incredible that it took nine years for anyone to question any of the claims Tom made in his presentations. It did happen eventually but, in the meantime, Tom made an absolute fortune. His biographer, Jeff Brownrigg, comments:

> The continuing success that Tom enjoyed by pretending to be what he was not was as much a mark of his skill as an actor as it was a measure of the gullibility of those who believed him . . . Life experience had taught him that it did not take much to manufacture credible truths from his lies.

Here are some of the claims made in his publicity while on the Chautauqua circuits.

War Wounds

Tom's publicity gradually increased his war service until it implied he had fought on the Western Front after Gallipoli. By the end of 1918, a printed biography, undoubtedly written by Tom himself, reads: 'After fighting through many of the fiercest and bloody struggles of the war and being twice desperately wounded, he was invalided home to his native land, bayoneted, blind and helpless.'

Having added bayonet wounds to his list of imaginary wartime injuries, Tom invented another complication to explain why he didn't visit Europe in 1922, as he claimed to have planned. In his copy of the biography of William Jennings Bryan, later given with hundreds of other books to the Hamilton Library, he wrote a notation explaining that he was reading the book:

In Hospital
Detroit Michigan
April 1922
The shell which blinded me did more—it shattered several bones on the left side of my face—notably the lower terminate, the left sinus, the mastoid, and the Ethmoid cells. For years they have

been decaying and causing me atrocious pain; and two weeks ago the specialist decided to operate—and here I am 'sick in bed with a nurse'—seven big surgical operations in a row. C'est La Guerre— Bang goes the trip to Europe.

He also took a leaf out of his old friend Bobby Pearce's book of lies in 1927. After appearing noticeably drunk on stage several times, he claimed that he was forced to take morphine to alleviate the agony caused when one of the 'four bullets lodged deep in his groin' began moving and causing excruciating pain.

Rupert Brooke

After the war ended Tom prepared a lecture about poets and writers who died in the war and were the inspiration for a new and better world. The title of the lecture was 'The New Elizabethans'. The title, and the ideas, were taken from a book by Edward Osborn. Tom never acknowledged the theft of the title.

In order to bolster his connection to his topic, Tom outrageously claimed to have held the British poet Rupert Brooke in his arms as he died. Brooke, whose patriotic sonnet, 'The Soldier', is the most famous British war poem, died of septicaemia on 23 April 1915 on the island of Skyros, while on his way to fight at Gallipoli.

In his biography of Brooke, *Red Wine of Youth*, Arthur Stringer relates a story told by photographer Eugene Hutchinson of Chicago, whose famous studio photo of Brooke, taken during the poet's visit to the US in 1912, was the frontispiece for his collected works.

Hutchinson told Stringer that a complete stranger visited his studio sometime in 1924 and told him:

My name is Thomas Skeyhill. I am an Australian. But years ago I decided that if ever I got to Chicago I'd look you up. For I was a nurse in the British Army and during the time of the Gallipoli adventure I was serving in the Eastern Mediterranean. And there, Rupert Brooke died in my arms.

This mind-boggling lie, repeated in Tom's lectures, is made all the more ridiculous by the fact that it contradicted often-published facts about Tom's role as a signaller in the AIF and the fact that he was on the troopship *Clan MacGillivray* at Lemnos on 23 April 1915. The story was obviously based on the published words of Brooke's close friend, William Denis Browne, who *was* present at Brooke's death:

> I sat with Rupert. At 4 o'clock he became weaker, and at 4.46 he died, with the sun shining all round his cabin, and the cool sea-breeze blowing through the door and the shaded windows. No one could have wished for a quieter or a calmer end than in that lovely bay, shielded by the mountains and fragrant with sage and thyme.

Russia

Although Tom can be definitely placed in Boston in May 1920, and was lecturing throughout the months of June, July and August, he was, in early 1921, claiming to have visited Russia which was then still in the last stages of the chaos and upheaval of the Bolshevik Revolution, in late 1920.

This led to a new lecture topic in 1921, with the pretentious title 'The Babylonian Finger', in which Tom expounded his ideas and opinions about Russia and the revolution.

He flagged the visit in various interviews in 1920, claiming he intended to 'bring back something the world will want to hear'. He then claimed to have been refused entry to Russia via Czechoslovakia and, disguised as a Swedish merchant and using a forged passport, to have crossed the frozen gulf of Finland by sled, entered the vastness of Russia and, his publicity later claimed, met Lenin and talked with 'high-ranking Communist officials'.

Just how he had managed to do this, in a huge country fighting a civil war, while being unable to speak Russian, Finnish, Swedish, German, or indeed any language other than English, is not explained.

Around this time Tom began to plant false clues about his where-abouts and movements in book annotations, in order to support the fabricated information in his publicity. On the cover of one volume of Russian history, he wrote 'Read in Esthonia [sic]'; another title, *The Eclipse of Russia*, by E.J. Dillon, is marked as being read on 20 November in Lithuania; another 'on a Swedish ferry'. He was effectively creating a false history of his travels and thoughts by appearing to annotate a vast library of books as he read them.

When he later presented part of his book collection to Hamilton Library, Tom thus left a trail of handwritten lies embedded in a publicly accessible archive, to support his spurious claims. The books also include handwritten philosophical comments relating to, or inspired by, the text. These are designed to look as if they are notes made of Tom's thoughts as he was reading. Many of these 'reflective comments' are hilariously pretentious and many are quotes stolen from other sources and uncredited.

Also found among memorabilia in Hamilton after his death is a postcard to his father marked 'Petrograd', explaining that he is in Russia. It carries no post marks, stamps or franking marks. A photograph of a forged passport to enter Russia for 'Albert Svenson' was also found in the memorabilia.

In spite of Tom's 'planted' evidence and a publicity photo for the 1921 speaking season, showing him dressed in furs, it appears certain to me that Tom was never in Russia, or even Europe, in 1920. I think he spent a few months reading books and writing false information in them.

Mussolini

Towards the end of 1925, desperate to find new topics for the lecture circuit that would make him look like an important figure in world affairs, Tom claimed that he had visited Italy and met Mussolini. When he advised the Redpath publicity department that he would lecture on his Italian experiences, his credibility was, at last, brought into question.

Harry Harrison, senior manager at the Redpath Bureau, wrote to Tom:

> Have just been going through your material. Do I understand that you had a personal interview with Mussolini? I want to be absolutely clear on this point. If you had such an interview it will be great newspaper stuff. If you didn't, we can get mighty good stories just the same. Please let me know definitely if I may use the statement that you had an interview with Mussolini.

We do not have Tom's reply. There is a letter of introduction from the Italian Embassy in Washington for Tom, noting that he *intends* to travel to Italy. Once again there is no documented evidence that he ever made the trip. The publicity for Tom's lecture on 'Fascism in Italy' claims he did make the journey and had 'seen' Mussolini. Even if he had watched as part of the crowd at one of the dictator's famous outdoor speeches, Tom wouldn't have learned much. Along with every other language, apart from English, he couldn't speak Italian.

The Plays

Tom's theatre connection was through his friendship with Laura Justine 'Jessie' Bonstelle. As a young actress Jessie appeared in repertory before becoming the manager of a theatre in Syracuse, New York. She secured the rights to stage a dramatic version of the classic American novel *Little Women* and wrote a book about the author of the novel, Louisa M. Alcott.

She and Tom probably met and became friends in 1918, when she was a member of the Stage Women's War Relief group. In 1925, aged 54, she established the Bonstelle Playhouse, also known as the Detroit Civic Theatre.

It appears Jessie encouraged Tom's aspirations to write plays and he is mentioned several times in the 'gossip' section of the theatre company's *Bonstellar* magazine as a guest at the theatre who 'intends to write plays'. Tom is also mentioned several times in a column in the magazine devoted to news about former members of the theatre company, who were known as 'AFBs'—'a former Bonstellar'. The column mentions, in one edition, that Tom's book on Alvin York has been released, but notes that: 'Tom Skeyhill is not, strictly speaking, an AFB, but he holds that rank as an honorary member, because of his great friendship and loyalty to "Bonnie" and the Civic Theatre.'

Whether his interest was in writing plays or courting the actress Marie Adele, who was part of the company and soon became his de facto wife and mother of his child, it's hard to say.

Tom certainly claimed to be writing plays and also claimed one of them, *The Unknown*, was in pre-production, requiring constant rewrites. The play, however, remains completely 'unknown' as there is no evidence of it, or any other play by Tom, ever being written, produced or staged.

There were many other lies and deceptions, including a claim that Tom was part-way through a degree in 'Pure Literature' at Oxford University when the war began and intended to complete it at some point.

A Career Change

Tom's relationship with Harry Harrison and the Redpath Bureau deteriorated rapidly throughout 1927. There were reports of Tom drinking and appearing drunk on stage. There was the nonsense of the four bullets and the morphine use and more and more war wounds and, finally, a report of 'improper behaviour' with a woman in a hotel used by the Redpath Bureau.

In August 1927 a letter from Tom to Harrison attempts to cover up and explain the 'drunkenness' reports with an almost pathetic bunch of lies:

> You have probably seen the reports that I have been in hospital with another attack of the old appendix troubles . . . I have been on an almost exclusive vegetarian diet . . . I have not had a single date—I never date on Chautauqua and I have not had a single drink—not one . . . I was able to limp out to my lecture each night—but I had a bitter and painful time. I will go on the operating table at NYC about September 15th. It will be a tough operation—four bullets and an infected appendix to come out . . . Pray for me a little.

The lies continued in a letter to Harrison dated 6 October 1927:

> The operation was a success. Four bullets removed. The surgeons described three of them as inconsequential. The fourth had moved and set up an abscess. This was the troublemaker. They did not remove the appendix because they felt the bullets and not the appendix for the cause of the trouble.

It was all to no avail. Others in the Redpath organisation had long held doubts about Tom's honesty and, on 16 December, Harrison replied:

Dear Skeyhill,

Things have come up that make it seem unwise for us to book you this next summer on our circuits. I'm wondering what you would take to cancel the agreement . . .

    With the compliments of the season,

    I beg to remain, Sincerely yours.

Tom's attitude to Harrison changed to one of defiance. Contradicting his earlier claims, he tells Harrison:

I cannot be responsible for what others tell you . . . My own life is my own affair . . . Therefore if I take a highball or date with a pretty girl . . . that is my business . . . and it is going to be.

There is no record of Harrison's reply, but Tom's reply to the missing letter was indignant:

Mr Harrison simple truth is I have lost faith in you . . . You have only yourself to blame. After the way I worked my heart out for you last summer. Twice I was in such pain that I had to have a morphine injection before I could even go on the platform.

On 27 February 1928, Harrison graciously replied:

We will accept your cancellation of the contract, and, believe me or not, I sincerely hope that you are right and I am entirely wrong.

By April 1928, Tom had once again fallen on his feet and been paid a $30,000 advance by publishers Doubleday-Doran, to write a biography and edit the war diaries of Sergeant Alvin York, America's greatest war hero of World War I (then known as the Great War).

Tom wrote a gloating letter to another Redpath manager, Elmer Person, which was passed on to Harrison. Tom crowed malignantly: 'The Doubleday-Doran book should be a best seller. They own over 120 bookstores and are spending $50,000 advertising it . . . Wouldn't I have drawn crowds in your circuit. But, alas, I cannot be in two places at once.'

Samuel Cowan had already written a definitive biography of York in 1922, but Tom was to have access to the hero's war diaries and was also contracted to write a version of his story for children.

York was one of the eldest in a backwoods family of eleven children. After the death of his father, he worked as a blacksmith and helped raise his younger siblings. In his youth he was known as a pugnacious drinker and fighter. In 1914 he was converted to pacifism and religion. When drafted he initially requested conscientious objector status on the grounds that his church forbade violence. His claim was refused and, finally persuaded that his religion was not incompatible with military service, he went to France as an infantry private in 1918.

In October 1918, as an acting corporal, he led a group of seventeen soldiers to attack a German machine gun division. They captured 35 machine guns and killed some 25 Germans. York then accepted the German officers' offer of surrender and took 132 prisoners. He was promoted to sergeant and awarded the Congressional Medal of Honor and the Croix de Guerre.

Tom, as you might expect, used Cowan's biography and York's diaries, with additions of his own and much embroidery, to produce two bestsellers: *Sergeant York: His Own Life Story and War Diary*, in 1928, and *Sergeant York: Last of the Long Hunters*, in 1930. The former of these two volumes is written in the first person, with Tom being the voice of Alvin York, which led to much criticism of Tom's exaggerated backwoods accent, unrealistic phrases and misinformed terminology.

Alvin York's most recent biographer, John Perry, is scathing about Tom's efforts, criticising him for lack of respect for history and accusing him of making claims, in the *Last of the Long Hunters*, that were 'almost certainly not true but impossible to prove or disprove', which sounds very much like Tom's *modus operandi*!

York himself was rather philosophical about the fictional childhood and family history created for him by Tom in *Last of the Long Hunters*. Writing to his friend, Arthur Bushing, in 1937, to invite him to attend a talk York was giving about the book, York tells him: 'I've got a dandy of a speech on the Long Hunters. I want you to be there so you can hear me spread some bull.'

As mentioned earlier, York was very much against Tom getting any credit at all when the cinema version of York's story was filmed in 1941.

Marie Adele sued Warner Brothers and settled out of court for a sum believed to be $3500, the amount that York had said Tom's estate should definitely receive 'no more than'. The film's end credits show a small, brief, almost subliminal credit stating that Tom edited the York diaries.

A Legacy of Lies

Tom died on 22 May 1932 as a result of a blood clot caused by a broken leg after the plane he owned, flown by Marie Adele's brother Louis, had engine failure and flipped over as it glided in to land on Tom's property, after a joy flight to view Tom's house from the air.

Tom was an extremely wealthy, popular and successful performer, author and poet, much renowned and respected as a former war hero throughout the US and Australia, except perhaps for parts of western Victoria.

Tom had returned to Australia in 1921 and toured with great success, giving performances and lectures and talking about his 'adventures' in Russia. In his article in *The Age* on 10 March 1969, headlined 'Skeyhill—Man of Mystery', Michael Ryan wrote: 'When Skeyhill, decades later, returned from the United States for a lecture tour of Australia, crowds in the thousands turned out to hear him. Everywhere except the hometown, that is. Not more than a dozen people heard him lecture in Hamilton.'

Ryan interviewed retired librarian Stella Bayley, who obviously, like many other locals, did not believe that Tom was blind when he returned home at the end of 1915: 'I saw him at the Hamilton races,' she said. 'As a supposedly blind man he had an assistant to guide him around. We were in the stand watching a race when he turned around suddenly and said, "Good day, Stella. How are you?"'

Ryan's article was written in response to general requests to news media for information about Tom's family, from the Glenelg regional library:

> The Glenelg regional library has a collection of 200 books which he owned. The rest of the collection, about another 500 books, is in America. The librarian, Miss F.K. Robertson, wants to trace any Skeyhill kin or admirers in the hope that they will pay to ship the books back to Hamilton. No Skeyhills remain in the Western District.

The Hamilton Library collection of books donated by Tom had once numbered 318. After his 1921 tour of Australia, Tom had sent several shipments of his books from the United States. The Melbourne *Age* reported, on 2 March 1925: 'During the year Hamilton Mechanics' Institute and Free Library added 400 books to the library, and spent £75 in improvements. Further gifts of valuable books from Mr. T. Skeyhill were received, and the Skeyhill library now contains 318 volumes.'

What happened in 1969, evidently, was that Marie Adele had passed away and those in charge of her estate were attempting to dispose of the rest of Tom's books as she knew Tom had wanted.

When I called the Hamilton Library, in early 2022, no one on the staff had ever heard of Tom Skeyhill, or his books. The mystery was solved by a diligent librarian who did some fine detective work and called me about a week later. At some point the Hamilton Mechanics' Institute and Free Library collection had become part of the Hamilton Library catalogue. Sometime in the 1960s Tom's books had been sent to the council's central library in Portland. Subsequent council area boundary changes had resulted in Hamilton no longer being part of Glenelg Shire, so Hamilton Library was no longer in the shire that had custody of the books.

In 2005 Portland Library, having no real desire to keep them, gave the 200 remaining books to the Hamilton History Centre. In 2014, the History Centre donated the books to the National Library of Australia.

It is with some sense of satisfaction that I note that the National Library official biography of Tom does mention that Jeff Brownrigg believes that Tom's blindness was 'probably fabricated'. It is also gratifying that the biography contains, as almost all biographies of Tom do, several mistakes. It claims that Tom 'earned a significant reputation as a reciter in his teenage years' and died 'after a plane he was piloting crashed'—neither of which is true.

What happened to the 118 books that had disappeared between 1925 and 2005 from the original collection Tom sent to Hamilton, or the 500 books, which nobody seems to have been willing to pay to have freighted to Australia in 1969, we will probably never know.

Who knows what fabricated snippets of misleading information and pretentious, borrowed, faked philosophical musings by Tom Skeyhill, master conman and pathological liar, might be scribbled in their margins?

1Ø

EUGENIE FALLINI—THE WOMAN WHO MURDERED HIS WIFE

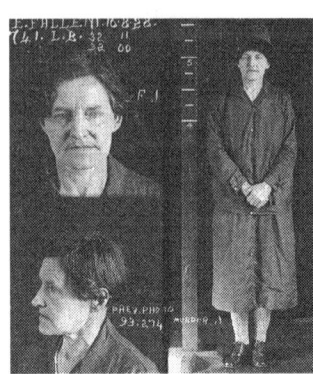

'A man trapped in a woman's body.'

Eugenia's Secret

On 7 October 1920 the headline in the *Sydney Morning Herald* announced:

EUGENIE FALLENI FOUND GUILTY—SENTENCE OF DEATH

This was the news for which all the curious and pruriently minded citizens of Sydney had been waiting. It was the culmination of one of the most talked about murder trials in Sydney's history, and one of the strangest legal cases Australia has ever seen.

The article went on to explain:

At the Central Criminal Court yesterday, before the Chief Justice (Sir William Cullen), the trial was concluded of Eugene Falleni, 45, who was charged with having, on September 28, 1917, at Lane Cove, feloniously and maliciously murdered Annie Crawford.

Now, the more observant among you will have already noticed something either odd or erroneous in the newspaper report, for it is 'Eugenie' who is found guilty in the headline, but 'Eugene' who was charged with the crime.

This is how one reporter described the defendant in court:

> The accused woman is strangely interesting. She bore an extraordinary resemblance to a man, for facially she is masculine. She wore a man's clothes. While in the docks she appeared distinctly nervous. She wears a gold band ring on the little finger, and she 'fiddled' with the dock rail. In her right hand, she carried a grey felt hat. Her hair is almost black and clipped short. It was neatly brushed and parted on the left side of her head.

That final piece of information may be lost on younger readers who don't know that, up until the 1960s, it was customary for males to part their hair on the left, and females on the right.

'Eugene Falleni' was indeed 'Eugenie Falleni', although she was probably born Eugenia Falleni. She also may have been Eugenia Martelli, Harry Leo Crawford, Eugenia Innocente, Jean Ford and, according to the *West Australian* newspaper, 'Eugenie Callini'.

Eugenia married three times, once to a man who was already married and twice to women who believed she was a man. One of the women, Annie Birkett, was brutally murdered by Eugenia.

In Western societies today there is widespread understanding and acknowledgement of those who are transgender, and protections for their rights have been legislated. A century ago, however, there was nothing but ignorance and morbid curiosity about trans people.

Eugenia Falleni committed a foul murder and considered another. She can be seen, however, as a victim of society's almost total ignorance about her true nature. She was also a victim of poverty and lack of education, and suffered badly from her father's lack of understanding and brutal attempts to make her 'normal'. She was also probably the victim of repeated rape as a young woman.

Eugenia, who was illiterate, was also a victim of her own belief that posing as a member of the opposite sex was a criminal offence and, if discovered, she would be gaoled. This led to a paranoid fear of detection, which was partly the reason for her brutal crime.

Her Italian Catholic father was hostile and uncomprehending about her 'masculinity' and possibly told his daughter that posing as a man was a criminal offence in order to force her into behaving as a female. He may even have believed it himself, although no such criminal law ever existed.

Eugenia feared being gaoled more than anything, for obvious reasons, and, in attempting to prevent it from happening, she performed a criminal act that led to it happening.

After four years of married life together, her wife, Annie, had discovered Eugenia's 'secret'.

Murder, Most Foul

The *Sydney Morning Herald* summarised the facts of the case this way:

> It was stated that the accused, while wearing male attire and passing herself off as Harry Leo Crawford, went through the form of marriage in 1913 with the deceased, Annie Birkett, a widow, who then became known as Mrs. Crawford.
>
> The charred remains of a woman, subsequently identified as Annie Birkett, or Crawford, were found on October 2, 1917, in the bush some distance from Chatswood, on the Lane Cove River.

It was three years before someone contacted the police with 'certain suspicions' and the body was exhumed and identified but, once it was, 'Harry Crawford' was soon arrested—and was discovered to be biologically female. Amazingly, when arrested, Crawford had remarried and was living with his second 'wife', Elizabeth 'Lizzie' Allison, who was a few years older than her 'husband'. They had married in September 1919 and she described him as a model husband.

The case caused a sensation. Transgenderism, as we now know, has been around as long as mankind has walked the planet, but there was blanket ignorance about it in Australia in 1920. The only words in the common vocabulary that could be found to label Eugenia's condition, such as 'homosexualist', 'pervert' and 'hermaphrodite', were all completely inaccurate.

To the newspaper readers of 1920, Eugenia was not only a freak, she was also a murderer, and that coincidental link made her 'condition' seem decidedly 'evil'.

For most people this morbid curiosity about the strangeness of the case focused on one main mystery: How could a woman posing as a man practise the physical deception of what many then still called 'the marriage act'?

The most sensational piece of testimony came when Constable John Henry Walsh presented a record of an interview conducted during the search of Harry Crawford's home, where the accused lived with his second wife, Elizabeth. It was read in court.

As the constable was searching the bedroom, the accused said, 'You will find it, something there that I have been using.' The following conversation then took place.

Detective: 'What is it, something artificial?'
[Falleni] replied: 'Yes, don't let her see it.'
Detective: 'Do you mean to say that she doesn't know anything about this?'
[Falleni] said his first wife had not known about it either, 'Not until the latter part of our marriage.'

At the risk of being disrespectful and frivolous in the midst of a serious narrative, this part of the story always brings to my mind the limerick that we found so hilarious as teenagers, about the poor policeman from Tottenham Junction. According to the limerick, the unfortunate policeman in question 'lost the use of his sexual function' but managed the situation ingeniously in the following manner: 'For the rest of his life he deceived his wife, By dextrous use of his truncheon.'

Eugenia Falleni did almost exactly the same thing as that mythical policeman from Tottenham Junction, although not 'for the rest of his life'. She also had more to hide than a mere case of male sexual dysfunction.

The 'article', found 'among male clothing in a locked leather suitcase' in Eugenia/Harry's room at the Stanmore house where she/he lived with her/his wife Lizzie, was later exhibited in court. It was 'made of wood and rubber bound with cloth in the shape of a phallus or dildo'.

What led to the murder, evidently, was that Annie Crawford, née Birkett, had discovered her husband's secret. It was reported later that Annie had been told 'by a neighbour' that her husband was a woman;

or maybe she had discovered the truth for herself. In September 1917 she told a relative, when talking about 'Harry', that she had 'found out something amazing about him', but Annie kept the details to herself and was killed a few days later.

Eugenia eventually admitted that Annie had discovered the truth and they argued about it. It seems that was why she planned a fatal picnic at Lane Cove on the 'Eight-hour Day' long weekend in 1917.

Reports in the *Sydney Morning Herald*, during the trial in 1920, gave the basic evidence from the scene of the crime:

> Evidently the woman had been burnt to death. With the exception of her stockings and shoes all her clothing had been destroyed. The body was intact, but the injuries by burning were most noticeable on the upper portion. None of the features was recognisable. There were signs of fire on the rocks, the ground, and the trees, but nothing could be seen of a made fire for cooking or any other purpose. The lower part of the body was almost untouched. The fire seemed to have extended about 100ft in another direction.
>
> During a search near the charred portions a carryall, a drinking glass, a mug, and a hatpin were found, also the broken parts of a glass bottle. A brooch and a greenstone pendant, which were on the body, had since been identified by the dead woman's son, Harry Birkett, as her property.

Eugenia/Harry was arrested and the evidence was overwhelming in favour of 'guilty'. The *Sydney Morning Herald* reported that:

> Police-sergeant Gorman stated that the day after the dead body was removed in 1917 he found a bottle containing a small quantity of kerosene a few feet from the spot . . .
>
> The accused, in a statement from the dock, said that she was unnerved by three months' detention in Long Bay gaol, and could not speak as she wished in declaring her innocence of the crime with which she was charged. She knew nothing, she said, about what happened after the woman with whom she had lived for four years disappeared. They had had words from time to time, but no serious quarrel.

Annie's son, also named Harry, gave evidence of the events leading up to the murder. He said his mother met the accused when they were both employed by Dr Clarke, of Wahroonga, where his mother worked in domestic service and Harry Crawford worked as a handyman.

Harry Birkett said that the accused 'was so persistent about his mother marrying him that she at last consented'.

Evidently Crawford, claiming to be a 38-year-old widower born in Scotland, was a considerate and generous suitor and took the widow and her son on outings to the circus and on picnics. Annie had a nest egg from her first marriage and the couple decided to quit working in service and use the money to open a corner store in Balmain, which they did prior to their marriage in February 1913 at the Methodist parsonage in that suburb.

Young Harry, whose father died when he was three, was nine when his mother remarried and remembered that they lived at Balmain for about six months after the marriage, but the couple 'did not seem very happy in their married life'.

The couple then separated and Annie and her son lived at Kogarah with her sister until the marriage was patched up and they moved to Drummoyne, where Crawford obtained menial work in hotels and factories. Harry Birkett testified that on 'Friday morning not long before Eight-hour Day in 1917, he went to work as usual, and never saw his mother again'.

Witnesses were called who said they saw the accused near the scene of the crime at the time of the murder. Mrs Ethel Carroll said that she saw 'a man sitting on a rock near the hill, with his head buried in his hands', not far from where the body was afterwards found. Ethel testified that the man 'appeared to be excited, and startled' when he saw her and later, as she returned from her walk, he had 'jumped over a rock and walked behind her for about six minutes, until he came to another track branching off from the one she was using'. This was obviously, the jury decided, the action of someone making sure a passing stranger didn't notice something. Ethel identified the 'man' in the dock was the one she saw that day.

Two dentists testified that dental evidence proved it was Annie Birkett's body that was found.

It really was a very obvious case of murder and the accused was rather obviously the murderer. Eugenia was found guilty and sentenced to death.

The Truth Will Out

You may be wondering by now why the crime took three years to solve. There are several reasons.

Firstly, the murder took place during World War I and at a time when the newspapers were full of war news. Things were going badly on the Western Front and almost 40,000 Australians died or were wounded in the four months between June and November 1917. An unidentified body at Lane Cove didn't seem such a big deal.

Secondly, it was not until 1919 that Annie was reported missing by her sister and son. It was known that Annie and her husband quarrelled and his story that she had 'cleared off' with a plumber' seemed to satisfy the neighbours, although there was no history of adultery in Annie's life and she was a shy, reserved woman.

'Harry Crawford' then sold the furniture and moved with his stepson to a boarding house in Woolloomooloo. At first he told his stepson that his mother was visiting friends but later he switched to the 'cleared off with a plumber' story with him also.

It appears that after a while the landlady, a certain Mrs Schieblich was 'on to' 'Crawford' and scared him enough to get him out of her house several months after the murder.

By that time Harry Birkett was living safely with his aunt at Kogarah and 'Crawford' was drinking heavily and was often in a deranged mental state. Evidence at the trial revealed that, during one bout of hysteria, he told Mrs Schieblich his room was haunted and she apparently replied, 'It's your wife that's haunting you, I think you killed her.' She later lied to him, saying that detectives had called looking for him, and he moved out of the house.

Why didn't Mrs Schieblich report her suspicions to the police? Well, as you can tell by her name, she was German and it was wartime. There was massive anti-German sentiment in 1917 and Frau Schieblich wanted no trouble with the authorities. She just wanted her suspicious boarder to be gone.

There were very good reasons why Harry Birkett had left to live with his aunt. His stepfather's behaviour was extremely weird after Annie 'left' and there were two incidents involving the young lad that shed a very ghastly light on the deranged mind of Eugenia Falleni.

It seems that Eugenia, deranged, despairing and suffering depression, actually contemplated killing her stepson and herself. There is very good evidence that on at least two occasions she set out to do this, only to have fits of remorse and change her mind.

On one occasion, soon after the murder, Eugenia took young Harry to The Gap, the notorious suicide spot near Watsons Bay in Sydney. According to Harry Birkett's account, they climbed over the safety fence so that they could throw rocks into the ocean and his step-father sat near the edge and encouraged him to sit with him. The boy, however, was nervous and refused, and they returned home.

A few days later the two took an even more bizarre journey. Leaving Mrs Schieblich's boarding house, they walked in pouring rain to the tram stop and caught the tram to Double Bay, where they alighted and walked into the bush.

What really scared Harry, apart from being dragged out at night in a thunderstorm to take a tram ride for no apparent reason, was that his stepfather was carrying a brand new shovel. What the boy didn't know until later was that there was a bottle of brandy in his stepfather's pocket. What Harry never knew was that there was almost certainly also a five-shot revolver in the pocket, with two bullets in the chamber.

These days, bushland is at a premium in Double Bay and 'secluded clearings in the bush' are non-existent, but in 1917 Eugenia soon found one and started to dig. The bottle of brandy was produced and Eugenia started drinking and told the boy to dig and offered him brandy also. This continued for some time, with the poor kid getting more fright-ened and the adult getting almost hysterical, until Eugenia suddenly threw the shovel into the bush and took the boy home.

The police found the revolver, still loaded with two bullets, when they found the dildo. Eugenia had stolen the gun while briefly employed as a payroll guard.

The theory is that, on the first occasion, Eugenia intended to suicide and take the boy with her by grabbing him and jumping off The Gap, or in the second attempt, shooting him and then herself.

The Whole Sad Story

Let me finally go back and start where I should have—at the beginning of the whole sad story of Eugenia Falleni.

Eugenia Falleni was born on 25 July 1875 in Italy (either in Florence or Livorno—accounts differ). She was the eldest of the Falleni family's 22 children, seventeen of whom survived. All but two of the children were, however, born in New Zealand, after the family moved to Wellington in 1877.

Eugenia was, apparently, always 'a man trapped in a woman's body'. She grew up as what might be called a 'tomboy', although there are two versions of her relationship with her father, a fisherman who also owned a horse and cart and sometimes worked as a carrier.

It seems most probable that a sympathetic grandmother and sister helped Eugenia to lead a double life during her teenage years. She would leave home dressed as a girl then change and become, to all intents and purposes, a young man often engaged in manual work in stables, brickyards or on the docks.

There is another version of the story that implies that Eugenia's father, knowing full well that his oldest child behaved as a man, exploited the fact by allowing her to do menial manual work as a man in order to earn income for the family.

What we do know is that Eugenia's father, seemingly in an attempt to force his nineteen-year-old daughter to be a woman, arranged her marriage to Braseli Innocente in September 1894 in Wellington. The poor girl was taken to Auckland by her husband, where she discovered that he was already married. She then fled back to Wellington, avoided her family, decided to live her life as a man and went to sea as a cabin boy.

Eugenia spent three years at sea as 'Eugene' but at some point her true identity was revealed. There is an apocryphal story that the cover was blown in a drunken conversation with an Italian-speaking captain when she was talking about her childhood and used the female form 'piccolina', rather than the male form 'piccolino', in referring to herself as a small child.

Whether she was repeatedly raped, as some versions of the story have it, or consented to sex for self-preservation or other reasons of her own, she was abandoned, destitute and pregnant in the port of Newcastle in 1898 and later that year in Sydney she gave birth to a daughter, Josephine.

Josephine was left with an Italian couple and raised by a woman she knew as 'Granny De Angeles', who told her that Eugenia was her mother and her father was a sea captain. She appears to have been a troubled and troublesome child and, having met her mother when she was seven, she knew Eugenia's secret.

Not long after 'Harry Crawford' and Annie Birkett were married, Granny De Angeles, whose husband had apparently deserted her and returned to Italy, died and twelve-year-old Josephine came to live with her mother. If this had not happened, it is quite probable that Eugenia may well have 'maintained the deception'.

The situation was like this: Eugenia/Harry was now living with three people as a family in the same house. Two of them were a 'wife' and stepson, to whom she/he was a male. They both believed she/he was Josephine's father, while Josephine knew that Eugenia/Harry was her mother. Confused? You should be!

After the disappearance of Annie and the move to the boarding house at Woolloomooloo, it didn't take long for both teenagers to quit living with 'Harry Crawford'. Josephine had 'shot through' by the time young Harry had left to live with his aunt at Kogarah and Mrs Schieblich had scared 'Harry Crawford' out of her premises.

Josephine was used as a hostile witness in the court case. Her statement read:

I first remember my mother when about seven years of age. She always wore men's clothing, and was known as Harry Crawford. I was brought up at Double Bay by Mrs. de Angeles, whom I used to call 'Granny.'

Granny told me that Harry Crawford was my mother, and that my father was the captain of a boat. My mother was very cruel to me when I was a child, and often forgot me.

Granny told me that my mother tried to smother me when I was a baby. Mrs de Angeles died when I was about 12 years of age, and my mother took me to a little confectionary shop in Balmain, kept by a Mrs. Birkett, who had a son named Harry.

My mother told me Mrs. Birkett had some money, and always thought my mother was a man. I said to my mother, 'She'll find you out one of these days.'

My mother replied, 'Oh, I'll watch it. I would rather do away with myself than let the police find anything about me.'

My mother told me always to call her father, and not let Mrs. Birkett nor anyone else know that she was a woman. I did not know that my mother was married to Mrs. Birkett, but they occupied the same bed-room. They quarrelled a great deal, and mother used to come out and say, 'More rows over you. I cannot get any sleep.'

I replied to my mother, and she said, 'Oh, a lovely daughter I've got.'

I said, 'What can you expect? A lovely mother I've got.'

In 1917 I met my mother, who told me everything was unsettled and upside down, as Mrs. Birkett had discovered she was a woman. My mother seemed very agitated, and was always reticent about herself.

Josephine's statement was given after police tracked her down, after they had arrested 'Harry Leo Crawford' at the Empire Hotel, Annandale, on 5 July 1920. On arrival at Long Bay prison, 'Harry' shocked the guards by requesting to be admitted to the Women's Section. At first they refused, but a prison doctor was called who later said, 'I knew within a matter of seconds that she was a woman.'

Mrs Schieblich, feeling safe now the war was over, testified that 'Harry Crawford' told her his wife had left him and added, 'We had a jolly good row, and I gave her a crack on the head, and she cleared.'

Eugenia/Harry later gave an account of the fatal picnic in which she claimed that Annie slipped and fell, hitting her head on a rock and losing consciousness and, despite her best efforts, died within minutes, at which point she panicked and resolved to burn Annie's body to make it unidentifiable. The motivation being fear that if Annie's body was identified, she would be arrested and her gender would be revealed.

The last part of Eugenia's statement was the only part anyone believed.

Annie Birkett's remains, which had been exhumed from the grave in which she had been buried as 'unknown', in 1917 at Rookwood Cemetery, were reburied by her family at Woronora Cemetery.

Meanwhile, Eugenia/Harry's second wife, Lizzie, who was quoted in the media as stating that 'Harry Crawford was an ideal husband' and they had 'a very happy married life', was forced to move home when the case started because she was 'so pestered by calls and sensation seekers'.

Harry Birkett, who was working in a tailoring business at the time of the trial, seemed to have survived the horrors of losing both natural parents and almost being murdered by his deranged transgender step-father. He was described as a 'bright young man'. I have no idea what happened to the troubled and unruly Josephine, who seems to have been the main cause of all the rows between Annie and her 'husband'.

Eugenia was sentenced to death, which was commuted to life, and served eleven years in Long Bay prison, during which time she lived as a woman, having lived the previous 25 years as a man.

Sympathisers petitioned for her release and, in February 1931, following a visit from Joe Lamaro, the minister for justice, she was released. Eugenia was nearly 60 years old and 'not of robust health'. She was taken by car to an unknown destination and disappeared without a trace.

On 9 June 1938 Mrs Jean Ford, the proprietor of a small boarding house in Glenmore Road, Paddington, stepped off the kerb in front of a car in nearby Oxford Street and was run over and badly injured. She had just finalised the sale of the premises and had £100 cash in her purse.

It was uncertain whether the event was a suicide attempt or merely an unfortunate accident, but Mrs Jean Ford died of her injuries the next day in Sydney Hospital. When all efforts to trace her family failed, the hospital authorities, in desperation, passed the matter on to the police, who came and took fingerprints.

The dead woman was Eugenia Falleni.

PART THREE
THE RATBAGS

'Ratbag: Australian colloquial. A person of unconventional or discreditable behaviour; eccentric. A person whose preoccupation with a particular theory or belief is seen as obsessive.'

Macquarie Dictionary

'Ratbags believe in the Divine Right of Kings, the Flat Earth Society, flying saucers and the Book of Revelations.'

Barry Humphries

11

JORGEN JORGENSEN—
THE KING OF ICELAND

'. . . now that I am free, I must take more care of myself.'

Jørgen Goes to Sea

The biography of Danish-born adventurer Jørgen Jørgensen reads more like the fictional and fantastical adventures of Baron Von Munchausen than a factual account of a life.

Jørgen was a sailor, explorer, warship captain, war hero, adventurer, gambler, spy, man of letters, political prisoner, expedition leader, entrepreneur, dispensing chemist, bushranger-hunter, policeman, convict and—wait for it—the King of Iceland!

There is no character in Australia's colonial history whose life is anywhere near as strange, bizarre, multifaceted, complex and confusing as that of Jørgen Jørgensen . . . or Jürgensen, alias John Johnson, alias Jorgen Jorgenson (with an 'o'—he changed it officially from 'e' while living in England in 1817).

What is really strange is that the roles he played in Australia's history occurred in two quite distinct episodes, which were separated by a quarter of a century.

In between his two Australian 'lives', Jørgen was a Danish naval hero in a war against Britain, a merchant, a British privateer, author, spy, inmate of Newgate, Tothill Fields and Fleet prisons (and several prison hulks)—as well as the ruler of Iceland.

He left us many writings, plays, political pamphlets, religious works and proposals, along with an 'autobiography' which, as Marcus Clarke so accurately stated, 'is written in a vain and egotistical strain, with much affectation of classical knowledge'.

If you find it hard to believe that the man who was a convict in Tasmania is known in Icelandic history as 'The Dog Days King'—you're not alone, but it's true.

Born in Copenhagen in 1780, the son of a mathematical-instrument maker, Jørgen received a good education. His parents were well off and keen to set him up in business, but he decided to 'go to sea'.

'When I saw a Dutch Indiaman set sail,' Jørgensen later wrote, 'with its officers on deck, dressed out in their fine uniforms, my heart burned with envy to be like them'.

His father did not approve of his son's notions and bound him for four years as apprentice on board an English collier, in an attempt to dissuade him from a seafaring life. Jørgen survived the ordeal and, at eighteen, in 1798, made a voyage to the Cape of Good Hope.

There he joined the British vessel *Harbinger*, bound for Algoa Bay on Africa's east coast, with a cargo of convicts. This was during the French Revolutionary War and the *Harbinger* narrowly escaped being taken by a French ship of 44 guns.

Back in Cape Town, in 1880, calling himself 'John Johnson', he joined another British ship, HMS *Lady Nelson*, a brig of 65 tons commanded by Lieutenant Grant, which was sent as a tender to HMS *Investigator*, commanded by Captain Flinders, on his surveying voyage round the Australian coast. They sailed to Sydney via Bass Strait then returned south and completed surveys of Port Phillip, Western Port, Port Dalrymple (on the Tamar River) and the Derwent River.

In Sydney Jørgen met the French explorer Nicolas Baudin, who was a guest of Governor King (during a brief truce between the two nations). He accompanied Baudin on an expedition as far as the Hawkesbury Valley and claimed the Frenchman's obsession seemed to be 'to advance further than any Englishman had ever been before . . .

returning to Paris and boasting that he had been where no traveller had been before him'.

Jørgensen claims that 'about 100 miles from Sydney':

> I had become so impatient at his incessant reasons, thus continually discovered, for penetrating further, with so futile an object as, that, espying a large white rock projecting from a little eminence, I ran forward, and, standing upon it, called out to him with a show of exultation that that was the point beyond which no white man had been. Baudin then marched about 20 paces further, and returned quite satisfied.

In 1803 the *Lady Nelson* set sail from Sydney to form a settlement at the Derwent River at Risdon Cove. The settlement was soon moved to the site of what became Hobart Town.

Growing tired of navy life, our hero captained a small vessel on a sealing voyage to New Zealand, returned to Sydney and shipped as chief officer on a whaler, the *Alexander*, which sailed for the Derwent. He wrote later, 'I can boast of having stuck the first whale in that river.' He also claimed to be the first European to climb Mount Wellington.

The *Alexander* spent a year whaling and sealing around Australia and New Zealand, and returned to London, via Tahiti, Cape Horn and St Helena. She docked at Gravesend in London in June 1806.

Jørgensen had convinced two Maori men and two Tahitians to sail with him. His vague plan was that they should learn European ways and Christianity and return home as 'ambassadors' for Britain. He presented them to Sir Joseph Banks, who paid their expenses and placed them in the care of Reverend Joseph Hardcastle, 'in order that by initiating them in the truths of the Christian religion they might be able to confer a similar boon on their own countrymen'.

All four of them died in England, within a year.

Jørgen, however, was off on other adventures by then. He went back to Copenhagen, and found it was being bombarded by his recent friends, the British!

Denmark and Norway had a policy of 'armed neutrality' during the Napoleonic Wars. However, in 1801 and 1807, the British attacked the Danish capital to ensure that the Danish–Norwegian fleet did not fall into the hands of the French. These wars were known as the 'Gunboat Wars' due to the Danish use of small heavily armed ships against the larger British vessels.

Having returned home a local hero, with exaggerated stories of his many adventures, Jørgen now decided to become a truly national hero and convinced his father and seven other merchants of Copenhagen, 'touched with a spirit of reprisal against the English', to purchase a small vessel, armed with 28 guns, of which Jørgen was made captain. With a crew of 83 men, the vessel, named *Admiral Juul,* broke through the winter ice 'a month before it was expected that any vessel could get out' and captured three British merchant ships.

Emboldened by his success, Jørgen took his ship along the Yorkshire coast and encountered HMS *Sappho* and *Clio.* HMS *Sappho* was a warship with a crew of 120 men, much faster and bigger than the *Admiral Juul,* but Jørgensen fought her for almost an hour—firing 17 broadsides. With his masts, rigging and sails shot to pieces and his ammunition spent, he finally surrendered.

Taken to Yarmouth, he was now a prisoner of the British but, as he tells it, he had 'chanced to obtain an interview' previously in Copenhagen with a 'public officer connected with the British Ministry'.

This mysterious person arranged for him to travel to London, where, in light of his past service in the British Navy, he was asked to become a spy. He then, evidently, suggested a scheme for the relief of Iceland.

The Dog Days King
Iceland, a territory of Denmark, was suffering from the Danish–English hostilities. The inhabitants survived on the export of wool and fish and trade with Britain, as well as Denmark. With supplies cut off by Danish ships, the island was starving. English merchants wanted to find some daring fellow willing to run the blockade. Guess who?

So, Jørgen, with support from Sir Joseph Banks, was given permission to take a ship from Liverpool, with goods provided by merchants of that city. In spite of predicted bad weather in the winter season, he departed on 29 December 1807.

The vessel was only 350 tons, yet the insurance on the cargo cost the speculators 1000 guineas. 'The enterprise was considered almost desperate,' Jørgensen wrote—and it was 'madness to attempt such a voyage which . . . must necessarily be made at that season of the year almost in the dark'. The ship made it through to Reykjavik and left its cargo with the local 'supercargo' (a merchant who specialised in managing cargo sales and distribution).

Inspired by his success Jørgensen returned to Liverpool, loaded two vessels with flour and provisions, and headed back to Reykjavik.

While this was happening, however, the governor of Iceland, Count von Tramp, issued a proclamation prohibiting trade with the British and, when the two vessels arrived, they were ordered to leave at once, without unloading.

Jørgensen pretended to prepare to sail, but was determined to land his cargo and reclaim what was already ashore. The next day was Sunday and most of Reykjavik's population was at church when Jørgen and twelve of his men went ashore. At the governor's residence, he stationed six men at the front and six at the back and, with a brace of pistols in his belt, he walked in and found only 'the cook, who was busy preparing dinner, one or two domestics, and a Danish lady', plus Count von Tramp, who was 'reposing on a sofa'.

The governor was taken captive and imprisoned under hatches in one of the ships, while Jørgen helped himself to the contents of an iron chest containing the island's tax collection. The people of Reykjavik came out of church and found that a revolution had taken place.

Jørgensen later noted:

I am not aware, unless some more deep-read historian than myself can cite an instance, that any revolution in the annals of nations was ever more adroitly, more harmlessly, or more decisively effected than this. The whole government of the island was changed in a moment. I was well aware of the sentiments of the people before I planned my scheme, and I knew I was safe.

The next day he issued a proclamation stating that the people of Iceland, tired of Danish oppression, had called on him to be the head of the government. The island's few British residents imagined that Jørgensen had the support of the Icelanders, and the Danes supposed he was supported by the British government. Most of Reykjavik seemed quite satisfied, so Jørgensen made some new laws.

He cut taxes by 50 per cent, released all people from debts due to the Crown of Denmark and compelled tax defaulters to make up deficiencies from their private estates. When a magistrate from a northern village, 150 miles (240 kilometres) from Reykjavik, refused to accept the situation or surrender the iron chest holding the local taxes, the 'king' and his crew piled brushwood round his house and lit it, at which point the magistrate 'immediately submitted'.

Jørgensen then advanced money for the benefit of public schools and fisheries, and placed a duty on the 'British goods' which he had himself imported. He established trial by jury and free representative government, and increased the salaries of the clergy, who then were 'not wanting in their gratitude' and 'preached resignation and content-ment under the new order of things'.

He also built a fort equipped with six guns, raised a troop of cavalry, and hoisted the ancient and independent flag of Iceland, pale blue with three salted cod in the top left corner. The population appeared quite happy with the new regime.

Before departing Liverpool, Jørgensen had written to New York requesting that a ship might be sent to Iceland with tobacco, and soon after his return to the capital from his royal tour, a vessel entered the harbour 'with a valuable cargo from New York' which the king exchanged for part of his (heavily taxed) British goods.

This commercial enterprise was so successful that Jørgensen decided to visit London and 'enter into an amicable treaty with Great Britain in order to permit vessels with British licenses' to trade in his kingdom. He set sail in one of the ships he'd arrived with, accom-panied by a ship belonging to the deposed Count von Tramp, which unfortunately caught fire and was burned with all her cargo.

This forced a return to Iceland, where a British warship, HMS *Talbot*, was waiting in the harbour. After transferring passengers to the British warship, Jørgensen sailed for Liverpool, arriving eight days later.

The warship had obviously been sent to find out what on earth was going on in Iceland, so Jørgensen hurried up to London and told Sir Joseph Banks what he'd done. Banks was furious and refused to have anything more to do with him.

The captain of the *Talbot*, in his report of the 'Iceland affair' to the British government, said that 'King Jørgensen' had 'established a republican government in Iceland, for the purpose of making that island a nest for all the disaffected persons in Europe', and added 'that he was highly unqualified to hold the command of a kingdom, because he had merely been an apprentice on board an English collier, and had served as midshipman in an English ship of war'.

When he got wind of this, Jørgensen went into hiding. He was arrested a week later at the Spread Eagle Inn in London and taken before the lord mayor, where he was charged with being 'an alien to an enemy, at large without the king's license, and with having broken his parole'.

Gaolbird, Author, Gambler, Spy

After spending five weeks in Tothill Fields prison, Jørgen was moved to a prison hulk where Danish prisoners were kept. A year later he was released on parole and lived at Reading, west of London, where he wrote *The Copenhagen Expedition Traced to other Causes than the Treaty of Tilsit*.

Ten months later, having returned to London, he got together with some of the political refugees he'd met in prison and took to living a Bohemian lifestyle, gambling, writing and living in an attic.

Although he claimed he was part of a syndicate of sixteen who won a lottery valued at £20,000, Jørgen gambled his share away and, in order to escape his debts, fled to Lisbon and then Madrid. He kept gambling and claimed he was robbed. However it happened, he was apparently left with only his jacket and trousers.

In desperation he then joined the crew of a British gunboat that was taking mail back to England. Evidently, his plan was to jump ship as soon as they docked. However, the gunboat never reached the shore of Britain. Having off-loaded the mail to a coastal ship at sea, the vessel was sent to cruise off Cape St Vincent, south of Portugal.

Back in the Royal Navy as 'John Johnson', Jørgen gained a promotion and the gunboat captured several privateer vessels, but he soon became restless.

At Gibraltar, in 1813, he either became ill or feigned illness and was invalided back to Portsmouth and placed on board the hulk hospital ship *Gladiator*. He claimed that: '800 persons were collected in this horribly pent-up place, which could not have afforded moderate accommodation for half of them, even had they been in good health.'

He was in a difficult situation. If he said he wasn't ill, he'd be accused of malingering, punished and sent back to sea. After much letter-writing to his superiors he was discharged and returned to London.

In a coffee house in the Strand, he met a 'friend' from prison days, Count Dillon, a member of an Irish rebel family. Thinking Jørgensen was still an 'enemy of England', Dillon talked openly about rebel plots and Jørgensen saw a chance to sell valuable information to the government.

The talk was about a plot involving the Americans and the French, 'to send out an armed expedition' to take possession of the Australian colonies. This idea was actually suggested by the zoologist François Peron, who was part of the Baudin expedition with the *Geographe* and the *Naturaliste*, visiting Sydney in 1801. Baudin might not have known Peron was a spy as the two men did not get on. Peron under-mined Baudin's authority and attempted to write him out of history after Baudin died in Mauritius on the way home.

According to Dillon, the idea was that two armed French and American vessels were to sail together into the South Seas, and 'plunder the colonies'.

Jørgensen hurried to the Colonial Office, and laid his intelligence before 'a gentleman high in office' who remarked that it was a 'wild scheme' and even if it was successful, England would lose little or nothing as those colonies were 'not worth keeping for they already cost the Government £100,000 a year!'.

(The secret expedition did sail, in 1813, when Britain was at war with the United States. The two French ships, commanded by Count Dillon, were wrecked off Cadiz but the Americans proceeded, and burned seventeen British whalers, which resulted in an enormous price rise for sperm oil in London.)

Jørgensen was far-sighted in his view of the Pacific and despaired at Britain's neglect of her Pacific colonies:

> It is indeed much to be regretted that the . . . trade of these seas has so long been looked over by the authorities at home . . . The pearl fishery is said to be more profitable and less hazardous than that of the sperm whale, and the sandalwood and beche-de-mer, which are produced so abundantly on the northern coasts of our New Holland, are known

to yield the Dutch, through the medium of the Malays, an immense revenue.

. . . The Christian religion, which is rapidly extending itself by the aid of our gospel missionaries, is doing much to raise these people in the scale of civilised society; and although the Americans are hourly taking advantage of our comparative supineness, the approach of an English flag is always, and we trust ever will be, hailed with superior satisfaction.

Meanwhile, once again in debt from gambling, Jørgensen was sent to the Fleet Debtors' Prison. When evidence of the destruction of the British whaling ships proved part of his story to be true, however, he was quick to remind His Majesty's ministers of the service he had rendered.

He was subsequently supplied with money to pay his debts but, instead, lost every penny gambling and was sent back to debtors' prison. There he 'amused himself' by writing histories, pamphlets and stories, and eventually made enough money to live on.

One day he was summoned to the Foreign Office, and 'had the pleasure to be engaged on a foreign mission to the seat of war'. In other words, he became a spy.

Amply supplied with money for expenses, and provided with an order to 'draw on London' for any funds he might require while travelling, he could have at once left London for Paris with money and credit. Instead, however, he went to a gambling house and lost the money, and even the clothes he had been given for his journey.

Totally broke, Jørgensen exchanged his only suit for a sailor's jacket and trousers, walked to Gravesend and signed on as crew on a transport bound for Ostend. There he met an officer who luckily knew him, and verified his identity, and managed to cash an 'order' on the Foreign Office.

Jørgensen wrote later that his spying mission was 'to ascertain what effect the subjugation of Napoleon was likely to have on British Commerce'. After the British victory at Waterloo, he was sent on a 'special mission' to Warsaw. On his last night in Paris, a visit to a gambling establishment resulted in the loss of all his money and he was forced to sell his shirt to a sergeant, for 7 francs.

According to his own account, he buttoned up his coat and made his way to Jonchery, some 170 miles from Paris, booked into the best hotel, and bluffed the local authorities into giving him money. For several months, using his diplomatic passport, he managed to extract money from those in charge under the new regime.

Returning to London, Jørgensen collected his pay and, predictably, lost every penny gambling. Several years later, in 1820, while living in Tottenham Court Road, he was arrested for pawning 'articles of bedroom furniture' belonging to his landlady—and sentenced to seven years transportation.

Luck was on his side for, while waiting to be transported, he was sent to Newgate Prison, where he became assistant to the surgeon, Mr Box. His behaviour and skill at the job were so good that he became the prison 'dispenser', and retained the post for nearly two years.

Then it was found that the items he was accused of stealing had been pawned by another lodger and he was pardoned, on condition that he 'quit the kingdom within a month'.

Sadly, he started gambling with the savings from his prison job and overstayed his 'month' by several weeks. He had signed on to a navy vessel and was on his way to catch the tender to the ship when he met an old prison acquaintance. Realising Jørgensen had 'outstayed his time' and expecting a reward, his 'old friend' called the police.

This time Jørgensen was sentenced to transportation for life, but spent the next three years in his former situation in the prison hospital. It was during this time that he wrote several books including *The Religion of Christ the Religion of Nature,* and an account of his spying adventures titled 'Continental Tour'.

Back to Van Diemen's Land

He finally sailed from Sheerness with 150 convicts and a detachment of military with their wives and children in the *Woodman*, which arrived at Hobart on 5 May 1826, 23 years after he had helped establish the island's first settlement at nearby Risdon Cove.

Some of his writings in Newgate make interesting reading. He noted, for example, that it was not a good idea to waste the court's time with arguments of innocence:

I well remember one day when five men were arraigned at the bar, the four most guilty of whom, being asked their plea by the court, answered promptly, 'Guilty, my Lord,' and were sentenced to a few months' imprisonment, while the fifth, sensible of his comparative innocence, pleaded 'Not guilty,' occupied the time of the court with his defence for three-quarters of an hour, and was sentenced to seven years' transportation.

Jørgensen had 'letters of recommendation' from two of the directors of the Van Diemen's Land Company and hoped that his services to Britain would count for something in Hobart. He was given a job as a 'prisoner clerk'. The work, copying letters, receipts, etc., all day, was tedious and hard, and the pay ('6 pence a day and 1 penny for rations; the former paid quarterly, and the latter every month') was hardly enough to live on.

When he heard a plan was proposed to explore the company's land, and to trace a road through the wilderness from the River Shannon to Circular Head, he applied to join and was not only accepted, he was made leader.

Each man carried six weeks' provisions and it was an epic journey. When no ford was to be found at the River Ouse, Jørgensen followed the stream for more than 30 miles until a ford was found by accident, when their dogs chased a kangaroo.

They found the source of the Derwent and then crossed unexplored snow-covered mountains, but failed to reach Circular Head. When their provisions ran out, Jørgensen led them back to a stock hut. (The provisions which were to have been left at Circular Head by boat were never delivered so, if they had gone on, they would have died of starvation.)

In the early part of January 1827, Jørgensen led another party of four, including the surveyor Mr Lorymer, along the western coast from Circular Head to the Shannon River. Along the barren coast they found many wrecks and 'a mountain of sand which . . . measured on the top seven miles in length'. In places the scrub was so dense that their progress slowed to 200 yards a day. They were caught in quicksand on the seashore and Lorymer was drowned attempting to cross the Duck River on a makeshift raft. When the three survivors at last reached Circular Head, their food had run out. Jørgensen lay ill for four days after they were picked up, and took months to recover.

Back in Hobart he received his ticket of leave. Free, but banned from leaving the island, he briefly became editor of a colonial news-paper, but argued with the proprietor and left.

Van Diemen's Land was then a brutal place and, by 1827, so many convicts had escaped that it was policy to hang all captured runaways. When this proved ineffective, a new scheme was introduced. Men were employed to act as 'field police', go-betweens for the Crown with the convicts and bushrangers. Jørgensen volunteered and was appointed constable of the field police and assistant-constable to the police magistrate for Oatlands.

The boundaries of the Oatlands district measured more than 150 miles, and the job involved visiting all the farms and stock huts in Oatlands, Clyde, Campbell Town, the Swan ports and the Richmond district to protect settlers from bushrangers and hostile Aboriginal groups. For two years he camped out alone at places called 'Murderer's Plains', 'Deadman's Point', 'Hell's Corner' and 'Four-square Gallows'.

After two years of that life, Jørgensen became part of the infamous 'black line' that attempted to gradually push all the island's Indigenous inhabitants onto the Forestier Peninsula. In September 1830, the whole population of the island was called to arms. All field police, ticket of leave men and convicts were ordered to join the line; and 2000 armed men moved slowly across the island. The operation achieved very little but eventually most of the remaining Aboriginal people were confined on Flinders Island.

Jørgen was given a conditional pardon in 1830 and, in 1831, was granted 100 acres (40 hectares) of land, which he immediately sold. We have no evidence that he gambled the money away, but you can't help but wonder.

In January 1831 then 50, he married a 30-year-old illiterate Irish convict, Norah Corbett. Both Jørgensen and his wife were granted full pardons in 1835.

There is an anecdotal story that the couple tried to run a dairy farm but they knew nothing about cows or farming, confused planting time with harvesting, and Jørgen soon decided to stick to writing.

He wrote a pamphlet on the 'Funding System', which paid the bills for a while, but was again broke when a letter from Denmark arrived (via the Danish envoy in London via Lord Glenelg via the governor, Colonel Arthur). It informed him that his mother was dead and that he had been left a modest fortune.

His wife, Norah, died in July 1840, and he followed her six months later, on 20 January 1841, dying in the Colonial Hospital from 'inflammation of the lungs'. He was 60 years old.

Writing of the Icelandic revolution Jørgensen, in a rare moment of truth, said of himself: 'I fully determined to seize the first opportunity to strike some blow to be spoken of . . . It was not love of liberty which influenced me on this occasion . . . I have in the course of my life been under the malignant influence of other passions.'

Apart from his writings Jørgensen's explorations in 1826–27 are considered great feats of endurance and colonial exploration.

Icelanders use the term 'Dog Days King' when referring to Jørgensen in their history, as his nine-week reign coincided with the period when Sirius, the 'dog star', is visible in the heavens over Iceland.

Jørgensen never called himself 'King of Iceland', though he certainly was, among many other things, the island's ruler and head of government for nine weeks in 1808.

Having taken so many risks, dared and ventured so much, and gambled so often with both his money and his life, Jørgensen finally began to mellow in his 50s. Towards the end of his life, he wrote about hesitating to cross a flooded river near Espie's farm:

I would not venture to cross. Mr Espie expressed some surprise at my backwardness, as he had formerly seen me cross without any apprehension. I replied, 'Yes, Mr Espie, I was then a prisoner, and life of little matter; but now that I am free, I must take more care of myself.'

12

HENRY JAMES O'FARRELL— THE CELIBATE ASSASSIN

'A large number of ladies fainted, others were seized with hysterics, and the whole multitude was convulsed.'

The Good Catholic Lad

Henry James O'Farrell was born in 1833 at Arran Quay, on the banks of the Liffey River in the heart of Dublin. He was the tenth of the eleven children of a successful butcher, William O'Farrell, and his wife, Maria. In 1841 most of the family migrated to Melbourne, where they had relatives. William opened a butcher's shop in Elizabeth Street and was soon doing well enough to send his younger children to private schools. Henry was enrolled in Reverend David Boyd's school.

Henry was only nine when his mother died in 1842. He was then educated as a boarder at St Francis's College, Melbourne. The under-funded pioneer Catholic diocese in Melbourne had its first bishop, the Irish Augustinian friar James Alipius Goold, appointed in 1847. Goold arrived in Melbourne in 1848, the same year that Henry, aged fifteen, left school and went to spend two years as an apprentice in a law firm in which his older brother Peter, then aged 22, was a junior lawyer.

At the end of 1850 Henry gave up his apprenticeship at law and entered the small seminary that Bishop Goold had set up to train priests at St Francis's. The Catholic Church desperately needed priests and Henry took deacon's orders, including a vow of celibacy in 1852. He was remembered as an industrious, genial student with strong Irish nationalist sympathies. He next spent two years in Europe studying and travelling. When he returned, in 1855, he was a well-educated, well-read 22-year-old who spoke reasonable French.

His father had died in 1854 and Henry was, apparently, showing signs of behaviour that made his superiors in the church consider him unsuitable for ordination as a priest. There are several reasons why they could have come to this conclusion. Possibly emotionally traumatised by his father's death, Henry was later accused of having developed 'proclivities' that were 'inappropriate to the calling'.

Unfortunately, the nature of these 'proclivities' was not spelled out, but the most likely possibilities are alcoholism, from which he certainly suffered in later life, or arguing over doctrine or Irish politics. Although he was accused of testing his vow of celibacy in a socially 'inappropriate' manner at times, there was no suggestion of inappropriate sexual conduct of any sort.

In 1854, Henry, along with others in his family, entered into a dispute with Bishop Goold over the settlement of the estate of his deceased father, William O'Farrell. According to Henry's older brother, Peter, now an up-and-coming Melbourne solicitor, several assets left as legacies to the church in accordance with the will were transferred to Bishop Goold before the estate was settled. When it was discovered that the estate's debts outweighed its assets, Peter O'Farrell explained the situation to the bishop, who declined to return any of the legacies the church had received.

Henry had evidently also clashed with Bishop Goold on one or more points of Catholic doctrine, and the two could not reconcile their differences. Perhaps this had played a part in Henry being considered unsuitable for ordination but, whatever the reasons, Henry developed an attitude of bitter resentment towards the Catholic hierarchy which deepened as the years went by.

Henry's sister Christina had married Timothy Lane, a wealthy squatter who was part-owner of Clunes Station, where gold had been found. Towards the end of 1855, Henry left Melbourne to work for his brother-in-law, who had established the mining company Lane, McDonald & Co. Henry gained experience in the rural industries of mining and sheep farming, and learned quickly. Within a few short years he had moved to Ballarat and, in partnership with a cousin Joseph Kennedy, set up a successful farm produce business, dealing in hay and corn. Locals remembered him as a shrewd, sensible, industrious businessman who was quick-witted, knowledgeable and quite skilled in conversation and argument.

Tall, well-dressed and gentlemanly, Henry was involved in the affairs of the local Catholic church in Ballarat and, by 1860, he was wealthy enough to make a second extended visit to Europe.

On his return, in 1862, he found his brother Peter involved in another legal dispute, connected to the building of St Patrick's Cathedral. As early as 1848 Bishop Goold had requested land for a cathedral and managed to get the colonial government to grant land for a site in 1851. A contract for the building was signed in 1858 and construction began that same year. Peter O'Farrell was the solicitor acting on behalf of the church.

Peter claimed that he had made business enemies among the builders and tradesmen involved in the construction of the cathedral because Bishop Goold had ordered him to default on payments. When it became public knowledge that St Patrick's College was unable to pay its debts, anonymous letters to newspaper editors made derogatory remarks about Peter O'Farrell and he sued the man he thought had written them, Michael Hanify, a clerk of Petty Sessions, for libel. Peter lost the case and was ruined financially and emotionally.

The outcome of the whole affair was that Peter O'Farrell lost most of his clients, who were almost all Catholic, ended up deeply in debt, and 'did a runner' from the colony of Victoria in 1864.

His brother's troubles added to Henry's struggle to reconcile his faith in the Catholic Church and his deepening resentment towards the church hierarchy. Someone who knew him well at the time wrote that he had developed 'a vindictive animosity towards the whole body of the Catholic clergy, vilifying them in a most outrageous manner whenever they formed the topic of conversation'. (Mr J. Tappin, letter to *Ballarat Star*, 19 March 1868)

His sister, Caroline Allen, observed in 1865 that Henry 'appeared restless, uneasy and excitable, and that he seemed deeply affected by financial losses which he said he had sustained through his brother's departure'.

Henry also had more troubles of his own at this period of his life. Adding to his mental stress and instability was the fact that his cousin and business partner, Joseph Kennedy, had descended into chronic alcoholism and died during a fit of *delirium tremens*, in 1865. Henry had had to work hard to compensate for his cousin's alcoholism and was himself drinking heavily. He had also invested in shares and property and was in debt. During 1865 and 1866 he began speculating in mining shares and sank more deeply into debt.

Henry was residing at his business premises in Ballarat and was still attempting to live according to his vow of celibacy. It was reported that he was in the habit of testing his vows by inviting young female neighbours to spend the evening with him to demonstrate that he was capable of 'conquering whatever failings he might possess, though his visitors were allowed, perhaps, greater liberties than were compatible with strict propriety'. (*Ballarat Star*, 26 March 1868)

Inevitably the business failed, causing Henry acute social embarrassment, as well as severe neurotic despair. In September 1866, while he himself was suffering an attack of *delirium tremens*, he threatened to kill a banking friend who refused to extend him further credit. The police were notified, and his sisters came and took him back to Melbourne to look after him.

Several months later he returned to Ballarat but, in January 1867, he was reported to have had several 'epileptic fits', suffered another severe attack of the 'DT's' and threatened to kill himself. He was placed in Ballarat Hospital on 23 March and his sisters were again called in to help. When the business was wound up, Henry was found to have debts totalling £600, and assets of £60. On 5 April he left hospital and again accompanied his sisters back to Melbourne.

While in Melbourne Henry suffered from severe bouts of depression, became obsessed with Irish nationalism and Fenianism, and began arguing vehemently, at any opportunity, in favour of Irish republicanism.

In April 1867, possibly to placate his family, who had no idea what to do with him, he wrote to the Bishop of Adelaide, expressing a desire to restart his career with the church, but the bishop was visiting Ireland and no reply came for more than a year. Between April and August of 1867, it seems Henry developed a different plan for his future. He planned a suicide mission.

In September 1867 Henry travelled to Sydney where he stayed at the Currency Lass Hotel, owned by Irish Catholic Daniel Tierney. In order to get the family to agree to pay for his passage to Sydney and his accommodation while there, he told relatives that he was keen to start a church career and was going to try for positions in New South Wales. A note, later found in a sort of diary he kept at the time, reveals that this was just a ploy to get to Sydney:

> Go in for the Church: The idea disgusts me. That is what they would have me do. And yet I cannot get money unless I lead them to believe I am studying for the Church. I did think of doing so once, and it plunged me into a fear—the having to decide on loyalty to a Church or to Country.

After two months at the Currency Lass Hotel, Henry was asked to leave. His drunkenness, erratic behaviour and habit of arguing with other guests about Fenianism were drawing far too much attention to Daniel Tierney's establishment at a time when the Irish question and Fenianism were rather delicate topics. Anti-Irish sentiments threatened to upset the uneasy harmony and acceptance that existed between Sydney's Protestant majority and the more than 20 per cent Irish-Catholic population.

Henry's sisters sent him money to enable him to board at the Clarendon Hotel. In December he used part of the money to purchase two revolvers: a small Colt model and a slightly larger, six-shot Smith and Wesson.

Henry had decided to assassinate, as a political gesture, a very important visitor with an Irish connection, the Earl of Ulster, who was to arrive in Sydney on 21 January 1868. The earl also happened to be the second son of Queen Victoria—Prince Alfred, Duke of Edinburgh—and the first member of the royal family to ever visit the colonies of Australia.

Queen Victoria's Favourite Son

Being the second son of a reigning British monarch in the 19th century did not carry a great deal of responsibility, unless your older brother took it upon himself to predecease you without having sons of his own.

Queen Victoria had nine children, including four sons. Alfred, her second son and fourth child, was born in May 1844. He remained second in line to the throne, behind his brother Albert Edward, Prince of Wales, until Albert Edward and his wife, Princess Alexandra of Denmark and Wales, began producing sons of their own in 1864, causing Alfred to slip further and further down the line of succession.

As a royal prince, Alfred, known as 'Affie' to his family, was not particularly colourful or remarkable. He joined the Royal Navy at the age of twelve and was, by all accounts, a competent sailor and naval officer who would later, in 1893, become Admiral of the Fleet.

In 1864, when he was twenty, Alfred apparently developed a passion for his sister-in-law Alexandra, Princess of Wales, whose husband, the future King Edward VII, spent most of his spare time visiting brothels in Paris and London and designing sexual pleasure devices. Alfred's passion for his brother's wife may have led Queen Victoria to suggest a round-the-world voyage as a method of keeping him out of harm's way and avoiding scandal.

Alfred was, evidently, Queen Victoria's favourite son and it was decided when he was quite young that he should eventually inherit the German Dukedom of Saxe-Coburg and Gotha from his father's older brother Ernst II, who had no legitimate offspring. Consequently, Queen Victoria insisted that he turn down an offer to become king of Greece upon the resignation of King Otto in 1862. He was made Duke of Edinburgh, Earl of Kent and, significantly, Earl of Ulster in 1866 and packed off on a seventeen-month round-the-world, goodwill voyage as captain in command of HMS *Galatea* in January 1867.

Today most Australians probably have no idea who Prince Alfred, Duke of Edinburgh, was. His name is, however, used by millions of Australians every day in speaking about such places and institutions as the Royal Prince Alfred Hospital (RPA) in Sydney, the Alfred Hospital in Melbourne, Prince Alfred Park in Sydney, Prince Alfred College in Adelaide, Alfred Street at Circular Quay and Prince Alfred Square at

Parramatta—and the story of his remarkable adventures 'down under' is truly one of almost unbelievable circumstances and coincidences.

Alfred, who probably realised from an early age that he was never likely to be bothered with the title of king, served as a midshipman on HMS *Euryalus* and as lieutenant on HMS *Racoon*. In 1867, at the age of 23, he was promoted to captain, given command of HMS *Galatea* and sent out on a voyage designed to 'show the flag' to the far-flung corners of the British Empire.

The *Galatea* arrived in Adelaide on 31 October 1867, and the prince also visited Melbourne, Sydney, Brisbane and Hobart during a stay of six months on our shores.

At that time, of course, Australia was made up of separate British colonies and the popularity of the prince's visit took colonial authorities quite by surprise. Planning and preparations appear to have been woefully inadequate and crowd control at times virtually non-existent. There are reports of several people being seriously injured, even trampled so badly that they died from their injuries, in attempting to get just a glimpse of his royal personage.

Perhaps Prince Alfred felt safely removed, in the far-flung colonies of Australia, from the problems caused by the Fenian movement in Ireland, but we should remember that around 30 per cent of the convicts and soldiers who originally populated our eastern colonies were Irish.

There was certainly a warm welcome from the majority of Sydneysiders who were pro-British to the core, and the prince also received a very warm welcome from Sydney's German population, 500 of whom paraded through the streets carrying torches to meet him and listen to his Royal British Highness address them with a speech in fluent German, which was, after all, the prince's first language, as it was for all Queen Victoria's family.

There was no doubting the loyalty of Sir William Manning, the man who planned the fateful picnic at Clontarf, which was to be the scene of Australia's first ever act of international terrorism. It was after the prince's return to Sydney, having visited Brisbane, that the event occurred.

Sir William was a wealthy pastoralist and politician. He had been attorney-general of the colony of New South Wales and a list of his honorary positions will show readers just how respectable Sir William was.

He was trustee and vice-president of the Australian Club, vice-president of the Civil Service Club, a steward of the Australian Jockey Club, member of the Royal Sydney Yacht Squadron, and a founding president of the New South Wales Rifle Association. He was elected to the senate of the University of Sydney in 1861 and was vice-president of the Horticultural Society of New South Wales.

You really don't get much more respectable than that!

Sir William was also President of the Sydney Sailors' Home, and planned to enhance his reputation and social status by hosting a picnic for the prince at the beachfront picnic grounds at Clontarf, ostensibly to raise funds for the Sailors' Home.

This was to be no ordinary picnic. It was a gala occasion with marquees on the lawn, the band of the *Galatea* playing on the shore and an Aboriginal group to provide entertainment consisting of 'native sports and dances'. There was a marquee for lunch, another for the ladies and, of course, a special royal marquee for the prince himself, should he feel the need for privacy or be overwhelmed by the excitement of the occasion and need a rest.

Attendance was restricted to 1500 and any respectable person was able to purchase a ticket in advance (£1 for gentlemen, 10 shillings for ladies) to support the fundraising for the Sailors' Home and attend the event on 12 March 1868, as long as they were suitably well dressed for the occasion, naturally.

Henry James O'Farrell, having practised target shooting with his two revolvers on a vacant block at Waverley the day before, was quite well dressed on the day of the picnic, and had purchased his ticket.

Henry had planned to assassinate Prince Alfred on the day the prince first arrived in Sydney, 21 January, and had rented a verandah room in The Custom House Hotel, at Circular Quay, planning to shoot the prince as the royal carriage passed below. He changed his mind at the last minute, however, because he did not wish to harm the governor, Earl Belmore, who was sitting beside the prince. The governor had shown sympathy to Catholics and had agreed to be the patron of the St Patrick's Day events in Sydney later in the year.

Henry had heard rumours about a plot to burn down the Hyde Park Pavilion during the Royal Ball on 5 February, so he hired evening dress and attempted to attend the event and put his own plan into effect before the supposed arsonists could strike. Unfortunately, he could not show an invitation and was refused entry, and the arson plot turned out to be just a 'furphy'.

Although he acted alone, Henry, who was almost certainly clinically insane during the six months he spent in Sydney, was not particularly good at keeping secrets or covering his tracks. As early as December 1867, Henry had told a casual acquaintance, Henry Lewis, that he had just purchased a revolver. When Lewis remarked that anyone hearing that might think Henry was a Fenian, Henry asked Lewis his opinion on the hanging of the three Fenians in Manchester (*see* Footnote 1), Lewis stated, later in court:

> I said that I thought it was well to have hanged the men at Manchester ... he asked me whether I was a Protestant or a Catholic, and I answered that I was a Protestant; on this O'Farrell said to me, 'That accounts for the answer which you have just given to me'.

Then, in early January, Henry actually wrote letters to the editors of two Dublin newspapers, the *Irishman* and the *Nation*, informing them of his intention to assassinate the prince on 21 January.

Timothy Sullivan, who co-edited the *Nation* with his brother, Alexander, showed his brother the letter when he visited him in Richmond prison, where Alexander was serving time for 'sedition'. The brothers noted that the assassination attempt had either happened by the time the letter arrived in Ireland, or the letter was just nonsense. Alexander advised his brother to burn the letter in case the attempt *had* happened, in which case they could be implicated. So, Timothy Sullivan burned the letter.

The Picnic at Clontarf
The picnic at Clontarf provided a third opportunity for Henry James O'Farrell to do what he had decided to do. What happened there was described in such melodramatic and colourful detail by the *Sydney Mail* newspaper that I cannot improve on it:

When the Prince left the luncheon-tent, at the Sailors' Home Picnic, he escorted the Countess of Belmore to the door of the Royal tent, and then turned to converse with his Excellency the Governor, the Chief Justice, and Sir William Manning. They remained talking a few seconds, and then his Royal Highness and Sir William Manning sauntered across the green towards the clump of trees bordering the beach, and under which the Galatea Band was stationed.

The subject of conversation was the Sailors' Home, and his Royal Highness, to mark his appreciation of the institution, handed Sir William a cheque as a donation to the institution. Sir William made his acknowledgments for the donation, and then asked his Royal Highness whether he would go round to Cabbage Tree Beach to see the aboriginals, as they were then ready for some sports.

Before his Royal Highness could reply a treacherous assailant, who had just left the crowd of persons congregated under the shade of the trees, stole up behind him, and when he had approached to within five or six feet pulled out a revolver, took deliberate aim, and fired. The shot took effect about the middle of the back of his Royal Highness, an inch or two to the right of the spine. He fell forward on his hands and knees, exclaiming, 'Good God, my back is broken.'

Sir William Manning, hearing the discharge, and seeing his Royal Highness fall, turned and sprang at the would-be assassin, who then jumped back and aimed the murderous weapon at Sir William. Seeing the pistol directed towards him, Sir William stooped to evade the shot, and, losing his balance, fell.

Fortunately the charge did not explode; but as Sir William Manning was in the act of rising, the ruffian took aim a third time; just at the moment Mr Vial, of Castlereagh-street, who happened to be behind, sprang upon the dastardly assailant, pinioned his arms to his side, and thus the aim of the pistol was diverted from the body of Sir William Manning to the ground.

The weapon was discharged, however, and the shot entered the foot of Mr George Thorne, senior, who fainted, and was taken away by Mr Hassall, and other friends.

. . . Mr T. Hales and a young gentleman named McMahon lifted his Royal Highness to carry him into his tent. It was evident from the demeanour of his Royal Highness that he was suffering great pain, and he asked his bearers to carry him gently. This wish was complied with as far as possible, and thus he was borne into his tent. Here he was taken in charge by Dr Watson, of H.M.S. Challenger, who together with Dr Wright of Sydney, Dr Powell of the Galatea, and Assistant-surgeon Waugh of the Challenger, were immediately in attendance.

The dress of his Royal Highness was removed, and upon an examination of the wound it was found that the bullet had penetrated the back, near the middle, and about two inches from the right side of the lower part of the spine, traversing the course of the ribs, round by the right to the abdomen, where it lodged, immediately below the surface. No vital organ, fortunately, appeared to be injured, the course of the bullet being to all appearance, quite superficial.

It was later ascertained that the bullet, fired from the Smith & Wesson revolver, had probably been diverted from its deadly course by striking the metal clasp and a rubberised portion of Prince Alfred's braces. This had, perhaps, saved his life and prevented the first royal visit to Australia from ending as the first case of royal assassination on this continent.

Prince Alfred was now safe in the royal tent and, although in a great deal of pain, he was receiving the best available medical attention and it appeared he would survive the incident.

Things were not looking quite so good for Henry O'Farrell, however. Let us return to the colourful account in the *Sydney Mail*:

While this painful examination was in progress another scene, which almost defies description, was going on in another part of the ground. No sooner had Mr Vial grasped the arms of the man who had fired the shots, than M. Benjamin Mortimer (an American gentleman), Mr Whiting (of the firm of Dryman and Whiting), A.L. Jackson, and other gentlemen seized him; and, had it not been for the closing in around them of the police and other persons, they would speedily have placed him beyond the reach of the Law Courts.

The people shouted 'lynch him,' 'hang him,' 'string him up,' and so on, and there was a general rush to get at him. The police, headed by Superintendent Orridge, got hold of the assassin, and they had the greatest difficulty in preventing the infuriated people from tearing him limb from limb. In this the police were ably assisted by the Chief Justice, Lord Newry, and the men of the Galatea Band . . . while Mr Orridge, with herculean strength, kept back the crowd as much as possible.

The task of putting the prisoner on board the ship was not an easy one, and it was fully ten minutes before they could get him on to the wharf. By that time all the clothing from the upper part of his body was torn off, his eyes, face, and body were much bruised, and blood was flowing from various wounds; and when he was dragged on to the deck of the Paterson he appeared to be utterly unconscious.

No sooner was he on board than a number of sailors had a rope ready to string him up, and it was only by the interference of Lord Newry that his life was spared . . .

The whole of the police on the ground were under the command of Mr Fosbery. The people, out of whose hands the prisoner had been rescued, immediately gave vent to their disappointment, and . . . determined to bring him back from the steamer, and dispatch him at the scene of his crime.

A rush was then made for the steamer . . . but the Hon. John Hay, who was on the bridge . . . ordered the captain to haul off . . . and the vessel accordingly proceeded on her way to Sydney.

To say that the loyal British citizens of Sydney attending the picnic were outraged, embarrassed, and on the verge of hysteria would be, perhaps, an understatement. This was the biggest thing to happen in the 80-year British history of Australia and the *Sydney Mail* reporter was at great pains to graphically illustrate the 'effect of this dastardly attempt to assassinate the Prince, among the immense number of persons congregated at Clontarf':

A large number of ladies fainted, others were seized with hysterics, and the whole multitude was convulsed.

Suddenly a joyous throng had been converted into a mass of excited people, in whose breasts sympathy for the Royal sufferer, and indignation for his murderous assailant, alternately prevailed; while pallid faces and tearful eyes told of the deep anxiety that was felt in reference to the extent of the injuries the prince had sustained.

People crowded by hundreds around the tent in which the sufferer lay, until they were informed that they must keep back, in order to allow free ventilation; they at once fell back thirty or forty yards, and formed a complete cordon around the tent, and anxiously awaited the result of the examination.

Meanwhile, inside the royal tent, the prince who had, according to the *Sydney Mail*, 'never lost consciousness, although feeling faint and weak from the shock to his nervous system, and from loss of blood', was telling his carers about the sensation of being shot at close quarters. It felt, he said, 'as though he was being lifted off the ground.'

When he was told of the near panic, grief and hysteria among the hundreds waiting outside, the prince gave instructions that someone should go out and, 'Tell the people I am not much hurt, I shall be better presently.'

At about five o'clock he was placed on a mattress, which was placed on a litter. He was then carried by officers of the *Galatea* to the wharf and conveyed by boat to the wharf at Government House, where he convalesced in the care of two British nurses from a group led by Sister Osburn. (*See* Footnote 2.)

The nurses stayed on duty all night and, thankfully, there was 'no appearance of haemorrhage'. The bullet had miraculously missed any vital organs on its passage through the prince, who was in great pain and could not lie down.

The condition of Henry James O'Farrell, now ensconced in Darlinghurst Gaol, was not too flash either.

O'Farrell was described by the *Sydney Mail* as 'a man of good education, and in manner not unpleasing, fair-complexioned, about five feet eleven inches in height, and apparently about five and thirty years of age' with a 'slight beard and moustache, and a military air' who was 'perfectly self-possessed'.

His condition, having been rescued from the lynch mob, might be described as rather battle-scarred:

His clothes were torn to ribbons by the excited crowd, and he received many severe bruises, his eyes being blackened, his nose, swelled very much, and his lips puffed out . . .

The *Sydney Mail* had found out quite a lot about Mr O'Farrell in a relatively short length of time and informed its readers that:

> According to his own statements—although he says very little and maintains much reticence with respect to himself and his dastardly deed—he is a native of Dublin, but left Ireland at a very early age. He has been in many countries, has spent a considerable time on the European continent, and in America, and about three months ago came from Victoria to New South Wales.

The *Sydney Mail* then goes on to inform readers of sundry facts that today would be expected to be left to the judge and jury:

> He has expressed a hope that the Prince would not die, and says that he did not mean to kill, but merely to 'frighten him'—a statement which is absurd on the face of it. Two revolvers were found on him, one of which had not been discharged, and every chamber of which was loaded. The other, the weapon with which the attempt at assassination was committed, was picked up by one of the Galatea's bandsmen after the prisoner's capture. The latter is a small Colt's revolver, such as could easily be carried in the pocket.

The article ends by telling readers that 'immense crowds' gathered at both Government House and the offices of the *Sydney Mail* awaiting news of the prince's condition and assures us that the prince's youth and strong constitution will help him survive.

Called Upon to Suffer

While Sister Osburn was nursing the prince back to health, the outraged people of Sydney were leaving no stone unturned in their efforts to show their undying support and loyalty to Britain and the royal family.

This was a period of great political and religious conflict between Irish Catholics and the non-Catholic establishment in both Britain and the colonies of Australia. 'Fenian terrorism' was reported regularly in newspapers and there had been a shooting incident between Orange Lodge and Catholic factions during the prince's visit to Melbourne, which had apparently begun as a sectarian disagreement.

The assassination attempt generated an outpouring of prejudice and racism against Catholics and the Irish. Many public meetings were held around the country with nearly 20,000 people attending a meeting in Sydney the day after the shooting. By the following week, there were daily 'indignation meetings' everywhere. A mob even threatened to burn down Tierney's Currency Lass Hotel, where O'Farrell had stayed.

Anti-Irish hysteria was evident even in parliament and the New South Wales government passed the *Treason Felony Act* on 18 March, six days after the assassination attempt, making it an offence, among other things, to refuse to drink to the Queen's health.

Newspapers and politicians tried unsuccessfully to paint O'Farrell's act as part of a conspiracy, although it was patently obvious that the man was seriously mentally ill. Some even found fanciful and sinister evidence of a plot to disgrace and destabilise New South Wales by the rival colony of Victoria, seen by many in New South Wales as a hotbed of Irish Catholic sentiment and independent thinking. After all, O'Farrell had travelled from Victoria to perpetrate the deed.

Queen Victoria herself was the target of seven assassination attempts during her reign and was clever enough to make sure that she created no martyrs to provide fuel for enemies of the Crown. Not one of the would-be assassins was hanged. Two were 'put under care suited to their mental condition', two were imprisoned 'at Her Majesty's pleasure', one was banished, another transported for seven years, and the other, hilariously, was sent to Dartmoor Prison and 'ultimately released on his promise to go to Australia, where he was working as a house-painter as lately as 1882'.

When O'Farrell was tried at the end of March for attempted murder, which was punishable by death in New South Wales, the premier, James Martin, prosecuted for the Crown. O'Farrell's counsel was a liberal-minded Melbourne barrister, Butler Aspinall, who had defended some of the Eureka rebel miners 27 years earlier, for no fee.

Aspinall's defence rested on the grounds of O'Farrell's obvious insanity and suicide threats, caused by financial and religious worries, heavy drinking and obsessive delusion. He used the English precedent of self-proclaimed subversive, Edward Oxford, who shot at Queen Victoria in 1840, and was found insane and committed to an asylum.

Anti-Fenian sentiment, along with colonial rivalry, was so rife and vehement in New South Wales that Aspinall was denied entry to any Sydney clubs, until the Australia Club realised that their rules could not exclude a member of the Melbourne Club.

James Martin easily convinced the jury that O'Farrell was perfectly sane when he committed the act and the result was really a foregone conclusion. The trial lasted two days and the jury took one hour to find Henry James O'Farrell guilty and the judge pronounced a sentence of death.

Clemency for O'Farrell was refused. His sister Caroline appealed directly to the prince, with further evidence of insanity, and the prince backed her appeal. Despite the prince's own proposal that the execution be delayed and the sentence referred to the Queen, the appeal was refused. The prince also pointed out that 'attempted murder' was no longer a hanging offence in Britain, but the judge, in consultation with the New South Wales Executive Council, decided that colonial law prevailed.

Henry Parkes, who was colonial secretary and minister of police at the time, commented, 'We did not think that His Royal Highness should interfere in the administration of our laws.'

The whole affair was certainly not Parkes's proudest moment as a politician. He and James Martin had joined forces to win power in coalition in 1866 and Parkes tried very hard to establish a conspiracy theory of dangerous Fenian plots and clandestine groups ready to attack all that was decent and British in Australia, in order to win over the Protestant establishment vote and stay in power.

However, Parkes's overreaction, and his attempts to prove O'Farrell was a dangerous Fenian, proved counterproductive and made him a figure of ridicule. He resigned in September 1868, while parliament was in recess, after the *Sydney Morning Herald* announced, on 12 August, that the British government had declined to submit the *NSW Treason Felony Act* to the Queen for royal assent, after British newspapers had condemned it as a 'monstrous production' enacted in a 'whirlwind of passion' by a 'bewildered and misled Parliament'.

So, in spite of O'Farrell being obviously mentally ill and failing to kill the prince, and in spite of the prince asking for clemency for his would-be assassin, Henry O'Farrell was tried, found guilty and hanged at Darlinghurst Gaol on 21 April 1868, just five weeks and five days after the shooting.

His confession, written the day before the hanging, tells us that his many rambling claims to be part of a Fenian network were figments of his imagination and unsound mind. It reads in part:

> I had no foundation for saying there was a Fenian organization in New South Wales. From continually thinking and talking of what I may still be allowed to call the wrongs of Ireland, I became excited and filled with enthusiasm on the subject. And it was when under the influence of these feelings that I attempted to perpetuate the deed for which I am most justly called upon to suffer.

The day after the attempted assassination, the people of Sydney began giving generously to a public subscription fund, originally intended to pay for the erection of some enormous memorial to affirm their loyalty to the royal family and the Crown—and celebrate Alfred's safe recovery.

Eventually some element of common sense prevailed and it was suggested that the 'perfect memorial' would be a hospital—and so the idea of the Royal Prince Alfred Hospital was born.

The monies collected were placed in a fund and, in 1873, the *Prince Alfred Hospital Act* was passed, establishing a board of directors responsible for planning and building the hospital on land belonging to Sydney University in Missenden Road.

Royal Prince Alfred ('RPA') was planned as a clinical school for the university's new medical faculty and, appropriately, as a training school for nurses. Florence Nightingale supplied advice on the design via her group of nurses now at the old hospital in Sydney and by sending copies of her publication, *Notes on Hospitals and Notes on Nursing: What it is and what it is not.*

The project offered the opportunity for Sydney to build a well-designed hospital with trained staff and modern technology. It was everything the old 'Rum Hospital' in Macquarie Street was not!

RPA opened as a 146-bed hospital and received its first patients in 1882 at the Missenden Road site. During that year 1069 patients were admitted. The hospital has since established a national and international reputation for excellence as a training and referral institution. The prince authorised his coat of arms to be used as the new hospital's crest and King Edward VII granted the hospital its royal prefix in 1902.

In an odd way, this wonderful hospital owes its existence as much to Henry James O'Farrell as it does to Prince Alfred, Duke of Edinburgh.

In 1881, thirteen years after the assassination attempt, Henry's brother Peter O'Farrell, in a suicidal state, attempted to shoot Alipius Goold, Archbishop of Melbourne since 1874, near the archbishop's residence at Brighton.

Peter O'Farrell, too, failed to achieve his aim as an assassin and shot the archbishop in the hand. He was sentenced to two years in prison for 'unlawfully wounding'. He served the sentence and returned to France, where he had lived for some time in self-imposed exile. He died there in 1898, aged 70.

Footnote 1:

The Fenians and Manchester Martyrs: Fenian is a term given to members of the Irish Republican Brotherhood (IRB) and Fenian Brotherhood in the USA. These organisations were formed after the failed Irish uprising of 1848 and the early leaders were James Stephens, living in Paris, and John O'Mahony in the USA.

Basically, they believed that Ireland had a natural right to be free and that this could be achieved by violence and armed uprising. In 1867 American members of the organisation, veterans of the American Civil War, landed at Cork expecting to lead a Fenian army against the British. The revolt failed and led to the suspension of *habeas corpus* in Ireland and a wave of anti-Irish legislation.

The leaders of the rebellion, Thomas Kelly, and an American civil war captain, Timothy Deasy, were arrested while living in Manchester, where they had been hidden and supported by the city's large Irish Catholic migrant community.

After being charged, Kelly and Deasy were being driven from the courthouse to Belle Vue Prison with four other prisoners when a group of some thirty Fenians armed with revolvers attacked the prison van and attempted to break into it and free the men. The unarmed police sergeant inside the van with the prisoners refused to unlock the door and looked through the keyhole just as one of the rescuers attempted to shoot the lock. He died instantly and the keys were taken from his pocket and handed through the barred window to the rescuers. Kelly and Deasy escaped and were never recaptured.

Although the killing was accidental, three men, who admitted attempting to free the prisoners, were charged with murder committed by the 'joint enterprise and common purpose' of a conspiracy. They were sentenced to death and hanged in front of a crowd of 10,000, that had celebrated all night waiting for the hangings. Father Gadd, one of the three Catholic priests who attended to the prisoners, described the crowd as, 'inhuman ghouls from the purlieus of Deansgate and the slums of the City'. The city's Catholics had been ordered not to attend by their priests.

The British liberal press was appalled by the hangings and attacked the decision. Some elements of the conservative press commented that the court decision to hang the men had given the Fenian Movement exactly what it needed . . . martyrs.

Footnote 2: Sister Lucy Osburn and the British Nurses

Who were those trained nurses who were on hand to care for Prince Alfred and give him the up-to-date modern medical attention that enabled him to recover so quickly?

Believe it or not, they were Sydney's first properly trained nurses and had arrived from England just one week before the prince was shot, on the clipper ship *Dunbar Castle*. Had the prince been shot during his first stay in Sydney, as Henry O'Farrell intended, there would have been no nurses to care for him.

In 1867, New South Wales Colonial Secretary Henry Parkes, despairing of the dilapidated state of the Sydney Hospital, had written to Florence Nightingale and asked for her advice and help. The hospital was decrepit, dirty and ill-equipped. It operated with decades-old technology and was run by men who had no concept of the recent advances in medicine.

Parkes pushed through an act requiring the inspection of hospitals and suggested that the government bring to Sydney nursing sisters trained by Florence Nightingale, who could modernise the hospital, run the infirmary and dispensary, and train other nurses.

Florence sent six trained nurses, led by her protégé and cousin, Sister Lucy Osburn, to work at the Sydney Hospital. Sister Osburn and

Sister Haldane Turriff cared for Prince Alfred and restored him back to health.

Lucy Osburn was born in 1836 at Leeds, her father was the famous Egyptologist, William Osburn. She was well educated and spoke several languages, her hobby was breaking in Arab horses but she was passionate about the new female career of nursing and worked in hospitals in Holland, Germany and Vienna. She studied midwifery at King's College Hospital and attended Florence Nightingale's Training School at St Thomas's Hospital—all against her family's wishes.

When, in response to Henry Parkes's efforts to solicit help from Florence Nightingale, Lucy was appointed lady superintendent of the Sydney Infirmary and Dispensary at a salary of £150 in 1867, her father disowned her.

Sister Osburn was appointed for three months and stayed sixteen years, fighting constantly all that time against bureaucracy, misogyny, prejudice, professional jealousy and rivalry. She is one of the true heroes of our colonial history.

On her arrival in Sydney she discovered that construction of the accommodation to be built for the nurses had not even begun. Even so, by the end of the year, she had managed to train sixteen new local nurses. Her attempts to modernise the hospital were constantly frustrated and obstructed by Alfred Roberts, the visiting surgeon whose cronies attacked her in the Legislative Assembly.

Lucy Osburn had the filthy kitchens cleaned and managed to rid the hospital of the prostitutes, vagrants and derelicts previously used to feed the patients. The hospital had become a dumping ground for unwanted books and, when Lucy, who worshipped at the small Anglo-Catholic Christ Church St Laurence in George Street, rather than Sydney's larger 'protestant' Anglican churches, had the old books burned, her enemies accusing her of 'Bible burning'.

A royal commission in 1873 completely exonerated her and accused the all-male management committee of the hospital of neglect and 'interfering between the head of nursing and her nurses'. In 1874 Sister Osburn's salary was raised from £150 per annum to £250.

The old centre building was demolished in 1879 and work began on a new hospital in 1881, when the *Sydney Hospital Act* abolished the infirmary's old name and set up new conditions of management.

Lucy Osburn resigned and returned to Britain in 1884. She was suffering from diabetes and had contracted several diseases, including dysentery, while working in the poor conditions at the hospital. She intended to return to Australia to live, as she had made many friends here and felt that Sydney was her home. Her poor health, however, made it easier for her to remain in London, where she worked as a district nurse and then became superintendent to the Southwark, Newington and Walworth District Nursing Association. She died of diabetes in 1891.

After many delays, the new hospital was completed in 1894. It contains a museum dedicated to the memory of Sister Lucy Osburn.

13

GEORGE HENRY COCHRANE—
PAST MASTER IN SCOUNDRELISM

'. . . more to be pitied than blamed.'

The Versifying Blacksmith

George Henry Cochrane (alias various versions of Grant Madison Hervey/Harvey) was born in 1880 at Casterton, in far western Victoria, just 25 miles (40 kilometres) from the South Australian border.

The son of a storekeeper, and grandson of a convict whom he claimed was a 'noble fellow' who was 'most unjustly used', young George was a tall, strong red-headed lad who became a blacksmith at a local coach-building business and then moved to Melbourne, where he worked in a foundry.

By the age of twenty he was contributing verse to the *Bulletin* and, sometime in 1900, he moved to Sydney looking for work as a journalist and changed his name to Grant Hervey (he later claimed this was merely a nom de plume but, in fact, it was the name he went by in his private life from around 1902). Before he was 23 years old, he had worked on newspapers in Melbourne, Perth and the Western Australian goldfields, and attempted to start his own literary magazine.

Hervey seems, in his verse writing, to have been heavily influenced by Henry Lawson's ideas and sense of nostalgia. Many of his poems contain ideas and even phrases from Lawson's verse. Like Lawson he began as a pro-Labor writer and worked on *The Worker* newspaper, as did Lawson. His later writings and speeches became vehemently anti-Labor. His collected verse, written in the decade between 1903 and 1913, covered all the standard 'bush verse' themes of the time.

Here he is talking about bush workers ending a spree in town:

> We have spent what we earned in the saddle,
> What we made with the pick and the shears;
> Now it's time for the bush-ward skedaddle,
> It's farewell to the bars and the beers!
>
> From 'Leaving the Town'

It seems that whatever Hervey was writing about at the time was the most romantic and nostalgic of all topics for him. For example, he wrote about the passing of the bullock drivers, whose cursing and swearing and bullock whips moved the loads across the outback. The piece of silk on the end of the whip—known as the 'cracker'—was what made the noise:

> Silk Cracker Days! through the steaming haze
> Do I see them drive the teams,
> The men whose lips and roaring whips
> Make thunder in my dreams!
> . . . The Days are Gone! The coaly train
> Has seized on all the land,
> Whereon the teams in cracking days
> Went cursing through the sand!
>
> From 'Silk Cracker Days'

The theme of this poem is very similar to Henry Lawson's idea that the coming of the railway ended the golden days of the bush—Lawson wrote 'the mighty bush with iron rails is tethered to the world'.

Not long after lamenting the arrival of the railway, however, we find Hervey writing a hymn of praise to the mighty railway and the men who work on it, in a poem called 'Rolling Her Home':

Lashing her, crashing her; footplates a-clatter,
Cranks swinging forward in maniac haste;
Leaving the darkness and silence a-shatter
The former in twain and the latter effaced!
Gigantic and frantic, she sways in her agony.
Her cars all a-beat like a vast metronome:
Driving her on in her mighty protagony,
Lo! we go gallantly—Rolling Her Home!

Actually that's not a bad piece of rhymed verse—if you can put up with the 'agony/protagony' rhyme.

The Scottish-born associate editor of the *Bulletin*, James Edmond, took a liking to the young aspiring poet and began publishing his verse in the magazine. From 1903 to 1914, James Edmond was being bombarded weekly with hundreds of poems by aspiring balladists and versifiers. I find it hard to believe that Edmond would have championed Grant Hervey's verse on the basis of admiring its nationalistic sentimentality—as he probably received a dozen examples of such stuff every week. It is my guess that he was attracted to the young poet's energy and use of rhyme. Perhaps he liked poems like this one, very reminiscent of the earlier verse of Breaker Morant:

Kisses and Sin
Kiss now! while the girl is handy,
You can't when she's far away;
Sin now! lest your life be sandy,
Oasis-less and grey . . .
Sin NOW! you are growing older,
Away with your doubts and fears;
For the greyest ghosts that moulder
In the vale of our latter years
Are the haunting apparitions
Of the sins we contrived to miss,
The uncommitted transgressions—
The girls that we didn't kiss!

Intent to Murder

It would appear that the young poet was writing from personal experience when he wrote 'Kisses and Sin'. A few days before his 25th birthday, the Melbourne *Argus* reported the event in detail on Saturday, 18 November 1905:

City sensation

Mr Walter Baker Fired At

Grant Hervey Arrested

A sensational incident occurred in Bourke Street East when Grant Hervey, well known as a writer of verse, drew a revolver and fired at Mr Walter Baker, the leading actor of Mr Bland Holt's company.

The article goes on to explain that around eleven o'clock Mr Baker was travelling on a tram along Exhibition Street, when he saw his wife arm in arm with Hervey. He alighted from the tram and confronted the pair:

'What are you doing with my wife?' continued Mister Baker and without waiting for answer struck Hervey heavily on the jaw. The man staggered back with the force of the blow, and as he steadied himself drew a revolver from his pocket. Mr Baker seized his wife, swung her around to face Hervey as a shield, and then dashed for the corner of Spring Street. As soon as Mr Baker was clear of his wife Hervey fired. The shot struck the steel pier at the side of the Imperial Hotel doorway.

Detective Howard, who had witnessed the whole occurrence, rushed from the middle of the road, and intercepted Hervey, who was in the act of following Mr Baker with the revolver in his hand . . . Howard held Hervey by the wrists and disarmed him. Hervey made no further resistance, and was removed to the Little Bourke Street watchhouse shouting insults after Mr Baker, who had in the meantime returned.

Hervey was charged with shooting with intent to murder, and lodged in a cell. He gave his age as 25, his occupation as a journalist, and stated that he had 'no religion'.

The outraged actor, while admitting he and his wife had separated, told the *Argus*:

> 'I allow my wife £200 a year,' he said. 'I bought a house which cost over £2000, and my two daughters live with her. She has everything she can desire while I toil, in spite of the doctor's express orders to the contrary. Without telling me she suddenly arrived in Melbourne the other day by the SS Ophir. I saw her on Monday. I remember having seen Hervey's photograph hanging in my drawing room in Sydney. When I saw him tonight I thought, "How can I stand this?" I went across to him as any man would and asked him his name and what he was doing with my wife. Then I hit him under the jaw with my left hand ... He pulled a revolver from his hip pocket. I ducked behind my wife who screamed out, "Oh Walter!" Pushing her aside I ran towards the corner of Spring Street. He fired at me—I heard the whizz of a bullet. I dashed around the corner into Spring Street.'

Hervey made a statement to the press, admitting that he fired a gun in a busy street but explaining:

> In a wave of excitement, which comes over all of us at times, I drew my revolver and fired at him. Baker—and I would like you to stress this point if you please—hid behind his wife.

Baker followed Detective Howard and his prisoner to the watch house and the two men continued to insult each other. When Hervey stated that he was an Australian and proud of it, the *Argus* reported:

> 'That's all you have to be proud of,' said Mr Baker.
> 'He is under arrest,' said Detective Howard to Mr Baker. 'It's no use rubbing it in.'
> Later, Mr Baker asked, 'What charge are you putting against him?'
> 'Shooting with intent to murder,' replied Howard.

At this point the *Argus* reported that Hervey yelled at the actor:

> 'Well? Well? Haven't you got something to say? This is the psychological moment. This is where we turn the limelight on.'
> 'A lot you know about the psychological moment,' retorted Mr Baker.

In light of later events, Detective Howard's statements and evidence at the trial are interesting. He told the *Argus* that:

> He had some difficulty in inducing Hervey to give up his revolver. Hervey fingered the trigger nervously, and exclaimed several times, 'It's alright I'm not going to shoot again. Did you see that man assault me?' He was laboring under intense excitement.

The Adelaide *Express & Telegraph*, reporting on the trial, gave further information that:

> Detective Howard said that when Baker rushed away Hervey followed him with a revolver in his right hand. He went up to Hervey and said, 'Are you mad?' Hervey tried to return the revolver to his pocket but somebody caught him by the left shoulder. The witness was able to take the weapon away.

On Thursday 14 December 1905, the case went to court. The *Sydney Morning Herald* reported the result the following day:

Grant Hervey Not Guilty.

Melbourne, Thursday.

Accused in defence made a long statement. He said he made a practice of carrying a revolver, because he had received a number of anonymous letters threatening to kill him, and because his work as a journalist led him into dangerous parts of the city. Mrs Baker was an old and esteemed friend of his and he was also well acquainted with her brothers and sisters. When walking up Bourke street with Mrs Baker he offered her his arm, as an act of courtesy due to all women from all men, and when he fired the revolver shot he merely wished to frighten Baker, and took extreme care to so fire that no damage was done.

The jury returned a verdict of not guilty, and in discharging the accused Mr Justice Hodges said, 'I may perhaps say that for your own safety and the safety of others that it is desirable you should not carry a loaded revolver. I will also make another remark with reference to your statement to the jury that beside the courtesy proper between man and woman there is also due a little fair dealing between man and man.'

So, apparently, the jury believed Hervey's side of the story and he was cleared on both charges and allowed to walk free. His only punishment being the night he spent in the watch house and the judge's insult in relation to what the judge considered his ungentlemanly behaviour.

Hervey made good use of the experience by writing a poem entitled 'The Night I Spent in Quad', in which he pontificated about injustices visited upon the downtrodden who find their way into the prison system. His lifelong obsession with his convict grandfather seemed to be the spur that led to this fixation. It is apparent that, around this time, Hervey was beginning to manifest signs of irrational thinking and impetuous behaviour, at best—and mental instability, at worst.

In the collection of verse, dedicated to James Edmond and published in 1913, certain of the poems reinforce Hervey's proud assertion made to the police in 1905, that he had 'no religion'. Another poem in the volume, however, is a hymn of praise to the Almighty.

The book's title, *Australians Yet, and Other Verses*, 'Ballads of Manhood, Work, Good Cheer, Mateship, Masculine Vigour and Nationalism', perhaps gives an insight into the odd mix of philosophies that were attempting to form themselves into some sort of cogent manifesto in the mind of George Cochrane, the ex-blacksmith who had now successfully transformed himself into Grant Hervey, poet and journalist.

A Danger to the Community

Not everyone in the publishing world shared James Edmond's enthusiasm for the literary works of Grant Hervey. Another Scottish-Australian journalist who knew him, Wallace Nelson, said of him: 'He turned out poetry by the square yard with mechanical regularity. When he had done a fair morning's work he used to put his coat on and go and have a drink.'

Hervey's religious beliefs moved easily between vehement atheism and prophetic Old Testament Christianity depending on his mood at the time. Similarly, his political stance varied, from working on the Labor newspaper *The Worker* for several years, to a tour around western Victoria for the People's Party, speaking against Labor's referendum proposals.

He was able to swear under oath in 1905 that he 'took extreme care to so fire that no damage was done' when he shot at Walter Baker in Bourke Street, and then swear again under oath ten years later, 'in a fit of insanity in Melbourne I shot at Walter Baker'. When arrested in 1915 he told police his religion was 'Greek' and later, during the trial, called on Almighty God to be his witness.

Hervey might have managed to talk his way out of a prison sentence in 1905, but he was unable to do so ten years later after managing to get himself entangled in a legal struggle with the infamous John Norton, notorious alcoholic, politician, scandal-monger and crusading editor and proprietor of the *Truth*, Australia's only national newspaper at the time.

Once again, there was a woman at the heart of the matter.

Norton was at the time living apart from his wife, Ada, and it was common knowledge that he was very keen to attain custody of their daughter. Sometime during the first week of January 1915 Hervey, who was employed by Norton as a journalist, told his employer that he had 'behaved indecently' with Ada Norton on Christmas Day 1914, and again on Boxing Day. He suggested that he could arrange to be caught in *flagrante delicto* with Mrs Norton for the sum of £200. This would provide Norton with the evidence he needed to gain custody of his daughter.

Unfortunately for Hervey, Norton contrived to have him say all this while two police detectives and a short-hand stenographer were secreted in an adjoining room. At the resulting trial Mrs Norton denied the accusation, Hervey recanted the story, was found guilty of attempted blackmail and false pretences, and was sentenced to two years hard labour. He always claimed to have been 'set up' by Norton, either because of his friendship with Mrs Ada Norton or some journalistic disagreement.

At the same time he was accused of committing another crime. In October 1914 someone sent a telegram to Edward Gazzard, proprietor of the *Casterton News and the Merino and Sandford Record,* the local newspaper in Hervey's hometown. Gazzard and Hervey were journalistic enemies and the telegram, sent under a false name, asserted that the Sydney press had just announced that Mr Grant Hervey had been declared bankrupt.

Hervey was charged with 'forging and uttering'. The assertion being that he sent the telegram hoping that Gazzard would publish the information, at which point Hervey would sue him for libel. Strong evidence was presented to show that the accused was seen to type the telegram and later imposed upon a colleague to drop parts of the typewriter he used into the harbour in order to prevent the police from linking the typed telegram form to his typewriter. Several witnesses also testified that he attempted to get them to send the telegram at various post offices.

Hervey was found guilty of both crimes but successfully appealed the 'forging and uttering' verdict on a technicality. A second trial was held. Hervey was again found guilty of the charges.

After the verdict was delivered he made an impassioned and long-winded statement, in which he claimed to be the victim of a vicious prank that was not perpetrated by Gazzard, but by his own colleagues in Sydney. His defence was not aided by the fact that, when the Casterton and Portland newspapers published the false story, Hervey had issued writs against them in the Supreme Court and then hinted that he would settle out of court for less.

When the judge, Justice Pring, told Hervey that he simply did not believe a word he said, the 34-year-old prisoner in the dock did something out of character—he pleaded insanity:

> I have tried to keep this part of my life hidden: but now I feel that I must lift the veil. When the Norton case began, the Crown Prosecutor said that the most charitable construction that could be placed upon my actions was that I was insane. Mr Norton said practically the same thing, and at one stage Judge Docker asked if I had been examined by a medical man. It is a very distressing subject to me, your honour, but I think it best to place certain facts before you. I think it is generally admitted that insanity is hereditary. There is a taint of insanity in my blood. My grandfather, William Cochran [sic], died insane; my uncle,

Henry William Cochran [sic], is at present in an institution for the insane at Ararat Victoria; and two years ago my brother committed suicide at Broken Hill while insane. The same taint of insanity is in my blood.

Hervey then attempted to explain the effect that his 'taint' of insanity had on his relationships with women and stated that 'whenever I got into trouble before, a woman has been responsible, or rather, a woman has been at the bottom of it'.

He then told the judge:

From six to nine months of the year I can go about my business and pleasure the same as any rational man; then there comes a time when I have to go away from the city, and into the bush, and hide myself from my fellow man. I must do this to keep my brain upon its balance.

Justice Pring was unmoved by the prisoner's statement. The judge said he had no doubt that Hervey was 'a past master in scoundrelism' and 'a great danger to the community' and he sentenced him to two more years of hard labour—to be added to the two he was already serving.

Hervey was telling the truth for once in his accounts of his family's insanity. His grandfather died in Ararat Asylum in 1873, having spent years there after being found guilty of attempting to murder his wife. His younger brother shot himself through the head in 1912 while of 'unsound mind'.

The appeal proved ineffectual, however, and the prisoner served his four years. How the 'past master in scoundrelism' spent his time in prison is unknown, but he evidently spent some of it dreaming up what became known as the 'Greater Mildura' scam because, just six weeks after his release on 19 June 1919, having purchased an astrakhan coat and brushed up his fake American accent, he headed to Mildura where he made his speech to the 2000 assembled citizens.

The 'Greater Mildura' Scam

According to a long feature article in the *Mildura Cultivator* on 6 August 1919, G. Madison Harvey, a tall imposing man who wore a full-length astrakhan coat and spoke in a broad American accent, had addressed a public meeting attended by 2000 people the previous Saturday to present his 'Greater Mildura' scheme for a new state for which he sought financial backing.

Mr Madison Harvey admitted he had never been to Mildura before but said that he was aware of the town's unique history and the self-reliant and pioneering spirit of its citizens and was, therefore, proposing that the district of Sunraysia and the Darling Valley should become an independent state, with Mildura as its capital.

He further proposed that he was just the man to make this happen and that, if everyone present donated £5 to the cause, he would take the proposal to Prime Minister Billy Hughes and then on to Westminster and make sure it was carried through. He only required, he said, to be paid £1000 every six months to devote his life to lobbying and advocating and negotiating with the relevant authorities until the goal of independence was attained for Sunraysia.

The speech was a doozy! Reading detailed accounts of it more than 100 years later, you cannot help but be impressed. To fully understand just how the tall and eloquent 'snake oil salesman' with the astrakhan coat and the fake American accent was able to manipulate the feelings and ambitions of 2000 good citizens of Sunraysia, we need to remember the district's unique origins and history.

The Mildura Irrigation Colony was the dreamchild of Alfred Deakin, solicitor-general and minister of public works in the Victorian parliament and later prime minister of Australia. In 1884 he visited the United States and investigated irrigation projects. He was impressed by the work of the Canadian Chaffey brothers, who had set up three 'irrigation communities' in California, and invited them to Australia. Mildura was eventually set up as a Chaffey-managed company town—an alcohol-free irrigation colony, a collective and company-run community of farmers and the first town of its type in Australia.

The project failed but, with government assistance and goodwill and perseverance, Mildura eventually prospered and the Chaffeys came to be seen as pioneers and visionaries.

In his impassioned address, delivered from the town's rotunda bandstand, to 2000 of those who had survived the turbulent years during which the town of Mildura had been established, G. Madison Harvey was fulsome in his praise of those who established the irrigation community, knowing full well that those present were the beneficiaries of the vision and endeavours of the Chaffey brothers, and that William Chaffey, who had chosen to remain in Mildura when his brothers returned to America, was at that time the shire president.

The speaker reminded his audience that they had been right about the Chaffey brothers when the rest of Australia had doubted and denigrated their vision. Now, he assured them, every right-minded person in Australia was aware that the people of Mildura had been right all along.

Having been introduced to the assembled citizenry by none other than the shire president, William Chaffey himself, the 'man with the plan' opened the meeting in prayer. Having asked the men present to remove their hats, he beseeched the Almighty to bless and protect the town and open the minds of those present to the soundness and wisdom of his proposal.

He asked those present whether they were 'lifters or leaners' and wanted to know if they were 'workers with minds and souls for a greater Mildura' or merely 'parasites on the backs of the pioneers'. He invited those present to consider other towns in the district that did not display the same enterprise, but benefited from the success of Mildura: 'If the Government of New South Wales had been alive to the possibility it would long ago have created another Mildura on the other side of the river.'

When a loud voice from the crowd replied, 'It hasn't got the guts,' Harvey was able to segue smoothly to the nub of his proposal. 'The expression,' he replied, 'if vulgar,' still, 'summed up the situation. It hadn't got the guts.' There was much more rhetoric and eloquence to come—along with some surprises—and the meeting lasted until 10.30 p.m.

Harvey's proposal took the form of the creation of a new state, the 'Soldiers' Memorial State' (or 'Greater Mildura'), to be settled by 100,000 returned servicemen, with Mildura (which would secede from Victoria) as its capital. This new state was to be an outback territory, peopled by a hardy breed of farmers and rural settlers, extending up the Darling River as far as Queensland and established on the principle of reward for hard work combined with entrepreneurial innovation.

As the speech went on, Harvey implied he was part of an organisation that could implement the plan and that he was the man for the job of promoting the concept. In the spirit of the Chaffey brothers, and imbued with good old Yankee know-how, he would give the region the kind of promotion and recognition it deserved.

At this point in the diatribe, it became obvious that Harvey was launching a daring public attack on the man who had become famous for promoting Sunraysia, as the district had become known, using funds provided by the local cooperative organisation—the Australian Dried Fruits Association (ADFA).

That man was Clement John 'Jack' De Garis, whose official title was Director of Publicity for the Australian Dried Fruits Association. (De Garis is the subject of Chapter 5 of this volume.)

It seems that Harvey had decided that his plan to ingratiate himself with the Sunraysia fruit growers and townsfolk of Mildura, in order to extract some financial gain from their gullibility, could only work if he called into question the competency and honesty of the man in whom they had placed their trust for the past year.

It is not quite certain why Harvey believed that an attack on De Garis was an essential part of his plan to extract money from the citizens of Sunraysia, but at some point he apparently decided that it was a good idea to call into question De Garis's credibility and the corporate governance and professionalism of the ADFA.

Harvey implied that De Garis had wasted £20,000 of the people's money on second-rate and unsuccessful stunts and announced that he had eighteen questions he would like the ADFA to answer if they could. At that point Jack De Garis appeared from out of the crowd and offered to answer them.

Now, Jack De Garis was a local and there were many in Mildura who thought he was a genius, but there were some who found his ideas and gimmicks a bit of an embarrassment and a little self-indulgent. The general consensus of the meeting was that it would be polite and fair to at least hear out this imposing American speaker.

Once De Garis was allowed onto the stage, Harvey read a series of accusations in the form of questions. De Garis heard him out and then replied that he could answer all the accusations but wanted first to refute one claim and then ask Mr Harvey a couple of questions.

In his one-and-a-half-hour speech, Harvey had boasted that the town was already £1 million richer when he stepped off the train that morning—because of the idea he had brought to them. He also said he was motivated to come and help after despairing of the ineptitude of De Garis's campaigns, which he claimed had achieved nothing.

Jack De Garis countered by saying that, as it was his publicity that had brought his accuser to town, he had obviously succeeded as the town was, according to Harvey himself, now apparently £1 million richer!

The locals enjoyed the joke and sympathy started to swing towards their local hero. De Garis then pointed out that the man Harvey had praised to the skies, the man who had in fact introduced him that evening, Shire President W.B. Chaffey, was the founder and life president of the ADFA.

Then came three simple questions from De Garis: 'Who are you?', 'Who do you represent?' and 'Where have you been for the past seven years?'

Now, anyone involved in political organisations at any level knows the golden rule of public debates and meetings—'Never ask an opponent a question unless you know the answer'.

Jack De Garis did know the answer to his questions—G. Madison Harvey was, of course, George Henry Cochrane, alias Grant Hervey; he represented no organisation except himself; and he had—for the past four years—been in prison for fraud, attempted blackmail and forging and uttering.

The *Mildura Cultivator* reported what happened next:

Mr Harvey, throwing off his overcoat, declared in impassioned tones that he had spent a good deal of the time mentioned in prison. He was sent to gaol on the 19th August 1915 (after eight months of trial) and he was released on the 19th June, 1919. His real name was Grant Madison Hervey . . . It was while in prison that he evolved the scheme of a Greater Mildura. He was an Australian not an American as he had represented. Knowing Australia as he did, he felt that the people would pay more attention to 'a man from abroad' than they would to an Australian. He believed in his scheme and had hoped to get it accepted.

There was, as you can imagine, quite an uproar in the crowd but they quietened enough to hear Jack De Garis refute some of the claims the now-exposed conman had made. He added a statement that the Sunraysia publicity campaign was now reaching its conclusion and a full report as to its success or otherwise would be published in due course by the ADFA.

Mr G. Picton, a soldier-settler, then addressed the meeting briefly and condemned Harvey for falsely criticising and denigrating organisations that had helped returned servicemen in the district.

Harvey denied he had done this and asked the chairman for permission to speak again. By this time, however, it was 10.30 at night and the president declared that he thought Mr Harvey had already said 'more than enough'. He then added that he personally resented the actions of the guest speaker and declared the meeting closed. With his proposal for a new state exposed as a pipe-dream at best, and a scam at worst, he beat a hasty retreat.

The *Mildura Cultivator* concluded its long report of the eventful meeting held on Saturday, 2 August 1919, with a short paragraph that read: 'Mr Hervey left by Monday morning's fast train.'

Tarred and Feathered

Evidently, Hervey found it hard to get work as a journalist after his run-in with John Norton and the law—and claimed later that he'd been blacklisted by editors and 'boycotted in his profession'.

His reaction to this situation was to set up his own newspaper. It seems that he harboured a strong grudge against De Garis for exposing him and this led to him establishing a very short-lived weekly newspaper called the *Mildura & Merbein Sun* in January 1921. It lasted 37 weeks.

Hervey used the paper to attack De Garis's successful newspaper, the *Sunraysia Daily*, question his integrity and belittle the success of the publicity campaign he ran to promote the district's produce.

He also published scurrilous personal attacks on the owners of local businesses that refused to advertise in his newspaper and generally scandalised the district with his 'gutter journalism'.

Jack De Garis was having financial problems in his businesses, which included orchards, processing and packing sheds in Mildura, a newspaper and a publishing business. Having successfully bought and established the Pyap farming settlement in South Australia, he was having trouble attempting to raise capital to set up an irrigation community on 50,000 acres (20,000 hectares) at Kendenup in Western Australia.

Hervey wrote long and regular articles attacking De Garis and claiming that he had defrauded the town and the ADFA. Many of Mildura's citizens took his claims to be an insult to the town.

The final straw came when Hervey printed a special edition of the *Mildura & Merbein Sun*, with the headline 'De Garis Bankrupt', which was a lie. He also had posters printed and displayed in Mildura and Melbourne on Monday 24 October, which proclaimed the same brief message.

Mildura had had enough of 'G. Madison Harvey' and many citizens felt the town's reputation needed to be salvaged. They decided to act— and they did.

The story was soon all over the wire service. The *Singleton Argus* reported it on Saturday 29 October:

Tarred and Feathered

GRANT HERVEY'S EXPERIENCE.

A MILDURA SENSATION.

Mildura was a centre of sensation on Tuesday last when it became known that a large number of citizens had decided to tar and feather Mr Grant Hervey, editor of the 'Mildura and Merebein [sic] Sun,' following on the publication of a statement regarding the alleged bankruptcy of Mr C. J. de Garis in a special issue of the 'Sun' on the previous Thursday. The statement was also circulated, by means of posters in Melbourne on Monday. After Mr Hervey's return from Melbourne on Tuesday morning about 100 men in some 20 motorcars assembled in front of Mr Hervey's house, but found the place barricaded.

At midday it was learned that Hervey had telephoned for a car to take him to Ouyen, and several carloads of men went to a spot on Deakin Avenue, two miles from Mildura, where there is a bridge over the main irrigation channel. When Hervey's car arrived he was seized by several men, bound, gagged, and placed in one of the cars, which immediately drove off to an aerodrome on the west side of the town. At the aerodrome Hervey was stripped naked, tarred from head to foot, including his hair, and covered with feathers. The aggressors then took away his clothes and left him to seek shelter and clothing as best he could.

Apparently, kapok was used—not feathers.

Later reports state that upon the completion of the operation the bell of the local fire station was rung violently for several minutes, as a result of which more than 1000 persons were soon in the vicinity, where Hervey was standing in the open with his arms stretched to the skies, calling on God to forgive his opponents, who, he said, had not realised what they had been doing.

Sixteen men were arrested.

As the case proceeded through the court system, it became apparent that some of the men charged were local businessmen who had legitimate grievances against Hervey. He had attempted to blackmail a few of them into advertising in his newspaper in order to prevent him from revealing 'skeletons' from their past private lives, or making accusations in the newspaper about their business dealings.

At first the men were charged with assault and grievous bodily harm, but then that charge was put aside and a more serious charge of conspiracy was laid against the group. If it could be proved that they planned and conspired together in order to attack Hervey, the punishment would be quite severe.

By the time the case, via the court process, had reached the Supreme Court at Ballarat, the number of accused had been reduced to twelve, there being insufficient evidence against the others.

The Melbourne *Argus* reported that Mr Maxwell, appearing for the accused, denied that the men had conspired to commit a crime as 'the mere fact of a number of people joining together did not necessarily constitute conspiracy'. He asked the jury to:

Consider the case of a bushfire breaking out in the township without any arrangements having been made. The men of that place would flock together to put out the fire, and anyone who arrived on the scene might say, 'This is a wonderful organised enterprise.'

. . . Hervey was a menace to Mildura, just as the bushfire was to the township. His last infamous act had set a match alight, and had had the same effect on the people of Mildura as the news of a bushfire would have. Hundreds of people have been stirred, and, by accord, had said, 'We are in it,' just as they would be in a case of fire. But that was not conspiracy. That day at Mildura, Grant Hervey was the bushfire, and the people, by impulse, had flocked out to deal with him.

The jury found the men 'not guilty' of conspiracy.

The charge of assault and grievous bodily harm was then laid against the men and they all pleaded guilty.

The *Argus* reported the judge's summation and sentence:

Mr Justice McArthur said that in his long experience at the bar he had come a great deal in contact with the 'gutter press', but never had he seen anything so foul and filthy as the articles which Hervey had published . . .

Hervey had convicted himself of blackmail and had exhibited repulsive hypocrisy in the witness box. His honour said that he did not believe certain things which the 'creature Hervey' had said in the box, but he wanted the whole community to understand that, despicable as Hervey was, that was no justification for men taking the law into their own hands . . .

Each of the accused would be fined £25 and sentenced to 3 months imprisonment, but the sentence would be suspended, upon them entering into a personal bond of £50 to be of good behaviour for 12 months.

The bonds were entered into, and a month was allowed in which to pay the fines.

Twenty-five quid was a lot of money in those days, but no doubt the men who were found guilty thought it a small price to pay for the pleasure of tarring and feathering G. Madison Harvey.

Most Vile Criminal

Grant Hervey's life became even stranger after he was tarred and feathered. In 1923 he stole a chequebook from the owner of an office he was renting in Sydney and forged signatures on two cheques. His defence was that he needed to feed his wife and child and could not afford to pay for heating or lighting, as he had been 'black banned' in his profession by John Norton. He was again convicted of forgery and sent to prison for two years. On his release he seems to have lived for a time in Melbourne, again posing as an American—this time calling himself G. Madison McGlashon. In 1929 he briefly edited a 'scandal sheet' newspaper in Sydney, called *Becket's Budget*.

He became well known for his political speeches at 'speaker's corner' at The Domain in Sydney and stood as an independent labour candidate against the Labor Party in the Queensland seat of Paddington at the Queensland state elections in 1926, losing heavily to the only other candidate, the Labor Party's Alfred Jones.

In 1931 he noticed an advertisement from a Mrs Mahoney, in Brisbane, in the classified section of the newspaper seeking information about her sister, a Mrs F. Hervey. At that time he was living with Fiona Lockwood, who some sources say he had married on 19 October 1920. Although he knew it was not his wife who was being sought in the ad, he sent a telegram asking for £20 from Mrs Mahoney. He signed the telegram form as Mrs F. Hervey and was again charged with forging and uttering.

In a bizarre speech in his own defence in court, Hervey launched a paranoid tirade against the Theodore Labor Government in Queensland, accusing Theodore of setting him up and calling himself 'the master journalist of Australia'. He concluded, 'I regard you as the fairest judge who has ever occupied the Bench.' To which Judge Edwards replied: 'And I think you are one of the most vile criminals I have ever come across. I sentence you to two years on each charge, concurrent, and I regret I cannot make it more.'

Hervey replied, politely, 'Thank you, your Honour.'

He became librarian while in Bathurst Gaol and wrote a novel, *An Eden of the Good*, published in London in 1934. According to his biographer Geoffrey Serle, author Nettie Palmer described him in 1933 (possibly in an obituary) as 'a bulky giant with a large reddish

beard . . . a caricature of those expansive young men of the nineties . . .
patriotic and Utopian'.

Hervey died on 6 November 1933 in Melbourne and was buried
in Springvale Cemetery. If there was a marriage in October 1920, it
may well have been bigamous, for there *is* a record of George Henry
Cochrane marrying his long-time friend, the widow Annie Crowe of
Casterton, at South Melbourne on 20 October 1918. Which seems odd
seeing that George Cochrane, alias Grant Hervey, was supposedly in
prison in New South Wales at the time!

I find myself mentally quoting Lewis Carroll: "'Curiouser and
curiouser!", said Alice.'

The *Australian Worker* commented in 1923: 'Undoubtedly Hervey
has a mental kink, and is more to be pitied than blamed.'

14
JOHN LEAK—INSUBORDINATE LARRIKIN

'. . . he was always the last to withdraw.'

The Queensland 9th Battalion

The National Archives of Australia show that a man calling himself John Leak enlisted as a private in the 9th Battalion, 3rd Brigade, 1st Division of the Australian Imperial Force (AIF) on 28 January 1915 in Rockhampton, Queensland. The 9th Battalion was recruited almost exclusively from Queensland. His army records show that he was born in Portsmouth, England, in 1892 and came to Australia sometime before the war began. His file shows that his parents were dead and his next of kin was listed as a brother living in Canada. His profession is given as 'teamster'—in other words, he was a bullock driver. There were still many teams of bullocks carting freight in that part of Queensland in 1915.

Private Leak embarked with the 5th Reinforcements for the 9th Battalion on the transport HMAT *Kyarra A55*, arrived at Gallipoli and joined his unit on 22 June 1915. He served there until the evacuation on 19 December. After the withdrawal from Gallipoli, the battalion returned to Egypt and was brought up to strength with reinforcements. They sailed for France in March 1916, disembarked at Marseilles and headed to northern France to engage in the Somme offensive in July on the Western Front.

The 9th Battalion spearheading the attack as the 1st Australian Division, flanked by British divisions, moved towards Pozières on 22 July 1916. Pozières, situated on a ridge overlooking the Somme, was a vital objective for the Allies and was taken after four days of savage fighting.

Private Leak survived the fighting at Pozières, but was severely wounded at the Battle of Mouquet Farm one month later on 21 August.

The Battle of Mouquet Farm was fought just 1 mile (1.6 kilometres) northwest of Pozières. The purpose of the operation was to extend British control of the strategic ridge that extended from Pozières to the ruined town of Thiepval by capturing a relatively small area of farmland.

The Australian divisions that fought in this battle were the three which had served at Gallipoli: the 1st, 2nd and 4th.

During the second week of August, the 4th Division led the attack and managed to gain a small amount of territory on the fringe of the farm. This small gain cost the 4th Division 4649 casualties, mostly due to the fact that the German artillery had well-entrenched positions within range of the farm and the shelling was constant.

The 1st Division replaced the 4th and took up the attack in the third week of August. Having lost one-third of its men during the Battle of Pozières a month earlier, the 4th Division made little progress and, in one week of fighting, lost another 2650 men, killed and wounded. One of the wounded was Private John Leak.

The 2nd Division, led by Major-General Gordon Legge, then took over. In a dawn attack on 26 August, they actually succeeded in reaching the farm, only to discover well-entrenched shelters, which had been reinforced by troops of the German Guard Reserve Corps.

The Australians were forced to retreat and suffered another 1268 casualties. The 4th Division was then brought back into the fray and captured the farm again on 29 August, but could not hold it against German counterattacks. The Australians recaptured the farm on 3 September but were again forced to retreat in the face of German artillery fire and counterattacks.

These two operations cost the 4th Division a further 2405 casualties. The farm remained an island of German resistance after the Australian divisions were withdrawn on 5 September and was not captured until British forces swept past and completely surrounded it some three weeks later.

In the futile attempt to capture Mouquet Farm, 11,000 Australian casualties were sustained. In the first six weeks of the Somme offensive, the three ANZAC divisions of the Australian Army had suffered casualties of 23,000. Of these 6741 had been killed. This figure is roughly comparable to the fatalities suffered by these divisions during the eight months of fighting at Gallipoli, when 5833 men were killed in action and a further 1985 died later from wounds.

Leak was hospitalised from the wounds he received in the fighting at Mouquet Farm and then repatriated to London for further treatment and recovery. He did not rejoin the 9th Battalion until 15 October 1917.

He continued fighting with the 9th Battalion until 7 March 1918, when he was gassed in Belgium, and was again hospitalised. During the time between his two bouts in hospital, he was constantly found to be in breach of army regulations and was punished on a number of occasions.

Insubordination

John Leak was a larrikin; throughout his army career he appears to have been a repeat offender when it came to such crimes as insolence, disobedience and, most commonly, going absent without leave. A look at his official record 'charge sheet' reveals a long list of offences and there is plenty of evidence to mark him out as what we might call 'an habitual offender'.

On his service record under the heading 'CRIME', which is written in bold capitals, the entries include: 'Entering sergeants' mess & demanding drink', 'Neglecting to obey RSM in that he refused to leave Sergeant's Mess when ordered to by the RSM' (for which he served fourteen days detention) and, in 1917 alone, being 'absent without leave' on at least six occasions.

The punishments handed out to Private Leak varied, from forfeiting his pay on three occasions, to detention in military prison on three other occasions.

Finally, in 1917, after Leak was absent without leave from 1 November to 6 November, he was called in to face his commanding officer, who told him that he was sick of handing out punishment after punishment and was passing the problem on to a higher authority. Within days Private Leak went before a field general court martial and was charged with being a deserter.

In his defence Leak gave his side of the story, which was that he and a mate, having been gassed in action, had requested permission from the company commander to seek medical treatment. Not only was this request denied but also, according to Leak's testimony, the two men were accused of malingering. Leak went on to say that, as he feared that his mate's eyesight had been permanently impaired, they both went to find the medical help that they desperately needed.

He was found guilty and sentenced to 'Penal Servitude for Life'. Had John Leak served in the ranks of the land of his birth, the British Army, he would almost certainly have been shot by firing squad. As it was, he served less than a month of the life sentence. Within days of the verdict being handed down, the sentence was commuted to two years and, soon after that, it was suspended and Leak rejoined his battalion in the trenches.

It does appear that the court martial was, perhaps, an attempt to scare the 25-year-old soldier into mending his ways. The most likely explanation is that Leak's commanding officers were fed up with his behaviour and, when their patience ran out, decided to change what would probably have been another 'absent without leave' charge into something more serious. So the charge was upgraded to 'desertion', in order to teach him a lesson.

If that is the case, the plan failed. On 25 April 1918, Leak went absent without leave again, deserting from hospital without permission and turning up again four days later.

(This particular desertion occurred, coincidentally, on the third anniversary of Anzac Day. That day may have marked the low point in the military career of John Leak, but it also happens to be the day that Australian troops recaptured the French village of Villers-Bretonneux and stopped the advance of the German Army once and for all, an action that was, perhaps, the crowning glory of the AIF in World War I.)

This time the punishment handed out to Private Leak was the forfeiture of eleven days' pay, but it was like water off a duck's back to the bullock-driver from Rockhampton. In June 1918, less than two months later, and within days of returning from hospital where he had been recovering from being gassed at Hollebeke, he was in trouble again, serving seven days field punishment for 'insolence to an NCO'.

Home

In spite of his clashes with army authority, John Leak served until the end of the war and survived the conflict, having been wounded three times, gassed three times and disciplined for breaches of army regulations on more than a dozen occasions. On 9 February 1919 he embarked for Australia on a troopship and was officially discharged from the AIF in Queensland on 31 May.

John then picked up the threads of his life in Australia. He returned briefly to Rockhampton before spending two years on the southern Darling Downs, where he took up a soldier-settler's block near the small village of Berat, north of Warwick.

After two years there he abandoned the block he had been given and moved south to New South Wales where he applied, unsuccessfully, to be given another soldier-settler's block. He appears to have drifted from place to place and job to job for two years before moving briefly to South Australia and then on to Esperance in Western Australia where he worked as a mechanic and ran a garage.

On 12 January 1927, using the name William J.E. Leak, he married Ada Victoria Blood Smith. The couple reportedly lived in a tent and had either seven or eight children before moving to South Australia where John worked drilling for water in rural areas before retiring to Crafers in the Adelaide Hills, where he died, aged 80, in 1972.

Bigamy and Mystery

On 30 December 1918, less than six weeks before his departure from England by troopship, John Leak had married Beatrice May Chapman in the Parish Church of St John the Baptist, in Cardiff, Wales. The couple were never divorced and Beatrice May Chapman was still very much alive, and recorded on the census, when Leak married a second time.

An article in the *Cardiff Times* gave a report of the wedding, complete with background details about the happy couple, on 4 January 1919.

It appears that Beatrice, commonly known as 'May', was possibly the motivation, at least in part, for Private Leak's frequent absences without leave. He was certainly in a relationship with her as early as 1916, when she was nineteen years of age.

There is a photograph, taken on 30 December 1916 and reproduced in the *Cardiff Times* article, of him holding her hand, surrounded by her family, outside Buckingham Palace and, at some point during the war, he changed his next of kin on his official army record to 'Miss May Chapman of 62 Bridge Street, Cardiff'. When he enlisted, he had given his next of kin as his brother George of Saskatchewan in Canada.

One version of the story, gleaned from comments made by Leak in a previous article published in the *Cardiff Times*, suggests that he first met Beatrice May Chapman when her father was helping him to trace his family during a visit the young soldier made to Wales early in 1916. This article suggests that John Leak was born in Queensland, although his parents were both Welsh. The article quite specifically states that he believed his father was from Bryn Mawr and his mother was from Mountain Ash, both of which are in South Wales.

This information is, of course, in conflict with the information given by Leak on his enlistment, which states that he was born in Portsmouth and implies that his parents were English and migrated to Australia at some unknown time before the war. It is also in conflict with the information, given on his second marriage certificate, which states that he was born at Peak Hill, in Canada.

John 'William' Leak was, and still is, a 'man of mystery'.

He gave his age on enlistment in 1915, as 23. Twelve years later, on his second marriage certificate, his age was given as 28. Perhaps this seven-year discrepancy indicates that, like many other young men, he lied about his age in order to enlist, and was just sixteen at the time.

On the other hand, he may have lied about his age, as well as his first name, on the Western Australian marriage certificate in order to disguise the fact that the marriage was bigamous and therefore illegal.

Those who have investigated the life of John Leak as thoroughly as possible, using all the military and public records available, have been unable to find any record of him being born anywhere at any time.

There is no record of his birth in Wales, Canada, Australia or at Portsmouth, and the best estimate of his date of birth that can be gained from circumstantial evidence is 'sometime between 1892 and 1899'.

Tom McVeigh, former National Party member for the Darling Downs in federal parliament, and a member of the Malcolm Fraser ministry, spent many years researching the life of John Leak and co-wrote a book about him. McVeigh is of the opinion that Leak certainly lied when he claimed to be a 'teamster from Emerald' on the day he enlisted. Even at the age of 23, according to McVeigh, the young Englishman would not have had the experience to lead a team of bullocks.

It could be that the young man lied about his age and profession as well as the name of the town he came from, choosing Emerald simply because it was far enough away from Rockhampton for the information he gave to be not easily checked, yet not so far away as to arouse suspicion about why he was enlisting at Rockhampton.

Another possibility to consider is, of course, that he also lied about his name.

On his first marriage certificate he gave his father's name as James Leak, no mother's name was required. He was consistent on the second marriage certificate, again giving his father's name as James Leak and his mother's name as Sarah Wilson.

There is, however, no evidence yet found in census records or birth and marriage registrations of these two people being born or married or living in Britain; nor is there any evidence, in shipping or migration records, of them ever leaving Britain or arriving in Australia or Canada.

Tom McVeigh was born at Allora, close to Berat where John Leak lived for two years after the war. Tom spent his life farming in the district and had heard stories about John Leak from people of his parent's' generation, although he himself was not born until almost a decade after the World War I veteran had left the district.

Evidently, the returned soldier was made welcome in the district at first and invited to many Sunday dinners. He soon proved to be shiftless and untrustworthy, however, and, according to Tom McVeigh, 'after about two years he just shot through, owing money all around the town'.

Tom's research also seems to indicate that John Leak 'pulled a variety of lurks' in the various towns he lived in briefly in New South Wales, after he 'shot through' from Berat.

What Tom McVeigh found particularly frustrating in his search for the truth was the fact that John Leak gave different accounts of his birth and background in different interviews over the years. It appears that he and his second 'wife' had eight children and seven of those survived their father. Unfortunately, his children's stories about their father's origins were also 'inconsistent and unsupported'.

It is true, of course, that, if you are bigamist, you have every reason to lie about your past, but it is also not beyond the realms of possibility that the man we know as John Leak did not know where his parents came from. It seems significant to me that the first thing he did when he arrived in Britain in early 1916 was to go to Wales and enlist the help of William Chapman, his first wife's father, to trace his Welsh heritage.

It is also interesting that the article in the *Cardiff Times* specifically mentions the fact that he could not find anyone who knew his parents in either of the two towns in which he thought they had lived. Anyone who knows anything about towns in Wales will know how ludicrously impossible it is that anyone could live in those towns for any length of time and not be known and remembered.

There is at least some possibility that the man who called himself John Leak didn't actually know who he was.

A Place in History

In an interview the year before he died the enigmatic war veteran indicated that his only wish on returning to Australia in 1919 was to forget the war and have nothing to do with the army or the memory of the conflict in which he'd served.

He told a story about arriving by train in Rockhampton, seeing a flag-waving welcoming party waiting for him on the station platform, and immediately jumping on a southbound train to escape the fuss. He claimed that he never returned to Rockhampton.

He never joined the RSL and he never marched on Anzac Day. In fact, he went so far as to say, 'I don't believe in war.'

The more cynical among us might be tempted to point out that the man who didn't believe in war was still happy to accept a soldier-settler block of land in Queensland and apply for another in New South Wales.

Further evidence that he did not entirely turn his back on his military past is the fact that, in 1951, he wrote to the army seeking payment of certain entitlements that he had not bothered to claim in 1919. The army received the letter but took no action for, unfortunately, although it contained his service number and details of his service, it did not contain a return address. It was filed away as 'no address supplied' and the army made no attempt to track him down.

Although there does seem to be ample evidence that John Leak was an unreliable, self-serving and dishonest opportunist, the more sympathetic readers of this story may find some reasons, or at least alleviating circumstances, for his behaviour.

He did at least make an 'honest woman' of Beatrice May Chapman before leaving Britain and there is circumstantial evidence to suggest that there was an understanding that he would arrange passage to Australia for her. Perhaps there was insufficient time to do this between the date of their marriage and his embarkation home.

Whatever the reason, however, the Australian government did not fund her passage and it seems certain that her husband could not afford to at the time, or at any time in the decade after he left her behind. She stayed in Wales and lived with her parents until at least 1935, when she was recorded on the census under her maiden name. After that, there is no record of her at all and she's not mentioned in her father's funeral notice in 1955, although the rest of the family are.

The lies and confusion that John Leak perpetrated about his past may not all be related to the fact that he was a bigamist, or often 'moved on' when he owed money. There is at least some evidence that he himself did not know much about his origins and heritage.

Private John Leak had been through the horrors of war and been wounded three times and gassed three times. He certainly suffered from emphysema and continual bouts of bronchitis in later life and, like so many World War I veterans, probably also suffered from untreated 'post stress syndrome' or 'shellshock', as it was known then.

There is no doubt that Private John Leak had experienced the distress and horror of war at first-hand. Which brings us, finally, to the whole point of this story.

Perhaps the inquisitive reader has wondered by now why we are bothering to talk about this enigmatic lay-about at all. Some of you may be wondering why he seemed to get off so lightly so many times when he flouted army rules so blatantly. Others among you might even have wondered how he came to be photographed outside Buckingham Palace with his girlfriend's family, and why a newspaper like the *Cardiff Times* had taken so much interest in an Australian infantry private.

Well, for those of you who don't already know, I'll tell you.

For actions performed in the heat of battle at Pozières on 23 July 1916, a month before he was severely wounded at the Battle of Mouquet Farm, Private John Leak became the first Queenslander, and the only member of the 9th Battalion in World War I, to be awarded the Victoria Cross for bravery.

The full citation reads:

> He was one of a party which finally captured an enemy strong point. At one assault, when the enemy's bombs were outranging ours, Private Leak jumped out of the trench, ran forward under heavy machine-gun fire at close range, and threw three bombs into the enemy's bombing post. He then jumped into the post and bayoneted three unwounded enemy bombers.
>
> Later, when the enemy in overwhelming numbers was driving his party back, he was always the last to withdraw at each stage, and kept on throwing bombs. His courage and energy had such an effect on the enemy that, on the arrival of reinforcements, the whole trench was recaptured.

While many acts of selfless heroism in war have been performed by men who were model soldiers—obedient, disciplined, well-trained men who put duty and service before self-preservation—not all acts of bravery are performed by such men. Some are, as Tom McVeigh has noted, 'the actions of a loner, a courageous individual who has no great regard for life. When he'd see a challenge he'd just respond to it, not thinking about the implications of what that action might be.'

It is, perhaps, possible to reconcile some of the more unsavoury and less socially acceptable elements of John Leak's character with his amazing and admirable act of bravery that occurred that day on the Western Front, and in who knows how many other similar instances in other battles in which he fought.

15

JOHN GILLESPIE AND THE RING-IN GANG

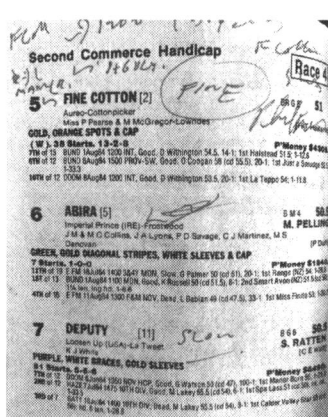

'It was the biggest farce of all time.'

The Cast

This is the story of a gang of five hilariously incompetent villains who resembled those Disney cartoon characters, the bumbling Beagle Boys, or, perhaps, the Three Stooges—plus two. The gang seemed to spend a lot of time discussing their lofty money-making ambitions while drinking beer in pubs or stubbies at various non-licensed locations. Then, on Saturday 18 August 1984, they perpetrated the most infamous horseracing scam in Australian history, known as the 'Fine Cotton Affair'. It was, as we now know, a complete shambles.

The five scoundrels were led by John Patrick Gillespie, who called himself a 'company director from the Gold Coast'. In fact, he was an inveterate petty criminal with many convictions for crimes, such as false pretences, stealing and armed robbery. While in Boggo Road Gaol, he had shared a cell with Pat Haitana, brother of a well-travelled jockey and trainer Hayden Haitana who was then residing at Coffs Harbour. They discussed a 'ring-in' plot and Pat suggested his brother as the trainer to carry out the scam.

Hayden Haitana was a likeable rogue and 'battling' racehorse trainer from New Zealand, who had trained in South Australia for more than a decade. Haitana moved from South Australia to Coffs Harbour and applied for a training licence with the local racing club. Although his licence had lapsed in South Australia, there was no objection to him being granted a licence to train at Coffs Harbour. According to an anonymous local racing identity, quoted in a *Coffs Coast Advocate* article by Greg White in 2009, Hayden was 'notorious for being a bullshit artist, particularly when he'd been drinking, which was pretty frequent'.

Then there was Robert North, a real estate agent and 'Brisbane socialite' who knew Gillespie and referred to him as 'a compulsive liar'. North later said they had discussed the ring-in idea many times and called himself 'the greatest fool' for getting involved and believing Gillespie, as he had 'never met a man who told lies' like him. North's home was used as the Brisbane headquarters for the gang.

Rounding out the gang of five was John Dixon, a video salesman and ex–Victorian police officer, and Tommaso 'Tom' DiLuzio, a Brisbane electronics engineer and small-time racehorse owner. Both Dixon and DiLuzio were involved in transporting the horses, as well as various other nefarious acts throughout the affair.

There was also a large supporting cast, including Mick Sayers, Sydney heroin dealer, gambler and 'SP' bookie, who helped finance the scam and was owed money by Gillespie and the gang.

Minor, but significant characters, played their roles, too: Pauline Pearse, a nurse and DiLuzio's live-in girlfriend, who nominally owned the starring racehorse in partnership with elderly Brisbane businessman Mr McGregor-Lowndes. A retired carnival operator who had made his money in fairground and sideshow attractions (including, according to some, the legendary 'dancing ducks' scam), McGregor-Lowndes had a conviction for selling sparrows painted yellow as canaries.

Wendy Smith and Bill Naoum were racehorse trainers caught up in the mess. Smith unknowingly harboured one of the horses involved, and Naoum innocently sold the gang the ring-in.

And of course there was the ring-in's rider, Gus Philpot, a naive young apprentice jockey, who was clueless about what was going on.

Lurking in the wings side-stage was a very dangerous, ruthless and clever character, Sydney master criminal George Freeman. A sworn enemy of the well-known Waterhouse family, Freeman may have used his knowledge of the ring-in to pull off the greatest 'double cross' scam in Australian gambling history, but was not implicated in the affair at the time and didn't suffer from any of the repercussions. For many years his name was rarely if ever mentioned with the ring-in, but one theory says he was almost certainly at the centre of the entire affair—like a spider in the middle of the web of intrigue which involved huge gambling debts and death threats.

The central characters in the story of Australia's best-known racing fraud were, however, none of these people—they were three completely innocent horses. Let's turn our attention to the equine 'fall guys'.

The horse who gave his name to the drama, Fine Cotton, was foaled in rural New South Wales on 29 November 1976, by the stallion Aureo from a mare called Cottonpicker whose sire was the Melbourne Cup winner Delta. He had won a dozen races at picnic meetings, and from 70 starts at registered meetings he had won just two races, at Wellington in the Central West of New South Wales.

Fine Cotton was a brown horse who had two white 'socks' on his back legs, just above his hooves, and a few white hairs on one side of his face and was branded with a 'K'. He was eight years old when he became Australia's most infamous racehorse.

The second horse, Dashing Soltaire, was a brown horse very similar to Fine Cotton, but he was faster and better-performed. He was part-owned by the famous British actor James Mason, Sydney racing identities Jack Ingham and J.B. Foyster, and the wife of another well-known owner and punter Don Storey. He had been trained in Sydney by noted trainer Vic Thompson Junior. As a two-year-old he had been one of the early favourites for the Golden Slipper after winning one of the lead-up races.

Dashing Soltaire was the intended ring-in and was bought by Gillespie in mid-1984 and sent to be trained at Coffs Harbour by Wendy Smith. Before his spell in Boggo Road Gaol, Gillespie, using the alias 'John Chandler', had met Smith, who was one of the first Australian female jockeys and a reputable trainer, and leased her a horse called Captain Cadet. Then Smith started getting strange phone calls from a man claiming he worked for a 'John Gillespie', telling her where and when to race the horse. As she had never heard of John Gillespie, she told the police and the calls stopped.

When he was released from Boggo Road, Gillespie again visited Wendy Smith, confessed his real name but told her he had been working 'undercover for the police'. Gillespie asked Smith to stable and train Dashing Soltaire and she looked after the horse until it was transferred to Haitana's training establishment on 4 August. Smith, who just loved horses and didn't drink or bet, later lost her trainer's licence, due to her incidental part in the saga.

The third horse was Bold Personality, foaled on 13 August 1977, by the American stallion Bold Aussie from a mare called Miss Personality. He had a white star on his forehead and no white markings on his legs. Being a classic 'bay' in colour, his lower legs were black. Bold Personality was a good class sprinter who had been trained by Tommy Smith and then sold to Bill Naoum, a successful milk vendor from Ballina on the New South Wales north coast, who had retired early and went into training horses. In August 1984 Naoum sold him to Gillespie.

Poor old Bold Personality suffered the greatest mistreatment and humiliation of the whole debacle at the hands of the incompetent ring-in gang. Dragged six hours north in a small horse float to a suburban backyard in Brisbane, with severe dehydration, then a nose bleed, undergoing a 'make over' with hair dye and house paint, then thrown into a race the next day.

The miracle is that he won the race—well, actually he didn't, though he was first past the post—just!

The Cunning Plan

In Boggo Road Gaol in 1983, John Gillespie chatted to Pat Haitana and a criminal named Bert Kidd, who was associated with Sydney gangster and SP bookie Mick Sayers, about a scheme for a ring-in. Pat suggested that his brother, Hayden, might be interested.

A former used-car salesman, Gillespie spent a lot of time in prison and had already been caught running 'ring-ins'. In 1982, at Doomben, he'd arranged for Apparent Heir to race impersonating Mannasong, which resulted in trainer Bill Steer being disqualified for life.

In early 1984, Gillespie, released from prison, met Pat and Hayden Haitana in Grafton, then continued on to Sydney and met up with Sayers in Bondi. Gillespie borrowed $8000 from Sayers and planned to buy two similar horses that would pass for one another at a glance. In July he paid $2000 for Fine Cotton, a poorly performed picnic galloper from Central New South Wales, and $10,000 for Dashing Soltaire, a Sydney sprinter who had performed well at a much higher level. Gillespie arranged for both horses to be transported to Coffs Harbour, where Fine Cotton went to Hayden Haitana's stable and Dashing Soltaire to Wendy Smith.

Haitana then proceeded to over-train and race Fine Cotton, mostly in southern Queensland. Although Haitana drank a lot and talked a lot, it seemed there was no notion around the Coffs Harbour racing fraternity that anything surreptitious was afoot when he arrived in the town and started training a horse that ran very poorly north of the border.

Asked why no one in the district had prior knowledge of the scam, one local racing identity who appeared as a witness in the resulting court case told the *Coffs Harbour Advocate*, anonymously, that Haitana was such a 'bullshit artist' that he 'could have sat around the bar and described the plan down to the tiniest detail and not a single person would have believed a word'.

Gang member Tom DiLuzio, a small-time racehorse owner, found two relatively disinterested parties to nominally own Fine Cotton. One of them was his live-in girlfriend, Pauline Pearse, and the other was businessman Mr McGregor-Lowndes. Haitana sold them Fine Cotton on 30 July for $1200; neither had seen the horse (and never would).

Fine Cotton ran at Bundamba on 1 August and again on 4 August, after being galloped hard on the morning of each race day to ensure he would not run well later in the day. He was then raced again at Doomben on 8 August and transferred to John Thompson's racing stables on the Gold Coast. Thompson's wife, Marie, later said the horse was not trained at all in the days leading up to his next race, and looked 'in poor condition and dehydrated'.

All went well for the gang and the ringing-in was planned for the Wednesday meeting at Eagle Farm on 15 August. Mick Sayers, who had bankrolled the venture, was arranging the money to finance the betting plunge with some of his Sydney underworld connections.

Ten days before the plan was to be activated, however, disaster struck. Dashing Soltaire had been transferred from Wendy Smith's care on 4 August to Haitana's stable. On 5 August the horse ran his hindquarters into the barbed wire fencing, injured himself severely and required stitches. He would be unable to race.

When Gillespie heard the news the next day, he rang an employee of Sayers and said the ring-in would have to be postponed.

What the gang didn't seem to realise was that they were only the pawns in the game. The ring-in was the lynch-pin of a well-planned betting plunge orchestrated to make huge amounts of money for some very dangerous people. Sayers' man told Gillespie that he was in serious trouble.

It is quite likely that, during their phone conversation, Gillespie was reminded about the gruesome fate of Sydney trainer George Brown. On 31 March that year, Brown took his poorly performed filly Risley to Brisbane. It is believed that Risley was to either be part of a 'form reversal' plunge or a ring-in at Doomben Racecourse. Backed heavily, from 14/1 to 4/1, Risley ran poorly and Brown returned home very agitated and worried and told his girlfriend, Pat Goodwin, that 'it had gone wrong'. On 2 April Brown's body, with his arms, legs and skull broken, was found in his burnt-out car at the top of Bulli Pass.

Gillespie returned ashen-faced to his fellow gang members, who were drinking that day at his Gold Coast home, and informed them that they had to find another horse within days and go ahead with the ring-in, or 'someone is going to die'.

Gillespie owed Sayers $8000, and Sayers was a dangerous man to owe money to. Further up the pecking order, however, Sayers was also in trouble. He owed George Freeman a 'substantial' amount of money. One theory about the ring-in having to go ahead when it did is that Sayers had told Freeman about it in order to save his skin and ingratiate himself with Freeman to buy time to repay the debt. We'll get to that later.

Whether Gillespie thought *he* was going to die or Mick Sayers was going to die, I don't know—maybe both. Gillespie certainly claimed he was marked down to die after the race.

With no option to abort the ring-in, the gang needed another horse. They hurriedly began looking for any horses for sale that might, just might, pass for Fine Cotton at a pinch. There were very few to choose from but there was a horse roughly the same age and height which was for sale at Ballina, near Lismore on the New South Wales north coast.

This horse was Bold Personality, owned and trained by Bill Naoum. Bold Personality's colour was bay, not brown, and he had different markings from Fine Cotton, but he would have to do.

Gillespie knew this horse and had tried to buy him previously. But Bill Naoum valued him at $20,000 and neither Gillespie nor the gang had that sort of money. The gang had long since exhausted their borrowed budget.

Undeterred by such trivial matters, Gillespie wrote out a dud cheque and Tom DiLuzio, who knew nothing about horses except that he'd part-owned a few, set off in his Toyota Corolla pulling a borrowed horse float. The transaction was completed and the horse suffered a six-hour trip in a closed-in trailer, wearing a thick rug, and arrived at Robert North's suburban home at Wellers Hill in Brisbane severely dehydrated.

Hayden Haitana then rather clumsily 'flushed' the horse—a process normally performed by a vet—in order for it to be rehydrated. This involved Haitana shoving several metres of garden hose up the horse's nose and into his stomach, which was then filled with water. As the hose was inexpertly extracted, a blood vessel in his nose ruptured. Any horse known to have bled is automatically disqualified from racing for three months, so they couldn't call a vet. Instead, they tied the horse's head to the stable rafters to stop the bleeding.

The next day, the gang had to deal with another, very obvious problem. They had to make Bold Personality, a bay with black legs, look like Fine Cotton, who was brown with white socks. So, apparently without consulting Hayden Haitana, John Gillespie did a tour of the district's chemist shops and bought up as many packets of Clairol henna hair dye as he could find.

Years later Haitana recalled:

They thought that if they got enough hair colouring to fill up a couple of buckets, you could cover the horse with it to make it look like Fine

Cotton. But, as it turns out, it doesn't take to horse's hair; there must be a chemical disbalance [sic] there . . . The horse came out red like a Hereford bull. I couldn't believe it.

At that point Haitana had had enough. He just wanted out of the whole thing, so he drove back to Coffs Harbour. Haitana later claimed, in a secret *60 Minutes* interview, that he went into hiding because 'a man with a gun' said to him, when he wanted 'out' of the whole thing, 'Do you want to end up like trainer Brown?' We'll never know if Haitana returned of his own accord or if he was 'brought back' at gun point, but he was again at Robert North's house early the next day.

On the morning of the race the whole gang assembled at North's home and decided to wash the horse to remove the dye as best they could. But they also realised they had yet another problem—Bold Personality wasn't wearing racing shoes. They hurriedly called a farrier, who arrived without realising he was to shoe a racehorse as the gang had neglected to tell him. The farrier only had trotting shoes, so these were fitted onto the horse.

Haitana remembered:

I was in the shower and you would hear the horse out in the backyard being very agitated jumping around. I looked out the window and here's these guys trying to paint its legs and the farrier trying to shoe it.

I said to them, 'Why are you doing this? You don't change the horse's colouring, you change the papers to fit the horse.'

Of course I shouldn't have done that because the papers disappeared immediately.

Years later Robert North, who claims he regretted getting involved in the scam almost as soon as he had agreed to it, told *Nine News* that he hoped they would abort the idea and cut and run on the day of the ring-in. He said that Gillespie 'was running around the back yard like a blue-arsed fly trying to spray the horse's hooves. It was unbelievable.'

In their attempt to replicate Fine Cotton's white socks on Bold Personality's black legs, the gang used Taubman's high-gloss white paint. Haitana also bandaged the horse's back legs so the paint would not show, but the paint would not dry on the wet horse and was running off slowly for the rest of the day.

The gang then decided to take both horses to the races. This move was based on the ridiculous notion that they might be able to swap them after the race had been run and won. Dixon brought Fine Cotton to the house in a horse float. So Fine Cotton went along for the ride and spent the day in the horse float in the car park at Eagle Farm.

In 2019, Robert North told *Nine News*, 'I just hoped that they'd keep driving anywhere but the racetrack, even if it was Timbuktu.'

But they didn't, of course, they drove to the track.

A Day at the Races

It was a nervous time for the racing game's most incompetent gang at Eagle Farm. The first scare of the day came when Hayden Haitana, who had been 'taken' to the races by Dixon, was called over the public address system to report to the steward's room. A terrified Haitana was relieved when he was fined $2 for the late announcement of the jockey.

The jockey was young Gus Philpot, a promising apprentice who was hoping to win race five, the Apprentices' Cup (which he did, on Goleen, at 4/1, after the fiasco of race four had unfolded). Philpot was apprenticed to trainer Bill Wehlow, the man who had trained the great Gunsynd, before the horse was sent to Tommy Smith in Sydney.

Wehlow's daughter had taken a booking over the phone late the previous day for Gus to ride Fine Cotton in race four.

The second problem to be dealt with was that, just before the race, they bumped into Bill Naoum, the man from whom they had purchased, with a worthless cheque, the horse that was about to run in the next race disguised as another horse! Naoum doesn't appear to have been suspicious that anything untoward was happening, perhaps he had not presented that dud cheque as yet, or the bank had not yet bounced it back.

One version of the story says that Gillespie took Naoum to the grandstand bar and kept talking to him while race four was run and won by a horse Naoum still technically and legally owned. Gillespie supposedly kept his head between the television screen and Naoum's line of vision and talked non-stop while the race was run.

Other versions of the day's activities have Gillespie watching the race with members of the Queensland police force.

While Gillespie was either ordering beers or chatting to police officers, Haitana was nervously legging Gus Philpot into the saddle on the back of a horse that was sweating rather odd-coloured perspiration, while white high-gloss paint ran out from under the bandages on his legs.

Years later Philpot recalled that he thought Haitana was nervous that day as he legged him up, but put it down to the fact that he was just a small-time country trainer unused to the 'big time' of Eagle Farm.

There was a huge pre-post betting plunge on 'Fine Cotton' that took his price from 33/1 to 7/2. This was not in the gang's plans at all, no one was supposed to know about the scam, but it seemed to them that all of Australia did. There were more people on course than usual that day and they all wanted to back horse number 5 in race four, although the form guide read: 'Hard to recommend after 8len 10th La Teppo Dbn Inter 1200m Aug 8. Earlier form not encouraging.' (Which meant that he had run tenth, 8 lengths behind the winner, in a restricted 'intermediate' handicap ten days earlier; and was a 'donkey' in racing parlance.)

Gus Philpot was unaware of the fuss in the betting ring. He simply got on board a horse he thought was the poorly performed 'hopeless case' called Fine Cotton. Not long after he also thought he'd won the race.

The beleaguered Bold Personality, pathetically disguised as Fine Cotton and skilfully ridden by Philpot, battled head to head with Harbour Gold, the horse who would otherwise have been a short-priced favourite for the race. Rather miraculously, Philpot's mount won by a short head.

No sooner had he done so than a large section of the crowd began booing and hooting, led by a man (or possibly 'a few men') near the winning post, yelling, 'Ring-in!' The stewards were startled into action and within 30 minutes Harbour Gold was declared the winner and 'Fine Cotton' was disqualified—although he was not declared a non-starter, which meant that no one who had backed him was entitled to a refund and the bookies kept the lot.

In his *Sun-Herald* column the next day, racing journalist Max Presnell commented that it hardly seemed fair that 'innocent' punters who had simply 'followed the money' in the betting avalanche had lost the lot. He said that the 'general feeling . . . was that Fine Cotton should have been declared a non-runner'.

In an interview with Patrick Bartley for the *Sydney Morning Herald* in 2014, Gus Philpot said he was so naive at the time that he didn't even know the horse's odds. He recalled that, when the crowd started booing and yelling, 'I thought they were booing me because my ride was a roughie and I must've beaten the favourite.'

Luckily for Philpot the stewards were either not very good at their job or genuinely realised how naive young Gus was. He said himself, in the *Sydney Morning Herald* interview:

> It was refreshing actually now I think back, the stewards immediately exonerated me and I was still a bit dazed when I got back to the jockeys' room and some of the older blokes were pointing out the window, saying you've just ridden a ring-in.
>
> And I pulled one of them aside and said, 'What's a ring-in?'

Philpot said his association, albeit innocent, with the scandal made him unpopular with trainers and cost him a successful career in Brisbane. His ambition to be a top rider in Brisbane was never likely to be realised after the 'Fine Cotton Affair'. He eventually became a trainer in Victoria.

Gus Philpot's life certainly wouldn't be the only one to be adversely affected by the failed scam.

Underneath the headline 'Police Guard Plunge Horse', the *Sun-Herald* next day published a photo captioned 'Jockey Gus Philpot brings Fine Cotton back to scale'. The photo quite clearly shows Bold Personality, complete with a small white star on his forehead (which Fine Cotton didn't have), being led back by the clerk of the course to weigh-in.

According to the *Sun-Herald:*

> Officials became suspicious of Fine Cotton's identity when he showed a glaring form improvement to win.

He had finished 10th in a field of 12 at the Brisbane Doomben track at his previous start.

Soon after the race stewards had asked trainer Haitana to produce Fine Cotton's registration papers.

He was escorted to the horse's stall but a search of the gear failed to produce the papers.

Haitana then told stewards he was certain he had brought the papers to the track but someone must have removed them from his race day gear bag.

The papers, of course, had never been in the bag. Haitana, as he revealed years later, had actually precipitated the 'disappearance' of the registration papers when he chastised the gang members for trying to alter the horse instead of the papers.

If the stewards had been doing their job more diligently that day, they might have noticed a horse parading before the race with the wrong brand, the wrong colouring and the wrong markings. The betting ring was going crazy as the horse's price tumbled from 33/1 to 7/2 and he had been backed all day all over Australia.

It would not have been hard to notice that the horse was Bold Personality, as he was actually in the race book—as a starter in race six. He had been entered for the Open Flying Handicap and scratched quite late. His name still appeared as a starter in the morning newspapers. That probably explains why Bill Naoum was at the races that day.

Commenting years later on the quality of the Queensland Turf Club (QTC) stewards' 'due diligence' on that day, Gus Philpot said: 'I reckon you could have put a rhinoceros in the race and no one would have noticed.'

Not long after the failed search for the papers, a public address announcement was broadcast, asking trainer Hayden Haitana to visit the stewards' room for the second time that day. The announcement, like the search of Haitana's gear bag, failed to produce what was being sought—it failed to produce Hayden Haitana!

The whole fiasco had become too much for Hayden's nervous system. As soon as he was out of sight of the stewards, Haitana headed to the bar and had a beer to settle his nerves. He realised that, for once in his life, it was no good just getting drunk and letting things run their course but he hid in a corner of the bar until correct weight was declared. He then collected a payout on a betting ticket and high-tailed it to the car park, jumped into his car with his old friend Fine Cotton in the horse float, and drove off into the sunset.

I mean this quite literally, for, having made a slight detour to leave Fine Cotton happily munching grass with a bunch of other horses in a paddock he had often noticed, not far from the Eagle Farm Racecourse, Haitana headed west, towards the sunset and the state of South Australia.

Also called to the stewards' room were Fine Cotton's registered owners, one of whom, 75-year-old retired businessman Mr McGregor-Lowndes, duly appeared and told the stewards he was as surprised as they were at the horse's form reversal and 'didn't think he could win' and 'didn't have a penny on him'.

Repercussions

At the QTC enquiry ten days later, Mr McGregor-Lowndes said that Hayden Haitana talked him into buying the horse. He also said that he believed he was the sole owner of Fine Cotton until he met Pauline Pearse on the day of the race, and that he had never seen the horse or Miss Pearse until that day (of course, he never actually saw the horse that day, either—he saw Bold Personality!).

There were three gang members missing from the QTC enquiry on that Monday, although all three had been 'required to attend'. According to his girlfriend Pearse, Tom DiLuzio did not attend because of a 'family commitment'. So the hearing was adjourned.

DiLuzio did attend on the following Friday and read a prepared statement in which he said he could only answer questions about a horse he did own, Zardulu. According to him, he didn't own Fine Cotton and refused to answer questions about the affair. He asked for proof of the QTC's legal right to question him and would not answer questions without legal advice.

Unfortunately for Tom, Pauline Pearse had given evidence on the Monday that she had never signed anything to acknowledge she owned Fine Cotton and she had identified Tom's signature on three entry forms for the horse in various races. She said Tom had been paying all the horse's expenses and she had 'little knowledge of racing' and had 'not really known what was going on'.

At the end of the QTC enquiry, all five members of the gang were banned for life from racecourses and the racing industry. They were then all charged by the police with the criminal offence of 'conspiracy to defraud'. Haitana, Gillespie and Dixon were also charged with falsely pretending that Bold Personality was Fine Cotton in order to defraud the QTC. Warrants were issued and Dixon, DiLuzio and North were arrested.

Meanwhile, Hayden Haitana and John Gillespie were on the run and couldn't be found by the police. However, much to the embarrassment of the police, Haitana gave a secret interview to *60 Minutes* while in hiding. In the interview he precipitated a string of far-reaching events by mentioning bookmaker 'Bob' Waterhouse as a 'possible' connection to the scam.

At his trial in December 1984, Robbie Waterhouse commented that it was odd that Haitana, in the *60 Minutes* interview (for which Waterhouse claimed Haitana was paid $20,000), referred to 'Bob' Waterhouse as a bookmaker he suspected was involved. Robbie pointed out that he had never been known as 'Bob'.

Haitana was finally arrested by South Australian police while he was having a beer in the pub at Truro, just east of the Barossa Valley, on 21 February 1985. He'd been previously spotted wearing dark glasses shopping in Woolworths at Renmark, in the Riverland district of South Australia.

After being interviewed Haitana refused to sign any statements and said: 'It's got nothing to do with you. It all happened in Queensland and there are plenty of heavies in this. I only want to talk to the Queensland police.'

The trial lasted six weeks and concluded on 13 November 1985.

Surprisingly the judge, Mr Justice Loewenthal, discharged Dixon as not having a case to answer. He accepted that Gillespie, who had skipped bail and was still on the run, had conceived the idea and was 'instrumental in organising and arranging substantial betting on the race in question'. Tom DiLuzio was found not guilty. Haitana and North were found guilty and sentenced to twelve months hard labour.

Two weeks later the *Sydney Morning Herald* announced:

The alleged mastermind of Queensland's Fine Cotton ring-in conspiracy, John Patrick Gillespie, 45, formally of Benowa on the Gold
Coast, was flown out of Melbourne yesterday under police custody . . .
    Gillespie was arrested by detectives on Tuesday during a dawn raid
on a house in the Victorian town of Cobram.
    Police alleged Gillespie had been found hiding in a cupboard in his
sister's home.

Gillespie was found guilty and given four years in prison. He served
most of his sentence and was soon in trouble again.

Haitana served six months, returned to South Australia and
somehow eked out a living outside of racing for 25 years. In an interview in 2010 with Simon White of the Adelaide *Advertiser*, he said he
kept a few cows and chickens, grew his own vegetables, fixed bicycles
for backpackers, bought and sold old cars, and sneaked into racecourses when he could. He spent his spare time with his grandkids,
helping men in prison and looking after those just out of gaol—making
sure they met parole requirements while looking after their money for
them so they didn't gamble it or have to steal. He was finally allowed
back on racetracks in 2013, almost 30 years after the event and fifteen
years after most of the others involved. He died, aged 72, in 2017.

At the time of the Fine Cotton fiasco, Gillespie had already been
labelled, quite rightly, 'The King of Cons' by *Sydney Morning Herald*
journalist Roger Crofts. Ten years before Fine Cotton he had defrauded
flood victims of the 1974 Queensland floods by scamming the official
relief scheme. Then, in 1977, he held up a TAB with a plastic pistol.
Just before the ring-in in 1984, he had bought $100,000 worth of opals
from eight different dealers in Lightning Ridge just as the banks closed
one Friday. Three dealers compared the cheques and discovered they
all had the same serial numbers. Gillespie served two years for the
fraud, concurrent with his sentence for the ring-in.

Before 1990, when he turned 50, Gillespie had accumulated more
than 350 convictions, and he has been adding to the total ever since.

In 1992, he became a founding director of the International
Millionaires' Club and the International Horse Owners' Club, both

incorporated in the British Virgin Islands and struck off in 1995. He was involved in a scheme in 1996 buying horses from a stud in Shropshire in England to be imported into Thailand. All that eventuated was that the stud's owner, Peter Hume, ended up with £50,000 less in his bank account.

In November 1998 three 'officials' from the imaginary nation of 'Melchizedek' were charged in the Philippines for selling 'internationally recognised Melchizedek passports' to hundreds of local Filipinos, Chinese and Bangladeshis for US$3500 each. Others paid large amounts of money to be guaranteed 'government work' on a Pacific territory of the 'Dominion of Melchizedek'.

Two of the men were arrested: an Australian named Dennis Oakley, who was Melchizedek's 'minister of the navy and the coast guard', and a Malaysian national, Chew Chin Yee, whose business card identified him as Melchizedek's 'honorary consul in Hong Kong' and 'minister of public works and gaming'. According to Philippine police, the ringleader, a brother-in-law of Chew Chin Yee, had managed to get away. No prizes for guessing—yes, it was John Gillespie.

In 2008 Gillespie 'ripped off' ex–rugby league player Greg Mullane, who he managed to con into being the front man for a property scam that left a Forbes farmer $150,000 poorer over a non-existent $10 million feed lot development to be financed by a non-existent multi-million-dollar collection of famous artworks, which was also used to attract investors into a $250,000 anti-wrinkle cream marketing scheme and another similar scheme for 'anti-arthritis' cream for horses. All the projects—surprise, surprise—left investors broke.

As late as 2016 Gillespie was involved in the offshore tax scam known as 'The Panama Papers Affair'.

John North, who says his family have never been able to shake off the shady reputation gained by him having been involved in the ring-in, explained the key to the whole sad farce to *Nine News* in 2019, when he commented ruefully, 'I think Gillespie owed a lot of favours to people.'

Gillespie certainly owed something to Mick Sayers, who had bank-rolled the entire ring-in scheme. More importantly, Sayers owed money to George Freeman.

Freeman, who described himself as 'a professional punter and commission agent', was called a 'crime boss' in the Woodward Royal Commission into Drug Trafficking (1977–79) and was named under parliamentary privilege as a leading figure in organised crime. He had also been detained in the US as an 'excluded person' and banned from entering Britain. He was reputed to have killed at least two men, and had several others killed. He ruined harness racing in Sydney by fixing almost every race and he ran the city's SP betting, illegal casinos and prostitution rackets. He lived in a heavily guarded mansion at Yowie Bay, south of Sydney.

Freeman's rather blatant involvement in a race-fixing scandal, involving a horse called Mr Digby, had shocked a lot of decent racing people. Mr Digby started in a 1600-metre race at Randwick on Bank Holiday, Monday 3 August 1981, and finished ninth. Two days later he stormed home, winning by 7 lengths over 1900 metres in a higher-class race at Canterbury. Mr Digby had never run a place before in his life. What scared racegoers was the fact that he was backed in to 11/8 favouritism to win more than $400,000 in the betting ring.

The reluctance of the Sydney Turf Club (STC) and Australian Jockey Club (AJC) to take action also gave many grave fears about the industry's future credibility. When investigations came up with evidence that George Freeman was involved, many racing club members were worried that thoroughbred racing was descending to the inglorious shonky level of trotting races, which were believed by many to be so crooked that they were commonly known as 'the red hots'.

Bookmakers and punters complained but the AJC decided not to open an enquiry. When Freeman, divorced and 46 years old, married a 24-year-old model, Georgina McLaughlin, on 6 August 1981, Freeman openly boasted that the money he'd won on Mr Digby was paying for the reception at the Hilton Hotel. Mr Digby's trainer, Harry Clark, was a guest at the wedding, as was Sydney solicitor, racehorse owner, big-time punter and STC board member Don Storey.

When the AJC finally did open an enquiry into the 'Mr Digby Affair' on 12 August, crusading MP John Hatton asked if it was true that Don Storey had backed Mr Digby and two other horses (one of them hilariously named Wilpado) to win $1.3 million.

Storey said he had backed Mr Digby every time it ran, as the horse had shown some ability. He added that he saw no harm in attending Freeman's wedding and mentioned that at least one member of the AJC board also attended. The STC passed a vote of confidence on Don Storey's integrity as a board member.

The AJC stewards' report concluded that they were unable to discover any evidence of cheating and stated that the betting had been 'normal'. They were concerned, however, that Peter Black, Mr Digby's registered owner, was not actually paying the training fees.

The horse's ownership was immediately transferred to the wife of the horse's trainer, Harry Clark.

Time form analyst Don Scott challenged the AJC's conclusions after studying the horse's improved sectional times from 3 August to 5 August and pointed out that it was not 'normal' for a midweek race to take half a million dollars out of the betting ring.

Then the AJC opened another enquiry, found Harry Clark and jockey Keith Banks guilty of 'not allowing a horse to run on its merits' and disqualified both for a year, which ruined their careers. Whoever planned the scheme, however, remained unpunished.

So with George Freeman now involved in the seedy side of racing, Mick Sayers enters the story with his 'ring-in' proposal. Mick Sayers owed Freeman a 'substantial' amount of money, often said to be more than $500,000 and at other times as low as $8000, which was still 'substantial' to most people in 1984.

The Theories

There are conflicting theories as to why Mick Sayers planned and funded the Fine Cotton Affair. The most plausible is that the scheme was an attempt to clear his debt and Sayers told Freeman about it to reassure him that he was attempting to get the money to pay him.

Another, rather more complex theory is that the ring-in was an attempt to get revenge on Freeman for the fact that the money Sayers owed him had been won when Freeman 'fixed' a race and placed a huge bet with Sayers, knowing he couldn't lose. Sayers then planned to *pretend* to fix a race, get Freeman involved financially and then back the most likely genuine winning chance and let the scheme backfire on Freeman.

Whatever his motives were, Sayers, having told Freeman about it, either in order to save his skin and buy time to repay the debt or set Freeman up as the fall guy, had to ensure the ring-in went ahead without delay.

Armed with the knowledge of the scam, Freeman apparently made plans of his own and, when Sayers called him to say it was postponed, he saw a chance to make even better plans.

The 'George Freeman pulling the strings' theory, developed by some who have studied the events closely, is that Freeman forced the ring-in to go ahead by threatening to kill Sayers if it didn't. He then spread the word about it and cunningly tricked Robbie Waterhouse into believing it and betting on it. According to this theory, Freeman then backed Harbour Gold, whose price had drifted out to 6/1, knowing the pathetic ring-in attempt would fail, and made sure that it was exposed. It is claimed that the man (or men), yelling 'Ring-in!' at the track that day, was sent there by Freeman.

George Freeman was far more powerful, intelligent and ruthless than Sayers, and way more intelligent than Gillespie and the rest of the 'Ring-in Gang'. Knowing that the plan was bound to fail one way or another, it's just the kind of thing Freeman would have thought up. There was long-held enmity between the Waterhouses and Freeman and the crime boss could have seen this as a chance to not only make money but to 'get the Waterhouses'.

In his memoirs Bill Waterhouse admitted that he once bought a gun because he feared Freeman would have attempts made on his life. He always claimed George Freeman set Robbie up over the Fine Cotton Affair and the implication is that Freeman had enough influence within the AJC to make sure the Waterhouses 'took the fall'.

All that was ever proven against Robbie Waterhouse was 'prior knowledge' of a rort at Eagle Farm, yet he was banned from racetracks for life and served a prison sentence for lying to the Racing Appeals Tribunal, apparently to protect those for whom he had arranged the bet.

Bill Waterhouse's only 'alleged' crime was the accusation, never substantiated, that he put a false bet in his book so it appeared he had at least taken some money on Fine Cotton.

No one had ever heard of the racing 'crime' 'prior knowledge' before, and the concept had certainly never been used to ban people

for life. The AJC was justifiably annoyed that the industry's reputation had been dragged through the mud by the incompetence of
the Queensland management of racing, and a scapegoat was needed.
Robbie was implicated by gossip of being involved in a few suspect
racing results and it was time to clean up the image of the sport
of kings.

Up in sunny Queensland, racing minister Russ Hinze blamed
unsavoury elements 'from down south' and the QTC were rather
miffed when the AJC set up a separate enquiry.

One thing that doesn't quite 'gel' with the theory that Freeman
pulled off a cunning double-cross and backed Harbour Gold is the
fact that the horse's price drifted out but never firmed back in. If
Freeman did win the reputed $1.5 million on the horse, it certainly
wasn't on the TAB or an Australian racetrack where the amount of
money needed to be invested to win that much (around $300,000)
would have affected the betting to at least some degree (actually a
large degree) and shortened the odds. It was Fine Cotton (alias Bold
Personality) whose odds shortened hugely, not Harbour Gold's. So
there is a flaw in that theory.

Another, less popular, theory is that George Freeman did back the
ring-in horse, not Harbour Gold, then blamed Robbie Waterhouse
for the failed scam and dumped on him.

On the other hand, John Gillespie, after his release from prison for
his part in the ring-in, claimed that the double-cross scam was exactly
what *he and Sayers* had done—*not* Freeman.

In 2010 Gillespie claimed the whole scheme was designed by
Sayers as payback on Freeman, who had previously placed a huge bet
with Sayers then paid off every jockey in a race to get the winning
result. Sayers then planned the entire Fine Cotton Affair to scam the
money back by getting Freeman to 'fall in' to Fine Cotton, while *they*
backed Harbour Gold.

One suspects that perhaps Gillespie knew Freeman did something
of the sort to him and Sayers, and decided to claim it was the other
way around to save face.

'I don't mind if people think it was a joke, or whatever,' Gillespie
told Queensland's *Sunday Mail* reporter Adam Shand in May 2010,
'because I walked away with $1.8 million.'

Naturally, no one believed Gillespie for a minute. AJC Chief Steward John Schreck said, 'Dick Francis could not think up something like that . . . With great respect to Mr Gillespie, anything he says you would have to take with a great big pinch of salt.'

Gillespie also claimed he was marked down to die after the race. In the 2010 *Sunday Mail* interview, he gave his version of a phone call to Robert North's home after the race:

> Bob handed the telephone to me and Freeman said to me: 'We know what you have done and I am sending two men to Brisbane to fix you up.' I replied that they had better be your best blokes otherwise they wouldn't be coming back. Then I hung up on Freeman . . .
>
> I looked around and Bob, who had the heart of a split pea, had fainted and fallen to the ground.

Gillespie went on to claim that he deposited his $1.8 million in an offshore account and Sayers had hidden up to $12 million in winnings in a Swiss bank account.

He also claimed, in the same interview, that he fled to the US in 1985 after famed 'big man' of Queensland politics and minister for racing in the Bjelke-Petersen government, Russ Hinze, told him the police had information that Gillespie would be killed if he attended court on the fraud charges. The 'hitman', according to Gillespie, was to be Chris Flannery, who had murdered other people for Freeman.

Given that it was impossible for Russ Hinze, who passed away in 1991, or Mick Sayers, who was gunned down and killed in the driveway of his Bronte home in February 1985, to corroborate the story in 2010, and given that taking $14 million dollars out of a betting pool in Australia in 1984 without affecting a horse's odds is a bit hard to imagine, and given that John Gillespie has more than 300 convictions for lying about things—one is tempted to agree with John Schreck's assessment of Gillespie. Maybe a ton of salt might be required though, rather than a big pinch.

Gillespie also claimed Mick Sayers was murdered for his role in the Fine Cotton Affair, while it is generally accepted that Sayers was killed for stealing heroin from big-time drug dealer Barry McCann. Sayers collected the heroin, went to get the cash, then came back dishevelled and claimed he'd been robbed. McCann gave him a few days to pay up and then Sayers was gunned down in front of his girlfriend in the driveway of his home. McCann himself was murdered in 1989.

In all the theories about the Fine Cotton Affair, there are always one or two annoying pieces of information that make you wonder.

One fact that makes you pause for a moment before you dismiss the double-cross theories is that Hayden Haitana, having accompanied the stewards to the horse's stall after the race and told them the registration papers were missing, didn't leave the racecourse at once. He claimed later that he went to have a beer after the race and waited until Harbour Gold was declared the winner before leaving the course.

This puzzled me until I realised that he also claimed later that he had $50 on Harbour Gold to win, and picked up the money before he scarpered. So maybe Hayden Haitana wasn't as silly as everyone made him out to be. Either he thought their ring-in couldn't win, or he figured that the scam would be exposed and Harbour Gold was the only other horse good enough to win.

Who knows?

One thing that is certain is that Gillespie's bumbling Gang of Five were totally out of their depth and had no idea what kind of people Sayers and Freeman were. They were lucky to escape with their lives.

Fine Cotton was finally located grazing peacefully where Haitana had left him. It was, in fact, a spelling paddock used by the Queensland Mounted Police. Television producer John Stainton, who created the Steve Irwin television series, bought him. Stainton bought the rights to the story and planned to use the horse to make a documentary mini-series about the affair but eventually gave up because 'it was a legal minefield'.

Fine Cotton was ridden recreationally until he was twenty and then retired to a paddock where he died in 2009, aged 32.

SOURCES

Research for these stories has been undertaken through:

Trove, National Library of Australia, newspaper records
Australian National Archives
NSW State Archives (police and court records)
Convict Records, Shipping Lists, British Court Archives
Ancestry.com.au
Australian Military Archives and Australian War Memorial
Smithsonian Institution Archives, USA
The *Bulletin* archive, National Library of Australia
Australian Dictionary of Biography, Australian National University, Canberra

Earlier versions of several of these stories have appeared in other collections by the author.

Select Bibliography

Amos, Keith, *The Fenians and Australia c.1865–1880*, (A thesis submitted for the degree of Doctor of Philosophy of the University of New England, Armidale, 1985) published 1987, Rune, UNE

Annear, Robyn, *The Man Who Lost Himself*, Text Publishing, Melbourne, 2002

Bateson, Charles, *The Convict Ships*, Brown, Son & Ferguson, Glasgow, 1969

Brownrigg, Jeff, *Anzac Cove to Hollywood*, Anchor Books, Sydney, 2010

Carlyon, Les, *Gallipoli*, Pan McMillan, Sydney, 2001

Clarke, Marcus, *Old Tales of a Young Country*, Mason, Firth and McCutcheon, Melbourne, 1871

Cobley, John (ed.), *Sydney Cove 1788, Vol 1*, Angus and Robertson, Sydney, 1963
— *Sydney Cove 1789–1790, Vol 2*, Angus and Robertson, Sydney, 1963
— *Sydney Cove 1791–1792, Vol 3*, Angus and Robertson, Sydney, 1963
— *Sydney Cove 1793–1795, Vol 4*, Angus and Robertson, Sydney, 1963
— *Sydney Cove 1795–1800, Vol 5*, Angus and Robertson, Sydney, 1963

Collins, David, *An Account of the English Colony in New South Wales,* Cadell & Davies, London, 1798

Coulthard-Clark, Chris, *The Encyclopedia of Australia's Battles,* Allen & Unwin, Sydney, 1998, 2001, 2010

Dorries, Ben, *Inside Story,* (Lester Grimmet's Retirement), Racenet website, 2020

Haynes, Jim (ed.), *Cobbers: Stories of Gallipoli 1915,* ABC Books, Sydney, 2005

Haynes, Jim, *The Book of Australian Popular Rhymed Verse,* ABC Books, Sydney, 2005

— *Australia's Best Unknown Stories,* Allen & Unwin, Sydney, 2014

— *The Best Gallipoli Yarns and Other True Stories,* Allen & Unwin, Sydney, 2015

— *Great Australian Scams, Cons and Rorts,* Allen & Unwin, Sydney, 2017

— *The Big Book of Australia's War Stories,* Allen & Unwin, Sydney, 2019

Hogan, James Francis, *The Convict King,* 1891, Aust Literature Gateway, University of Sydney, 2003

Jørgensen, Jørgen, *The Copenhagen Expedition Traced to Other Causes than the Treaty of Tilsit; with Observations on the History and Present State of Denmark by a Dane,* London, 1811

— *Travels through France and Germany in the Years 1815, 1816 & 1817. Comprising a View of the Moral, Political, and Social State of those Countries. Interspersed with Numerous Historical and Political Anecdotes, Derived from Authentic Sources,* London, 1817

— 'History of the Origin, Rise, and Progress of the Van Diemen's Land Company', (six articles), *Colonial Advocate* and *Tasmanian Monthly Review and Register,* Hobart, 1828, a revised version published in London in 1829 and republished in 1979

— *Observations on the Funded System; Containing a Summary View of the Present Political State of Great Britain, and the Relative Situation in which the Colony of Van Diemen's Land Stands towards the Mother Country,* Hobart, 1831

— *An Address to the Free Colonists of Van Diemen's Land, on Trial by Jury, and our Other Constitutional Rights,* Hobart, 1834

— 'A Shred of Autobiography, Containing Various Anecdotes, Personal and Historical, Connected with these Colonies', (two sections), *Hobart Town Almanack*, and *Van Diemen's Land Annual*, Hobart, 1835, and *Hobart Town Almanack*, and *Van Diemen's Land Annual*, Hobart, 1838

— 'Aboriginal Languages in Tasmania', *Tasmania Journal of Natural Science, Agriculture, Statistics*, Tasmanian Government Printer Hobart & John Murray, London, 1842

— Letter from Jürgensen dated 11 September 1835 to his brother Frederik (Fritz) Jürgensen, *Personalhistorisk Tidsskrift 9*, Copenhagen, 1928

Lyte, Charles, *Sir Joseph Banks*, AH & AW Reed, Sydney, 1980

Martin, James (ed. Tim Causer), *The Memorandoms of James Martin 1789*, (Fair copy), University College, London, 2014

McCormick, Tim, *First Views of Australia 1788–1825*, David Ell Press, Longueville Publications, Sydney, 1987

McVeigh, Tom, and Siebenhausen, Ron, *Our Restless Hero, Private John Leak, Queensland's First VC Recipient*, McVeigh & Siebenhausen, Clayfield, Queensland, 2015

Morton, James, and Lobez, Susanna, *Gangland Sydney*, Victory Books, Melbourne, 2011

Sellers, Travis, 'The Unofficial History of Brighton Cemetery', quoted in *J.C. De Garis*, Australian Variety Theatre Archive website, 2011

Serle, Geoffrey, 'Hervey, Grant (Madison)', *Australian Dictionary of Biography*, Vol. 9, Australian National University, Canberra, 1983

Smith, Stewart, *Prostitution in New South Wales: Law Reform Issues. Briefing Paper No 27/95*, NSW Parliament Library, Sydney, 1995

— *The Regulation of Prostitution in New South Wales Briefing Paper No 21/99*, NSW Parliament Library, Sydney, 1999

Stoker, Bram, *Famous Imposters*, Sturgis & Walton, New York, 1910

Straw, Leigh, *The Worst Woman in Sydney*, NewSouth Publishing, Sydney, 2016

Stringer, Arthur, *Red Wine of Youth*, Alfred A. Knopf, New York, 1921

Tench, Watkin, *A Complete Account of the Settlement at Port Jackson*, London, 1793

Terry, Paul, *The Claimant*, Echo Books, Melbourne, 2016

Twain, Mark, *More Tramps Abroad (Following the Equator)*, The American Publishing Co, Chicago, 1897

Vaux, James Hardy, *Memoirs of the First Thirty-Two Years of The Life of James Hardy Vaux, A Swindler and Pickpocket; Now Transported for the Second Time, and For Life, to New South Wales*, Murray, London, 1819 (republished as *The Memoirs of James Hardy Vaux*, John Hunt, London, 1827, 1829, 1830)

— *A New and Comprehensive Vocabulary of the Flash Language*, Murray, London, 1819

White, John, *Journal of a Voyage to New South Wales*, Debrett, London, 1790

Writer, Larry, *Underbelly – Razor*, Macmillan, Sydney, 2011

IMAGE CREDITS

Part One

Chapter 1: Charlotte Medal, Thomas Barrett 1788, Sydney Maritime Museum; Convicts embarking for Botany Bay, Thomas Rowlandson, 180-?, National Library of Australia, Rex Nan Kivell Collection, NK228.

Chapter 2: George Barrington by William Beechey, c. 1785, National Library of Australia, Rex Nan Kivell Collection, NK13; George Barrington pickpocketing, National Portrait Gallery.

Chapter 3: Harry Readford, State Records Office of WA; 'Homeward Bound', S.T. Gill, State Library of NSW.

Chapter 4: John Boyle O'Reilly, US Library of Congress; John Boyle O'Reilly, University of Exeter.

Chapter 5: Jack de Garis, *Green Room Magazine*, September 1920; *Victories of Failure* by Jack de Garis, 1925.

Part Two

Chapter 6: Portrait of James Hardy Vaux, originally published in Knapp & Baldwin's New Newgate Calendar, 1825; James Hardy Vaux, early colonial engraving.

Chapter 7: Arthur Orton—Tichborne Claimant, c. 1872, Maull & Co. Piccadilly; Roger Tichborne, daguerreotype, 1853.

Chapter 8: Kate Leigh, 1915, NSW State Archive; Kate Leigh, 1930, NSW Police Forensic Photography Archive, Justice and Police Museum, Sydney Living Museums.

Chapter 9: Tom Skeyhill, *Soldier Songs of ANZAC*, 1916; Tom Skeyhill, publicity photo, 1922.

Chapter 10: Eugenia Fallini, NSW Archive, 1928; Eugenia Fallini, NSW Archive, 1932.

Part Three
Chapter 11: Jørgen Jørgensen by Christoffer Wilhelm Eckersberg, c. 1830; Jørgen Jørgensen, carving on Ross Bridge by convict sculptor Daniel Herbert.

Chapter 12: Henry James O'Farrell, 1868, photograph by Montagu Scott; H.J. O'Farrell shooting Prince Alfred, newspaper drawing, National Library of Australia.

Chapter 13: George Henry Cochrane, 1927, National Library of Australia, 3085138; *Sunraysia Daily*, 1921.

Chapter 14: John Leak, 1915, Australian War Memorial; John Leak, November 1916.

Chapter 15: Cover—Eagle Farm racebook 18-8-1984; Page—Eagle Farm racebook, 18 August 1984, courtesy of Ben Dorries, Racenet.

ACKNOWLEDGEMENTS

Thanks to the following:

- Tom Bailey-Smith for smoothly managing the whole process;
- Rebecca Kaiser for fourteen years of good-humoured support and encouragement;
- Susin Chow for her perceptive copyediting and suggestions;
- Mika Tabata for the cover and family tree design;
- Pamela Dunne for proofreading;
- Jillian Dellit for research, suggestions and proofreading;
- Midland for the typesetting;
- all at Allen & Unwin;
- Ben Dorries of Racenet;
- Robyn McMillan.